How to Become a Web Developer

A Field Guide

Angel Garbarino

FULLSTACK.*io*

How to Become A Web Developer

A Field Guide

Written by Angel Garbarino
Edited by Nate Murray

Published by Fullstack.io.

Contents

Book Revision

- Revision 4 - 2020-01-24

Join The Book Discord Chat Room!

If you'd like to meet other readers, discuss the book, and help each other out, then join our community Discord channel.

To join the chat, visit: https://newline.co/discord[1]. See you there!

Bug Reports

If you'd like to report any bugs, typos, or suggestions just email us at: **us@fullstack.io**.

Be notified of updates via Twitter

If you'd like to be notified of updates to the book on Twitter, follow us at @fullstackio[2].

We'd love to hear from you!

Did you like the book? Did you find it helpful? We'd love to add your face to our list of testimonials on the website! Email us at: us@fullstack.io[3].

---

[1]https://newline.co/discord
[2]https://twitter.com/fullstackio
[3]mailto:us@fullstack.io

Download the Example Code

This book contains several example apps and code samples. Because you purchased the paperback version you can **download this code for free** at our website.

URL	https://newline.co/code/webdev
BOOK SERIAL CODE	AMZ-H8DN

To download the code, visit the URL above and enter your email and serial code and we'll email you the code download.

Learn more at: https://newline.co/code/webdev

About This Book

Preface

The audience for this book is me, five years ago, when I was starting to think about becoming a programmer. My path to get to where I am now - a Frontend Developer - was inefficient, convoluted, and often directionless. It was longer and more expensive than it needed to be.

My motivation to write this book is fueled, in part, by spite; I am still irked by the many false starts. I would spend time learning something, only to find out much later it did not get me closer to becoming a Web Developer. For example, I spent a lot of time learning WordPress - a tool to build websites - before understanding how WordPress fit into Web Development. At the time, I thought working on WordPress sites was the majority of Web Development - spoiler alert: I was wrong.

Additionally, I spent too much time trying to decipher tutorials written by Web Developers. Without intending to sound like a snob, professional developers are not the best teachers; especially for beginners. Not always, but often, advanced professionals have a hard time meeting beginners at their level. They make assumptions, intentionally or not, that lead to a lot of confusion. For example, I would read something like, "just SSH into this," and then spend the next couple of hours trying to figure out what SSH meant. Meanwhile, the article was explaining a different topic, but I was down a rabbit hole learning about SSH.

I know I am not the only self-taught programmer that has suffered unnecessary trials, but I still cannot find a reliable resource that meets beginners at this crucial stage. Yes there are a lot of "beginner coding bootcamps" or "HTML for beginners" books, but they all - in my opinion - fail to address the larger picture: **what is Web Development, and what does the path to becoming a Web Developer look like?**

I use the term **Web Developer** to describe any person who specializes in the development of web applications. Applications typically use HTML, CSS, JavaScript in combination with some server scripting language (we will discuss these terms throughout the book). Web pages, websites, web apps like Facebook, or Google Maps are all examples of Web applications.

Who You Are

I imagine that people reading this book will have little to no programming skills, but that they've considered joining a bootcamp or other online course. Or, as I discovered from conversations with a variety of people while writing this book, the reader is interested in being more versed and aware of the tech scene. Maybe they work in customer service, sales, or as a designer for a tech company and would like to better understand the fundamentals of the space they work in.

While writing this book, I avoided dry and overused code examples that I cannot read without suppressing an eye roll. I err on the side of humor, in the Exercises and the text. Hopefully, this humor is met with a smile and keeps the content more engaging.

Whether you're looking at becoming a Web Developer or would like to become familiar with the content for whatever reason, this book is the perfect place to start.

Acknowledgments

"A rising tide lifts all boats" was a saying I heard but never embraced, that is until *this* journey. Today, I have this quote front and center on a sticky note on my computer.

This book is not a reflection of my effort; it is a reflection of a lot of little efforts from everyone around me. In no particular order, here are some people that helped get this boat afloat.

Teton Tech Meetup Crew You're a cast of characters I never knew I needed. My life and this book have been greatly improved because of your ideas, thoughts, and opinions; the good and especially the bad ones. From debating the merits of what defines "code" to pointing out that I'm the only one who finds the word "sharding" funny, you have kept me afloat through this journey. Thank you.

Joji Davey My first in line to read through any content that was close to being draft-ready. Your thoughtfulness, devotion to see it through, and perspective helped me right the ship on several occasions. When I wrote, I always wrote with you in mind. You have truly gone above and beyond your best friend responsibilities.

Abby Broughton The illustrator and dear friend. I never thought our corny humor would find value in the workspace, but thank goodness it has. Your illustrations are more than entertaining and colorful; they bring to light concepts I struggled to explain with mere words.

Beta Readers I am so grateful for all of your insights and feedback. Time and attention might be the scarcest of humanity's resources these days, so when someone freely offers these to me, I am filled with gratitude, truly.

Nate Murray As this is my first effort with an engaged publisher, I'm not sure how valid the following statement is, but I'll make it anyways: Nate Murray is the best publisher in the World. He not only allowed me to write a book, but he also mentored me through it each step of the way.

Friends & Family And last but not least, my friends and family. You guys joined forces to keep me healthy, sane, and realistic. I fought you along the way, but as good friends and family do, you fought back. Thank you a million times over.

How to Get the Most Out of This Book

Overview

This book aims to be the first resource on your path to becoming a Web Developer. Consider this your prep course, getting you prepared with all the information you'll need to know about the Web Development field and the skills you'll need to break into it.

By the time you're done reading this book, you will have been introduced and have a baseline skill level in all the areas required to become a Web Developer. And more importantly, an understanding of how those skills fit into the larger picture of Web Development.

This book walks you through the crucial concepts that every developer will need to know. It ends with a "field-guide" of what the book covered and where to go next.

And if a career is not what you are after, you will certainly be more aware and better equipped to work in the tech space. I imagine that designers, customer support, and even sales folks that work in software/computer companies would greatly benefit from this book.

How much time is reading this book going to take?

This depends on how serious you want to take the book. If you go full-in and do all the Exercises, I anticipate the average chapter will take you about 4-5 hrs, which includes time spent on activities.

However, the book has been written so that you can still follow along if you choose not to participate in the activities. That is not to say the Exercises are not valuable, they are, and they really will drive the topics home. But I am aware time is a valuable resource, and not everyone has a schedule that affords them 4-5 hrs a chapter. Thus, if you skip the Exercises, each chapter should take you about 2 hrs. I recommend aiming to complete one chapter every two weeks; keeping the topics fresh from one chapter to the next.

At the end of each chapter, there is a "**Considerations for Further Study**" section. These are optional and are meant to equip you with follow up resources once you have completed the book.

Exercises

Every chapter includes Exercises. When you see yourself in an Exercise section, expect to be *doing* something on your computer. This book is meant to be read alongside a desktop computer, not a tablet or smart-phone.

I do my best to make the Exercises easy to follow. I use a *lot* of screenshots so you can focus on learning instead of spending brainpower figuring out *how* to follow along.

In the Exercises, I use various pink boxes and text overlaid on the screenshots to help point out specific things to look at.

Below are some of the various elements you can expect to see on the screenshots. I use them to draw your attention or point something out.

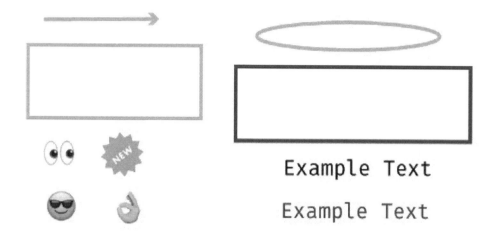

Example Text

Example Text

Running Code Examples

This book comes with a library of runnable code examples. The code is available to download from the same place you purchased the book. If you bought the book on Amazon, you should have received an email with instructions.

If you have trouble finding or downloading the code examples, email us at **us@fullstack.io**.

The code examples are organized by chapter. In the Exercises, I will link to the specific code example.

Getting Help

While I've made every effort to be clear, precise, and accurate, you may find something confusing or an Exercise step that does not seem to work.

Generally, there are three types of problems:

- An error in the book (e.g., how I describe something is wrong)
- An error in an Exercise.

- An error in your replication of the Exercise.

If you find an inaccuracy in how I describe something, or you feel a concept is not clear, email us! We want to make sure that the book is both accurate and clear.

If you suspect a problem with an Exercise, make sure that your version of the book's Exercises are up to date. We release updates periodically.

If you are using the latest Exercises and you think you've found an error we definitely want to hear about it.

Emailing Us

If you are emailing us for technical help, here's what we'd like to know:

- What revision of the book are you referring to?
- What operating system are you on? (e.g., MacOS 10.14, Windows 10)
- Which chapter and which Exercise are you on?
- What are you trying to accomplish?
- What have you already tried?
- What happened? (Including screenshots if applicable.)

When you've written down these things, email us at **us@fullstack.io**. We look forward to hearing from you.

Technical Support Response Time

We perform our free, technical support once per week.

Chapter 1: Setup and Tooling

There are a couple of key technologies that we will be using throughout this book. In this chapter, I will introduce you to these technologies, talk briefly about what we'll be using them for, and do a quick setup and walkthrough. The technologies are:

- **Web Browser**: Chrome and Chrome DevTools
- **Text Editor**: Visual Studio Code (VSCode for short)
- **Operating System**: macOS or Windows 10.

For each of these technologies, there are equal comparables. To keep the Exercises consistent, however, I will only be using the technologies listed above. For example, you won't see me changing from Chrome to Firefox.

It is true that these technologies are what I prefer. However, don't mistake this for a statement about them being the *best* technologies. By no means am I suggesting that Chrome is better than Firefox or heaven forbid I claim VSCode is the king of text editors.

In the end, what browser or text editor you decide to use should depend on what you like. If you don't have a preference than try the ones I am using here merely because it will make it easier to follow along.

I am a macOS user, and thus all the screenshots are done from a Mac. However, the instructions for most all the Exercises will be the same for Windows and macOS. Starting in *Chapter 6: The Terminal*, there are slight differences in the Exercise instructions between these two operating systems. In those cases, if you are a Windows user, look for the Window Users side-instructions in the Exercises. Both Windows and macOS users will be able to complete all Exercises.

Setting up the Technologies

Web Browser and Developer Tools

A good chunk of the Exercises in this book will require a web browser and developer tools.

We will be using the Chrome web browser. If you don't already have it installed, you can download it here[4]. It's free to download.

Developer Tools

Every modern browser comes with web developer tools (also called DevTools). These tools are used heavily by - you guessed it - Web Developers. The DevTools aim to help developers test and debug their code. For us, they provide a great place to explore the concepts we will talk about.

Here is a screenshot of the various DevTools for Chrome, Firefox, and Safari web browsers. They all do about the same thing but have slightly different looks.

---

[4]https://www.google.com/chrome/browser/

Chrome's DevTools

Firefox's DevTools

Safari's DevTools

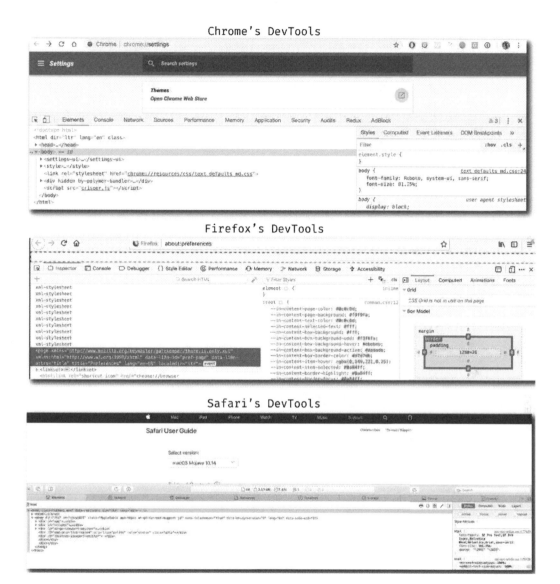

Exercise 1 of 2: Navigating the DevTools

1. Let's open the Chrome DevTools. Navigate to any web page via Chrome.

There are several ways to open the DevTools.

- You can open the DevTools via the Chrome menu. Click on View -> Developer

-> Developer Tools.

- A second way to open DevTools is to right-click on any web page, and select "inspect."

- The approach I recommend is a keyboard shortcut because it's the quickest and most convenient. With a web page open, hold command + alt + j. For Windows users, the command is ctrl + shift + j.

Once you have the DevTools open, you should see the following window pop-up. Depending on your settings, the DevTools may show up at the bottom of the screen, or on the right-hand side.

A couple of things to note:

- By default you will land on the **Console** panel. We will talk more about the Console panel in the JavaScript chapter.
- Everything inside the dark pink box is called a **panel**. To the left of the Console panel, for example, is the **Elements** panel.
- The red errors I show on my Console panel may or may not show for you. Errors like this are for Web Developers and are sent to the Console panel from the web page you are on. For our purposes, we can ignore them.

2. There are two main DevTool panels we will be using: Elements and Console. Let's navigate over to the Elements panel.

Click on the Elements panel just to the left of the Console panel.

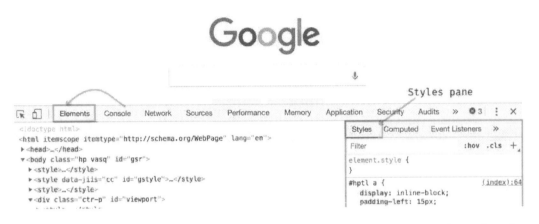

The Elements panel shows the web page as "code." A good way to visualize what the Elements panel does is to think of the web page as a stitching. The Elements panel would then be the backside of the stitches; they're the same, one is just prettier.

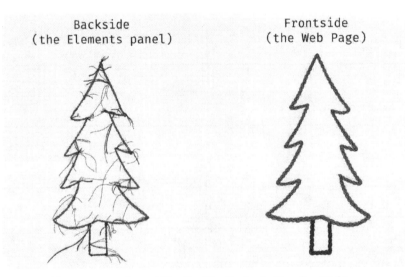

Elements panel would be the like the backside of a stitching

This is an overly simplistic analogy, but the idea is that the Elements panel is a reflection of the web page you are currently on. This will make more sense after the HTML and CSS chapters.

3. For now, that should get us familiar enough with the DevTools. I will talk more about what you're seeing and how to use the DevTools throughout this book.

4. If you'd like to modify the look or position of your DevTools I have provided some information below. If you'd like to skip it, jump to the next section: Text Editor.

By default, your DevTools window will show at the bottom of the web page, but you can modify its position if having it on the bottom of the web page is annoying to you. On the right side of the DevTools, click on the 3 horizontal dots to open the settings menu.

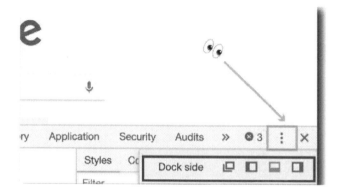

Once you open the menu, you'll see a section where you can select the "Dock side." Select a different Dock side. Play around and see if you have a preference.

Here's an example of the DevTools being docked on the right-hand side.

Another setting you can play with is a white vs. black background. Honestly, my preference is to have a black background. My screenshots all use a white background for printing purposes, but when not taking screenshots, I use the dark theme.

To change the background color, on the same menu, click "Settings."

Then in settings, change the theme from "light" to "dark."

A dark theme DevTools looks like the following screenshot:

Again, these settings are optional. These two options - dock placement and theme color - can have a significant impact on usability, so I thought them worth pointing out.

Text Editor

Every mainstream computer comes with what is called a **text editor**. A text editor is a program that edits text without adding markup, i.e., in plain text. Developers use text editors to assist in writing "code".

> **A Text Editor is not the same as a Word Processor**
>
> A word processor, something like Microsoft Word or Open Office, adds styling to text (e.g., margins, font-size, bold, italic, etc.). A text editor does not. When you write code, it's crucial that you *do not* use a word processor because the added styling will corrupt your code.

Technically, you could use your computer's default text editor to write code. However, because developers use their text editors so much, it shouldn't surprise you that they have developed fancy, sophisticated text editors for the sole purpose of writing code.

In this book, I am going to suggest you use the **VSCode** text editor. For several reasons: it's free, easy to navigate for beginners, and is a great first text editor that you can continue to use as you advance in Web Development.

Exercise 2 of 2: Setting up VSCode

In this Exercise, we are going to install VSCode, and practice opening and navigating around a text file.

1. Download VSCode here[5].

 VSCode is a Microsoft product and is often confused with Visual Studio, which you'll see with purple logo just to the left of the download screen. In short, Visual Studio is a more advanced, full-service type of text editor. Visual Studio is way more than we need, and is not free. Make sure you download the "Visual Studio Code" on the right-hand side of the screen, with the blue logo.

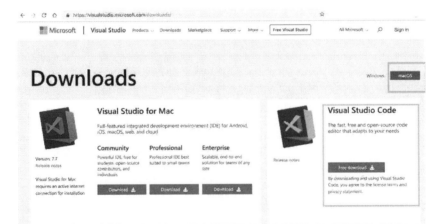

Click on the "Free download" under "Visual Studio Code." See the pink box in the screenshot. Also, make sure you are downloading the correct version. If you are on Windows, you will need to select "Windows," and not "macOS," as I have here.

---

[5]https://visualstudio.microsoft.com/downloads/

2. Once you click download, a zip file will start downloading. Open it when it's done. Once downloaded, move the VSCode application to your Applications folder.

3. Open VSCode like you would any other Application.

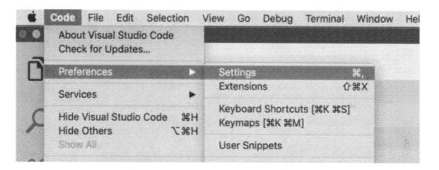

4. First things first, let's make this thing look good. The default theme in VSCode is pretty good, but I want to show you where you can modify these settings if you have different preferences.

Open VSCode preferences by clicking Code -> Preferences -> Settings.

Once you're in Preferences, search for "theme," in the search navigation (see the top-most pink box in the following screenshot).

After searching for "theme" an area will come up where you can select a different theme.

Out of the box, VSCode comes with a variety of themes. I am using a theme called "Verdandi" because it's light and easy to take screenshots from (Verdandi is not included by default. I had to download it). For now, play around with different themes and see which one you like best.

If you want to explore even more themes, you can find them in the VSCode Marketplace[6].

5. Now that we have our vanity taken care of let's open a simple text file using VSCode. Make sure you have downloaded the code that comes with this book. When you download the code, it will be downloaded as a zip file. You will need to unzip it.

Once you have downloaded and unzipped the code folder, click File -> Open, and

---

[6]https://marketplace.visualstudio.com/search?term=themes&target=VS&category=Tools&vsVersion=&subCategory=All&sortBy=Relevance

select the `1-setup/test-file.txt`[7].

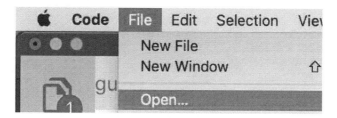

6. Once open, you should see something like the following screenshot. Remember, your theme is likely different than mine.

VSCode is just an application that lets you modify documents. Just like Microsoft Word allows you to edit word docs. The difference is, text editors are designed to modify documents of "code".

> **i** I keep putting "code" in quotes because the precise definition of code is a complex one. HTML and CSS, which we cover in the first two chapters are not technically code, but we will be editing .html and .css files in our text editor.

7. One beneficial thing about text editors is that they give line/row numbers. We will use these in our examples to describe where on the document you should look. So for example, if I say "on row 3," I mean the row with the sloth fact.

---

[7]code/src/1-setup/test-file.txt

≡ test-file.txt ✕

≡ test-file.txt

```
1    Hello there,
2
3 |  Did you know sloths only urinate/defecate once a week!
```

Use the keyboard shortcut control + g to navigate to a specific row. Once you hit that command, you'll be asked to type in a line number. Here I typed in 2, and you can see the line 2 is highlighted light-yellow.

```
:2|

Go to line 2
                                1   ottoere,
                                2
zero-to-web-devel...  M         3 |  Did you know sloths only urinate/defecate once a week!
```

You don't have to use this command, but it's helpful if you have a big file and want to navigate to a specific line/row number quickly. Try it out and see if you find it useful.

8. One last "how-to" that we should know for VSCode is saving. Saving here is just like saving in any other application. You can go to File -> Save, or as I prefer, use a keyboard shortcut command + s.

9. VSCode has a lot more bells and whistles, but there's no need for us to investigate those just yet. By the end of this book, revisiting VSCode's interface is recommended, but for now, know how to open VSCode, open files with it, and save files.

If you *still* want to learn more about VSCode, I recommend their "Getting Started" videos[8].

Operating Systems

There are 3 common Operating Systems for Desktop Computers: macOS, Windows, and Linux.

---

[8]https://code.visualstudio.com/docs/introvideos/basics

If you are on an Apple Computer, then you have a macOS, if you're on a Windows machine, then you're using a Windows, and if you're on a Linux, you already know it.

Without getting into too many details, Operating Systems are the core of your computer, dictating file structure, and commands; things we will encounter throughout this book.

I am using a macOS, and my examples will reflect that. However, that does not mean you need to have a Mac to participate in the Exercises of this book.

What's Next?

Up until this point, we've been getting ready and prepared. Tomorrow, the adventure starts. The next chapter, **What is a Web Page**, is an introduction to HTML. As you'll come to learn, HTML is the language of the web. We will learn what HTML is used for, and use Exercises in both the DevTools and VSCode to get more comfortable with the HTML syntax.

Chapter 2: What is a Web Page?

We're starting with the fundamentals; web pages. Ultimately, Web Development is about creating web pages. And though there is much more going on behind the scenes - as you'll come to understand throughout this book - we will start by looking at what a web page is.

Web page vs. Website?

People often talk about websites and web pages as if they are the same thing. This is fine for everyday discussions, but as a Web Developer, you should understand that they are different. A **website** is a collection of web pages, linking to other web pages. A **web page** is just a single HTML document.

Additionally, not everything you see on a web browser is a web page. Web browsers can load PDF files and image files in addition to web pages.

Have you ever been sent a PDF document in an email and then opened it in your web browser? This is an example of a web browser displaying something that is not a web page. If you're ever in doubt if something is a web page or one of these special file types, look at the end of the URL. Generally, any URL that ends in a file type like .pdf, .png, .jpeg is not a web page.

Open the following links and look at the end of their URLs.

- This is a pdf file[9]. It is not a web page.

🔒 ullstackreact.com/assets/media/react-from-zero/89ansd/table-of-contents/react-from-zero-book-table-of-contents.pdf

Notice the .pdf at
the end of the URL

---

[9]https://www.fullstackreact.com/assets/media/react-from-zero/89ansd/table-of-contents/react-from-zero-book-table-of-contents.pdf

- This image[10] is a png file. It is not a web page.

  tackreact.com/assets/images/react-from-zero/react-from-zero-book-mockup-shadow-facing-forward-cover-01-md.png

  Notice the .png at
  the end of the URL

Web Page vs. Website

A **web page** is an HTML document that can be displayed by a web browser.

A **website** is a collection of web pages linking to other web pages.

HTML

HyperText Markup Language, better known as HTML, is the language of the World Wide Web (WWW), and it has been since the very first web page, built-in 1991[11]. You can see the first web page at this link[12]. I encourage you to open it in a browser to see it in action.

It's rather incredible that it is still visible and usable today. This is possible because the first web page was built in HTML, and HTML continues to be the foundational language of all content on the web. Notice the .html at the end of the file[13].

---

[10]https://www.fullstackreact.com/assets/images/react-from-zero/react-from-zero-book-mockup-shadow-facing-forward-cover-01-md.png

[11]The first web page was created by the European Organization for Nuclear Research (CERN). This is the same organization that built the world's most powerful particle accelerator, smashing particles together at nearly the speed of light!

[12]http://info.cern.ch/hypertext/WWW/TheProject.html

[13]You don't generally see the .html in URLs, because by default when someone visits the main website's URL, the web page loads an index.html file.

← → C ⓘ Not Secure | info.cern.ch/hypertext/WWW/TheProject.html

World Wide Web

Here's what the first web page looks like:

World Wide Web

The WorldWideWeb (W3) is a wide-area hypermedia information retrieval initiative aiming to give universal access to a large universe of documents.

Everything there is online about W3 is linked directly or indirectly to this document, including an executive summary of the project, Mailing lists , Policy , November's W3 news , Frequently Asked Questions .

What's out there?
        Pointers to the world's online information, subjects , W3 servers, etc.
Help
        on the browser you are using
Software Products
        A list of W3 project components and their current state. (e.g. Line Mode ,X11 Viola , NeXTStep , Servers , Tools , Mail robot ,Library)
Technical
        Details of protocols, formats, program internals etc
Bibliography
        Paper documentation on W3 and references.
People
        A list of some people involved in the project.
History
        A summary of the history of the project.
How can I help ?
        If you would like to support the web..
Getting code
        Getting the code by anonymous FTP , etc.

 HTML started as a simple set of rules that let you add links and basic formatting to text. It was popular, but programmers wanted more, so they began creating their own versions. Things quickly got messy, with each browser supporting different versions of HTML[14]. In came The W3C organization (World Wide Web Consortium), which helped standardize HTML rules and still does to this day.

To better understand what HTML is, let's break down the acronym.

HyperText

The "HT," **HyperText** refers to a system of linking topics to related information. In short, it means a page that links to other pages.

When you have a web page linking to other web pages, you have a website. If you go back to the first web page, you'll notice it's just that: an HTML file that has links to

---

[14]https://www.wired.com/1997/04/a-brief-history-of-html/

other HTML files. Thus, technically it's a website, though granted it's a very simple one.

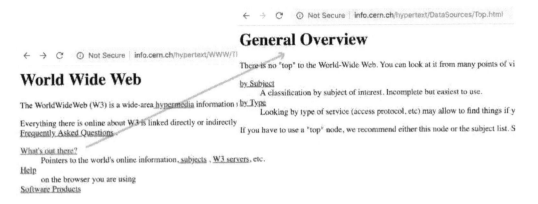

In the previous screenshot, each of the links on the "first website" link to other web pages. The pink arrow shows that the "What's out there?" link opens another web page called "General Overview."

Markup Language

The "ML" in HTML stands for **markup language**. Markup language is a generic term that refers to *any* language that tells you how to format a digital document. It does this via a standardized set of rules. These rules are different depending on which markup language you are using.

Markup is easy to take for granted because almost all the interactions we have with text have markup applied. When you are writing in a word processor, typing an email, or even looking at spreadsheets, you're looking at markup.

In the following screenshot, all these popular interfaces - Google docs, email, and Google Spreadsheets - are using markup.

Text that does not have markup is called **plain text**, and it's unlikely that you see it very often.

To help demonstrate what markup does, we are going to look at what the first website looks like without any markup, i.e., in **plain text**.

Exercise 1 of 8: Plain Text vs. Markup

1. Open the first website[15] in a browser window.
2. Select and Copy all the text on the web page.
3. Open the My Text Area[16] website in another browser window.
4. Paste the copied first website content onto the My Text Area web page.[17]

You should see the following:

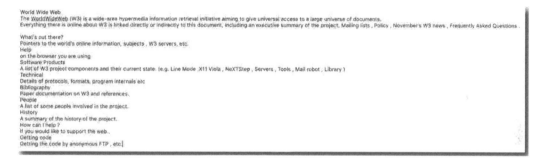

That is what plain text looks like. Without markup, there are no links, and all the text looks the same. Try this experiment with other text from a word processor, emails, or web pages. Seeing the markup stripped away will give you a better understanding of what markup does.

HTML is a Markup Language, not a Programming Language.

Programming languages allow you to run a process or execute an action, which HTML does not do. We will talk about programming languages later in this book.

---

[15]http://info.cern.ch/hypertext/WWW/TheProject.html

[16]http://www.mytextarea.com/

[17]My Text Area is a web page that only shows plain text. This can also be done on any plain text editor on your computer.

Exercise 2 of 8: Uncomment Examples Part I

I am going to introduce a process in this Exercise that we will repeat another 3 times as we work through the chapter.

The process will go like this: open an HTML file that has HTML examples on it. These examples are currently commented out, meaning they don't show on a web browser. You will remove the comments and then view the changes in a web browser.

I hope that by playing with HTML, as we discuss it, you will get more comfortable with the concept.

1. In the code that comes with this book, open up the `2-html/1-first-web-page.html` [18] in your text editor.

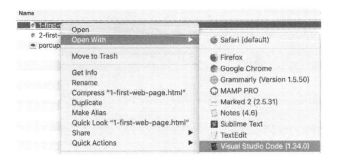

2. In your text editor, you'll notice that a lot of the HTML is greyed-out (my theme colors comments grey, but depending on your theme, the color may be different). That is because the majority of the HTML is commented out.

The "Uncomment #1" indicates the HTML snippet I want to uncomment here for practice.

---

[18] code/src/2-html/1-first-web-page.html

```
<html>
  <body>
    <!-- Uncomment #1
      <h1>test</h1>
    -->
    <!--Uncomment #2
    <b>keyword: b</b>
    -->
```

HTML Snippet #1

Comments wrap around the text you want to comment out, with an opening set of characters and a closing set of characters.

To comment around HTML, you use a less than character <, plus an open exclamation point ! followed by two dashes --. This opens the comment.

To close the comment, you use two dashes -- followed by a greater than character >. Here's an example:

The text in-between the opening and closing set of characters is what is commented out.

Comments are helpful because they allow us to write out HTML without it being displayed in the browser. When we're ready to display the HTML snippet, we remove the comments wrapping the snippet.

To delete a comment (a.k.a "uncomment"), you need to remove the opening <!-- and closing -->. So for example, the first comment we will uncomment is #1.

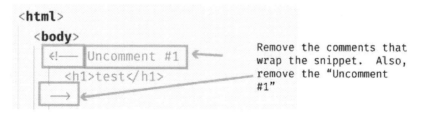

```
<html>
  <body>
    <!-- Uncomment #1
      <h1>test</h1>
    -->
```

Remove the comments that wrap the snippet. Also, remove the "Uncomment #1"

Here's what it looks like after uncommenting #1.

```
<body>
    <h1>test</h1>
```

I will, throughout the remainder of this chapter, refer back to this HTML document and ask you to remove the comments around a specific HTML snippet.

In my uncommenting demonstration, I asked you to remove the comments around #1. Later I will ask you to remove the comments from #2, etc.

3. Make sure you save your changes and then review them in the browser. On your computer, go to where the "1-first-web-page.html" file lives. Right-click on it and open it with Chrome.

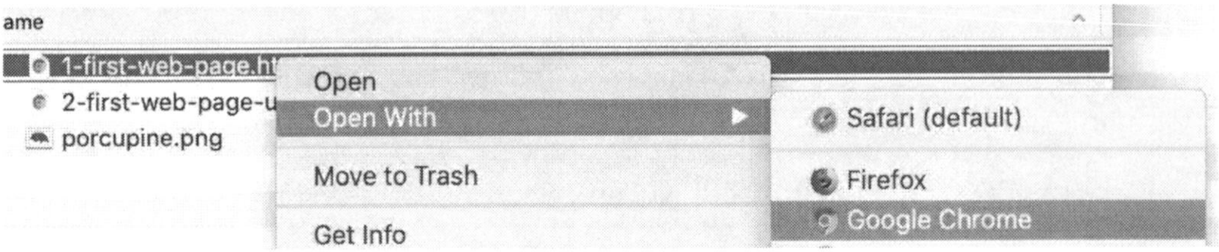

ame		
1-first-web-page.ht	Open	
2-first-web-page-u	Open With ▶	Safari (default)
porcupine.png	Move to Trash	Firefox
	Get Info	Google Chrome

4. Once opened in the browser, assuming you have uncommented #1, you should see something like the following screenshot:

← → C ⓘ File | file:///Users/

test

5. I would recommend keeping this HTML file open in the browser window as you work through this chapter. Anytime you uncomment another HTML snippet, just press save in your text editor and refresh the HTML document in the browser.

6. If at any time you want to view the whole "1-first-web-page.html" without any of the code commented out, open 2-html/2-first-web-page-uncommented.html[19] in

---

[19]code/src/2-html/2-first-web-page-uncommented.html

your text editor and browser. This file also has all the additional modifications I will ask you to make in the rest of the Exercises.

The HTML in #1 was to get you used to removing comments, as well as saving the HTML file and refreshing it in a browser. Now back to learning about HTML.

Using Markup

HTML is not the only language that uses markup. Markdown[20], for example, is a markup language that this book is written in. If I wanted to write a **bold word** in this book, I start and end the word with double asterisks `**bold words**`. In HTML, I would write bold words like this: `<b>bold words</b>`.

Each markup language uses its own rules to define blocks of text and assign formatting. HTML does this by using **tags** and **elements**.

HTML Tags

HTML **tags** are special keywords surrounded by a pair of angle brackets `<tag keyword>`. Most tags come in pairs, with an opening and closing tag. The closing tag is the same as an opening tag with the addition of a forward-slash.

HTML	In A Browser
`<b> keyword: b </b>`	**keyword: b**
`<em> keyword: em </em>`	*keyword: em*
`<h3> keyword: h3 </h3>`	**keyword: h3**

Some tags, like the tag used to display an image `<img >`, do not have a closing version. This is because you do not need to define an opening and closing to display an image, just a location of where the image can be found.

---

[20]https://daringfireball.net/projects/markdown/

HTML	In A Browser
`<img src="./porcupine.png">`	

There are close to 100 HTML tags[21]. Below are some of the more common ones. If they have a closing tag, I've included it.

Tag	Tag Name	Definition
`<p> </p>`	Paragraph	Define the start and stop of a paragraph.
`<h1> </h1>`	Heading 1	Headings can range from 1 to 6. The higher the number, the smaller the heading.
` `	Line Break	Inserts a single line break. Similar to hitting the carriage return key.
`<div> </div>`	Division	A division is a container that holds other elements. A division is helpful when separating blocks of HTML.
`<em> </em>`	Italic text	*Italic Text*, a.k.a., 'emphasized text'
`<a> </a>`	Anchor	You use the anchor tag to define what text should be clickable and where the click should take you. I navigate to the Fullstack.io website.

HTML Elements

HTML **elements** are individual components of HTML defined by HTML **tags**. At first glance, **elements** and **tags** can easily be mistaken for the same thing, but they are not the same. The key to remember is that elements are made up of tags, but tags are not made up of elements.

To help clarify, see the following examples of tags vs. elements.

---

[21]In total, there are around 100 different HTML Tags available. A list of them can be found here.

Tag	Element
`<p>`	`<p>` I am an element `</p>`
`<h1>`	`<h1>` I am a heading 1 element`</h1>`
`<img>`	`<img src='porcupine.png' />`

Where tags are used to define the start and stop of an element, elements refer to *both* the opening and closing tag and everything in-between. The elements that don't require a closing tag, like the `<img>` element, are called **void elements**. Elements are the building blocks of a web page and are a key concept that we will continue to revisit.

 ### Elements vs. Tag

Elements are made up of tags. Tags are not made up of elements. Elements are the building blocks of HTML. Example of an element: `<p>Paragraph Element</p>`, example of a tag `<p>`

Exercise 3 of 8: Uncomment Examples Part II

1. Let's test out the HTML elements we introduced in the previous section. In your text editor, open the `2-html/1-first-web-page.html`[22] document, if you don't already have it open.

2. Uncomment snippets #2, #3, and #4. These three snippets show the bold, italic, and heading-3 elements.

Remember to save after uncommenting and then refresh the HTML document in your browser.

In the following screenshot, I have three columned views: commented snippets, snippets uncommented, what it looks like in a browser.

---

[22]code/src/2-html/1-first-web-page.html

```
HTML snippets to uncomment        Snippets uncommented          What it looks like in a
<!--Uncomment #2                                                        browser
<b>keyword: b</b>
-->                               <b>keyword: b</b>
<!--Uncomment #3
<em>keyword: em</em>              <em>keyword: em</em>          keyword: b keyword: em
-->
<!--Uncomment #4                  <h3>keyword: h3</h3>          keyword: h3
<h3>keyword: h3</h3>
-->
```

I'll be the first to admit that the browser view does not look that good; the **bold** and *italic* words are squished onto the same line; hence, the vomit emoji in the screenshot. We'll fix this later.

3. Next, let's check out the image tag. Uncomment snippet #5.

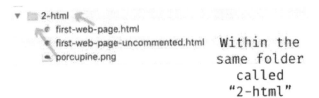

```
HTML snippets to uncomment        Snippets uncommented          What it looks like in a
<!--Uncomment #5                                                        browser
<img src="./porcupine.png">       <img src="./porcupine.png">
-->
```

Notice there is no closing tag on the <img > element. Everything you need to display the image is contained within the opening < and closing angle brackets >.

 If you don't see the porcupine image in the browser, make sure you have the porcupine.png file in the same folder as the "1-first-web-page.html" document. If you do, you should see the porcupine image come up.

```
▼ 📁 2-html
    first-web-page.html                 Within the
    first-web-page-uncommented.html     same folder
    porcupine.png                         called
                                         "2-html"
```

4. Next, let's uncomment snippet #6.

In addition to uncommenting #6, I want you to *add* another paragraph element below the snippet. You can replace the text with whatever you'd like, but the following screenshot will show you an example of a paragraph element you could add.

5. Next, let's uncomment snippet #7. This is a heading element. And it's the h1 heading, which means it's the largest of the heading tags. I want you first to uncomment it, and then *change* the heading element from an h1 element to an h4 element (h4 is a smaller heading element).

See the following screenshot for how to do this.

6. Lastly, we're going to return to the #2 and #3 snippets, and clean them up a bit. We'll first use the division `<div></div>` element.

Go back to the HTML snippet with the **bold** and *italic* words. Wrap both elements in opening `<div>` and closing `</div>` tags. See the following screenshot on how to do this.

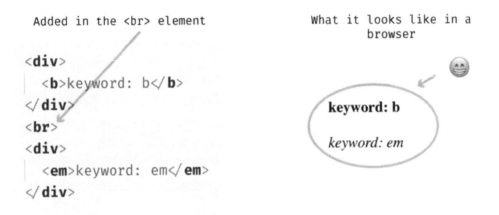

That looks a lot better. But I still want some spacing between the two lines. Let's use the line-break element to do that. Add the line-break `<br>` element in-between the 2 division elements. See the following screenshot on how to do this.

Added in the `<br>` element   What it looks like in a browser

```
<div>
    <b>keyword: b</b>
</div>
<br>
<div>
    <em>keyword: em</em>
</div>
```

keyword: b

keyword: em

You can see the `<br>` element added in a line-break, hence the element's name "line-break."

That's the last Exercise for now. We'll revisit this HTML document again shortly, so don't bother closing the text editor or browser window.

Attributes

So far, we have only talked about tags and elements, and have avoided talking about the extra keywords you sometimes see *inside* an element tag.

For example, in the following `<img>` tag, we see the keyword: src. The extra keyword src is called an **attribute**.

Attributes provide additional information. They are a part of the HTML language.

On the left side of the following screenshot is the HTML, and the right side is what the HTML looks like rendered.

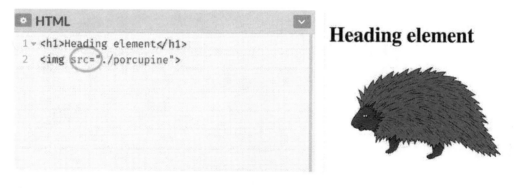

The **src** attribute - which I circled in pink - points to an external resource. In this case, it is pointing to where the porcupine image is located.

Here are some additional examples of HTML elements using attributes.

- An anchor element `<a></a>` uses the `href` attribute to link to another URL. Anytime you see a link in the text - like this[23] - it's the anchor tag at work. The attribute `href`, which stands for hypertext reference, indicates the link's destination.

```
HTML                                        This is a link
1 ▾ <a href="https://www.fullstack.io/">This is a link</a>
```

- The following header element `<h1></h1>` is using the `style` attribute to give it a blue color. You'll learn more about styles in the CSS chapter.

```
HTML                                        I am a header 1 element and I have a
1 ▾ <h1 style="color: blue">I am a header 1 element and I    style attribute that is giving me this
     have a style attribute that is giving me this blue      blue color
     color</h1>
```

---

[23]https://www.w3schools.com/tags/tag_a.asp

There are close to 200 different types of attributes, but in practice, you won't use but a handful. For our purposes, you do not need to know these attributes in detail. Just know that HTML elements use attributes to provide additional information.

Exercise 4 of 8: Uncomment Examples Part III

1. Let's test out the HTML attributes we introduced in the previous section. In your text editor, open the `2-html/1-first-web-page.html`[24] document if you don't already have it open.

2. Uncomment #8. This is an anchor tag that links to Google when you click on it.

```
    HTML snippets to uncomment              Snippets uncommented         What it looks like in a
                                                                                browser
<!--Uncomment #8
<a href="https://www.google.com/">       <a href="https://www.google.com/">       I'm a link!
  I'm a link!                               I'm a link!
</a>                                      </a>
-->
```

3. Try out the link. Take notice that when you click on the link, you are directed to Google in the *same* browser tab that your HTML document was in. To get back to your HTML document, you have to press the back button or reload it in another browser tab. Annoying right?

We're going to use another HTML attribute to solve this. It's called the **target** attribute, and it tells our link how to open it. If you set the target attribute to equal "_blank" that opens the link in a new tab or window.

Let's add the target attribute to our link element in the HTML document. See the following screenshot on how to do this.

```
<a href="https://www.google.com/" target="_blank">
  I'm a link!
</a>
```

Remember to save the changes, and then refresh the browser window. Try the anchor tag out again. You'll notice that it opens in a new tab.

This is a great example of what attributes do; they help out. Depending on the tag, attributes are not always required, or often have a mix of required and optional.

---

[24]code/src/2-html/1-first-web-page.html

Nesting

When an element *contains* another element, it is called a **nested** element. Nesting gives structure to your web page.

Take, for example, a bulleted list. You make a bulleted list using the HTML **unordered list** element: `<ul></ul>`. Wrapped between the opening and closing unordered list tags are the individual list items (the items you wanted bulleted). You use the HTML **list** `<li></li>` element to define these bulleted list items.

This is easier to see than to describe. In the following screenshot, you can see the opening unordered `<ul>` tag, defining the start of the unordered list. Next, come the individual list items. Closing the unordered list is the closing `</ul>` tag.

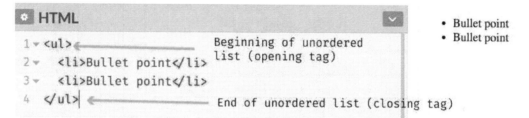

The `<li></li>` elements are *nested inside* of the `<ul></ul>` element.

If you want a numbered list, you use the **ordered list** `<ol></ol>` element. The `<li></li>` elements are then *nested inside* of the `<ol></ol>` element.

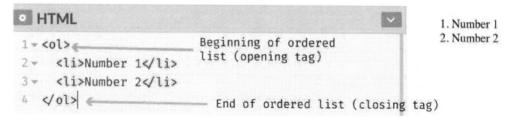

Child and Parent

When an element is nested inside of another element, it is referred to as a child. The parent is the element it is nested inside of.

The following are not real elements but should help clarify the relationship.

```
⚙ HTML
1 ▾ <parent>
2 ▾     <child>
3       </child>
4   </parent>
```

Here is another example, but this time with real HTML elements. Notice that one of the paragraph ‹p›‹/p› elements is both a child and parent? I have circled in pink elements that are parents and in blue where they are children. If an element is both a parent and a child, they are circled in purple.

```
⚙ HTML                                    ▾
1 ▾ <h1>I am a parent <em>I am a child</em></h1>
2
3 ▾ <div>
4 ▾     <p>I am a child</p>
5 ▾     <p>I am a child and parent<b> I am a child</b></p>
6   </div>
```

I am a parent *I am a child*

I am a child

I am a child and parent **I am a child**

KEY

☐ parent

☐ child

☐ parent and child

Framing elements' relationships to one-another as child and parent helps conceptualize the HTML structure as the nesting grows more complex.

For example, a parent element can have many children. The children of this parent now have a sibling relationship. Usually, programmers don't take it much farther than parent-child, but you could refer to an element as being a grandparent. However, that's about as far as you'll want to take the family tree terminology.

The following example does not use real elements, but hopefully, the fake element names help you better understand the relationship.

```
1 ▾ <grandparent>
2 ▾    <parent>
3 ▾       <child #1>
4          </child>          Siblings
5 ▾       <child #2>
6          </child>
7       </parent>
8  </grandparent>
```

Last In First Out (LIFO)

Nesting gets complicated quickly. It can be hard to keep track of where your matching closing tag should go. A tip to keep track of what tag closes what opening tag is to remember **Last In First Out (LIFO)**. For a paragraph tag that has a bolded word inside it, the bold tag is last in, so it would also be first out.

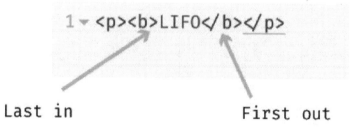

```
1 ▾ <p><b>LIFO</b></p>
```

Last in   First out

Indentations

In all of the HTML examples, the nested elements have used a system of indentations. Indentations make the HTML easier to read.

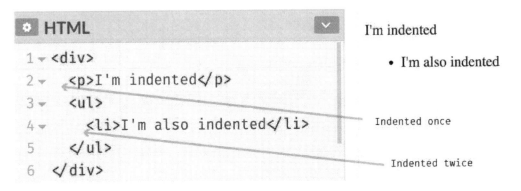

Indentations are optional; the browser can read the HTML file with no indentations. The browser can even read the page if all the HTML is squeezed into one line.

To a browser, the following two HTML snippets display the same thing.

One Line of HTML

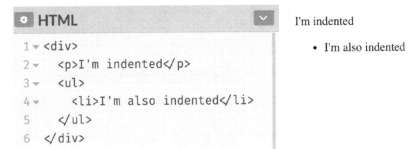

Same HTML but with Indentations

Which one is easier to read? If you're normal, then the second one should be your answer.

> A common saying in Web Development is: you will read code more than you will write it.

A good programmer is one that makes their code readable. Without proper indentation, HTML becomes unreadable, and you'll soon find yourself without any programming friends or an employer.

The specifics of how you indent may vary, such as the number of spaces you use for each tab, but as long as you stay consistent, you should be well on your way to writing readable HTML.

Exercise 5 of 8: Uncomment Examples Part IV

1. Let's play with the nesting, child-parent, and indentation concepts we introduced in the previous sections. In your text editor, open the 2-html/1-first-web-page.html [25] document if you don't already have it open.

2. Uncomment snippet #9. This HTML snippet needs some indentations to make it more readable. Look at the screenshot for how to do this. Go ahead and add the indentations and then see how it looks in the browser.

Use the Tab key

To make an indentation use the **tab** key. If you find yourself using spaces, you're doing it wrong. For two indentations, hit the tab key twice, etc. VSCode or any text editor will provide typing aids for indentations. If you'd like to learn more, here is a Stack Overflow discussion [26] providing helpful commands for VSCode. If you're using another text editor, a quick Google search will get you in the right direction.

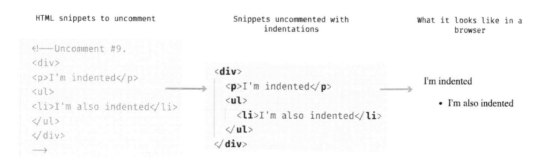

---

[25] code/src/2-html/1-first-web-page.html
[26] https://stackoverflow.com/questions/9012055/indentation-shortcuts-in-visual-studio

3. Let's add another bullet point. This bullet point is going to be a child element of the unordered list element.

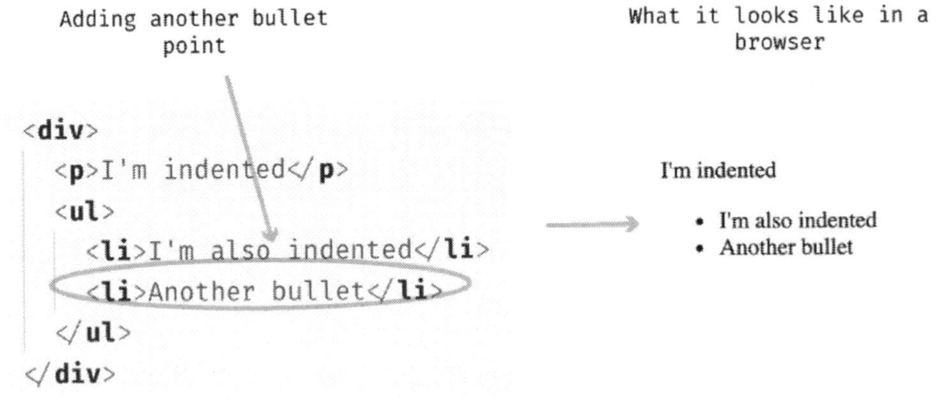

```
        Adding another bullet                    What it looks like in a
                point                                     browser

<div>
  <p>I'm indented</p>                            I'm indented
  <ul>
    <li>I'm also indented</li>                       • I'm also indented
    <li>Another bullet</li>                          • Another bullet
  </ul>
</div>
```

4. Let's make a word in one of the bullet points bold. The bold element will be nested inside the list element. See the following screenshot for how to do this.

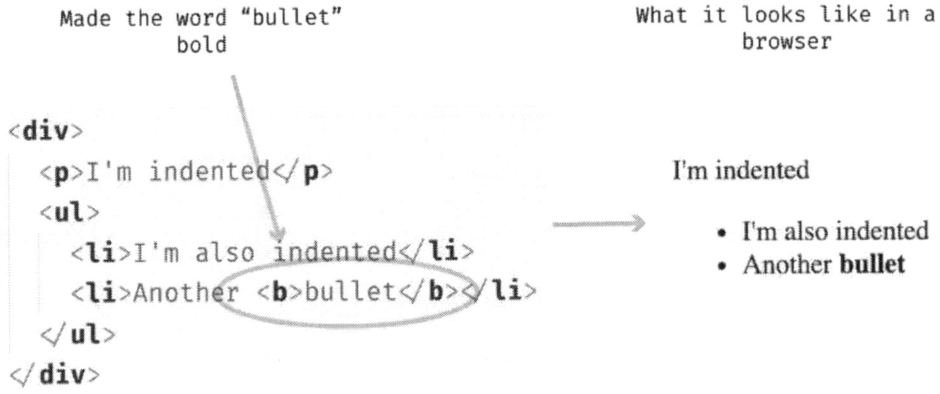

```
        Made the word "bullet"                    What it looks like in a
                bold                                      browser

<div>
  <p>I'm indented</p>                            I'm indented
  <ul>
    <li>I'm also indented</li>                       • I'm also indented
    <li>Another <b>bullet</b></li>                   • Another bullet
  </ul>
</div>
```

That wraps up our practice with the "1-first-web-page.html" document. Feel free to close both the HTML file in your text editor and browser window.

HTML in practice

We have covered the basics of HTML. We are now ready to look at the HTML of a web page.

Exercise 6 of 8: HTML in the browser

1. We are going to revisit the "first website" we looked at in the beginning of this chapter.

Open the first website[27] in a browser window.

2. Open the browser's DevTools (command + alt + j).

3. Navigate to the Elements panel in the DevTools. It's likely that when you open the DevTools, by default, you'll be on the "Console" panel. The Elements panel is just to the left of the Console panel.

---

[27]http://info.cern.ch/hypertext/WWW/TheProject.html

4. Under the Element's section is the HTML of the web page.

Some of the elements should look familiar, such as the heading1, anchor, and paragraph elements. I highlighted these elements in pink in the following screenshot.

 By default, the Elements tab will hide content if it's too long. For example, the content in the paragraph element is collapsed/hidden. To expand the element so you can see the full content click on the black right arrow next to the ‹p› tag.

5. A convenient feature in the DevTools is that when you're in the Elements tab, and you hover over elements, it will highlight the actual elements on the web page.

In the following screenshot, I am using my mouse to hover over the heading1 element, and Chrome is highlighting where that element is on the web page.

```
<html>
    <head></head>
...▼<body> == $0
    ▶<header>...</header>
      <h1>World Wide Web</h1>
```

I point this out, as I think it's valuable to spend a quick minute playing with this feature. Seeing the highlights as they correspond to the HTML element can be helpful when you're trying to make sense of everything you're seeing. Try it out!

6. If you're curious, below is a description of the other HTML elements on the web page. We haven't covered these elements, and though you'll eventually need to get familiar with them, they are not required for our purposes.

- The `<html></html>` element tells the browser that everything between the opening and closing tags are other HTML elements. This is why the HTML tag is referred to as the "root" of the HTML document.
- The `<head></head>` element generally contains elements that link to other resources the page is using. This web page is so simple it does not have any other resources it's using.
- The `<body></body>` element contains all the contents of the HTML document. Think of the body element as containing all the visible elements of the web page.
- The `<header></header>` element contains all elements that are involved in the introductory content of your website [28].
- The `<title></title>` [29] element tells the browser what to call the document. This is important because this is what search engines return when listing the document in the results. You can see from the following screenshot that when

---

[28] The nested `<nextid>` tag is no longer in use. It formerly served as a way to automatically create names for anchor tags.

[29] You may have to expand the header element to see the title element on the DevTools. You can do this by clicking on the right caret icon.

you search for "the first website," Google returns the text inside the title tag. The text inside the title element (pink box on the right) is the same as what Google gives the result's name (pink box on the left).

Exercise 7 of 8: Playing with the HTML

Now that we have a sense of the relationship between the web page and the HTML that we see in the Elements panel, we are going to use the Elements panel to make changes to the HTML.

1. Make sure you are on the same Elements panel we had open for the last Exercise.

2. In the Elements panel, double-click on the text inside the `<h1></h1>` element, and change the text from "World Wide Web" to "Your First Website." To see the change take effect, click outside of the Elements panel.

Now look at the web page and see that the text inside the `<h1></h1>` element has changed.

Your First Website

The WorldWideWeb (W3) is a wide-area hypermedia information retrieval initiative aiming to

Everything there is online about W3 is linked directly or indirectly to this document, including

What's out there?
    Pointers to the world's online information, subjects , W3 servers, etc.
Help

```
⌖  ▢   |  Elements  \  Console  \  Network  \  Sources  \  Performal
<html>
    <head></head>
  ▼ <body>
      ▶ <header>...</header>
···     <h1>Your First Website</h1>  == $0
        "The WorldWideWeb (W3) is a wide-area"
        <a name="0" href="WhatIs.html">
```

It is worth stopping for a moment to appreciate what you just did: you modified a web page!

Making changes in the DevTools doesn't modify the actual HTML. You are only modifying what your browser is displaying. In other words, you won't break anything. If you refresh the page, all your changes go away.

3. Back in the Elements panel, right-click on the `<h1>Your First Website</h1>`, and select "Edit as HTML."

```
        <head></head>
      ▼ <body>
          ▶ <header>...</header>
···          <h1>Your First We┌─────────────────────┐
            "The WorldWideWeb │ Edit text           │ a"
            <a name="0" href= │ Edit as HTML        │
            hypermedia</a>    │ Delete element      │
            " information ret │ Copy            ▶   │
                              │ Hide element        │
                              └─────────────────────┘
```

4. Go ahead and start typing in some HTML. You can add whatever you'd like. I added in a paragraph element, which you can see in the following screenshot.

```
<html>
  <head></head>
▼ <body>
  ▶ <header>…</header>
    <h1>Your First Website</h1>
    <p>I am adding a paragraph element</p>|
```

Remember when typing HTML you will need a closing and opening tag. If you'd prefer to copy-paste the same HTML, here is the snippet:

```
<p>I am adding a paragraph element</p>
```

Once you add in the HTML, click out of the editing box and you'll see the changes displayed on the web page.

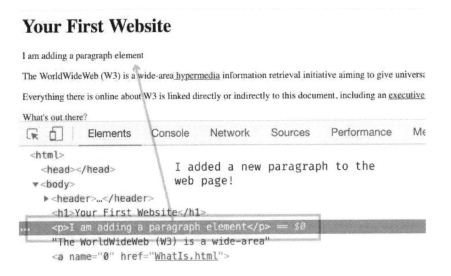

5. Continue to play around with the HTML in the Elements panel. Make changes and add or remove elements to see what happens. Whenever you want to remove all your changes, refresh the page.

The point of this Exercise was two-fold:

- First, to show you the relationship between HTML and a web page. The Elements panel is an excellent tool for demonstrating this relationship because it allows us to make changes to the HTML, which are then instantly reflected on the web page.
- Second, we got to practice writing HTML.

Hopefully, my earlier "stitching" analogy that I introduce in the Setup & Tooling chapter makes a little more sense. The Elements panel is like looking at the backside of the web page, if the web page were a stitching.

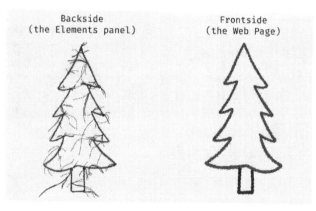

Backside
(the Elements panel)

Frontside
(the Web Page)

Web Browsers

How does the browser take HTML elements - like the following heading1 and image element - and turn them into more appealing text and porcupine image?

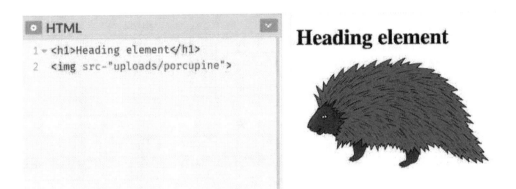

The browser does this through a process called **rendering**. The term render is used throughout programming, and in general, it merely means to display.

Granted, the details of the rendering process vary depending on the context. And in all honesty, there is a lot going on when the browser *renders* an HTML document. I will do a high-level overview of this process. But, I am going to treat the rendering process like it is a recipe for making sausages: I want to give you just enough so you have a general understanding, but I don't want to scare you off with too many details.

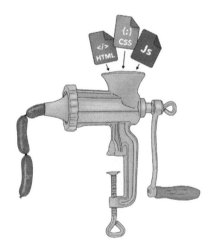

Rendering Engine

When a browser retrieves an HTML file, it uses its **rendering engine** to read the file from top to bottom. While reading the HTML file, the rendering engine **parses** the HTML. Parsing, put simply, is the browser working through the markup.

During the parsing process, the browser is checking for proper nesting structure, and loading any external resources the HTML file tells it to use.

In most web pages, the HTML document will include several ‹script› and ‹link› tags. These tags include links to external files[30] and indicate to the rendering engine that to display the web page, it will need to get these files and apply their instructions as well. We will cover some of these external file types in greater detail in the following chapters.

```
1   <head>                      Link tag to external file
2     <link rel="stylesheet" href="styles.css">
3   </head>              Script tag to external
4   <body>                       file
5     <script src="functionality.js"></script>
6   </body>
7
```

When investigating the first web page, we didn't encounter any of these external files because the first web page didn't require any additional styling, images, or functionality. However, we do run into these file types in the next chapter, so for now, take note.

Once the rendering engine is done parsing the HTML, it turns what it read into a model called the **DOM Tree**.

DOM

The Document Object Model, a.k.a. DOM (pronounced: Dom as in *Dom*inique), is the browser's completed model of what the HTML will look like. It's referred to as the

---

[30]We will cover external files in the CSS chapter.

DOM Tree because it looks like a tree diagram. Each HTML element is represented as a **node** on the diagram.

⚠ The DOM is an important concept

Get a general understanding of it now, and more difficult programming concepts will make sense faster later on. It's not the most intuitive concept, so take your time, and try and wrap your head around it.

I find that words are not enough to quite explain what a DOM tree is; it is best visualized. In the following diagram, hopefully, the connection between the HTML elements -> DOM -> web page comes through.

In the following example, the body element is the trunk of the DOM tree. Branching off of the truck, are the paragraph and heading1 elements. They are illustrated this way to demonstrate that each element is a *node*. Or, in the tree analogy, a branch.

The tree illustration should also help illustrate the elements' relationship to one another.

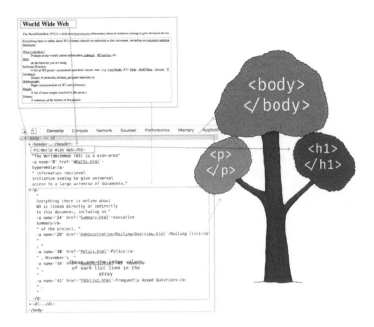

I have illustrated 3 elements as DOM nodes.

1. The body element is the truck of the tree. It is the truck because it is the topmost parent of the HTML document.
2. The paragraph is a branch coming off of the truck. It is a child of the body element. There are no additional branches off of the paragraph element, because it has no children.
3. The heading1 element is another branch. It would be considered a sibling of the paragraph element. Thus, it too is just another branch coming directly off of the truck.

Our body, paragraph, heading1 DOM Tree was pretty simple. Here is another DOM Tree that is just a little more complicated.

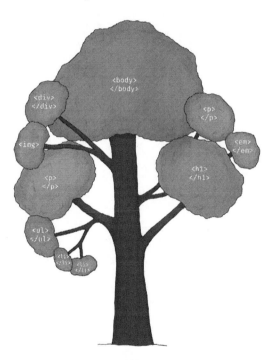

Of course, the real DOM Tree - the one the browser makes - does not look like something out of Dr. Seuss' Lorax. In fact, unless there's a resource I don't know about, I'm not sure you can *see* the DOM tree the browser produces. It's just one of those steps you need to know is happening, though you'll never actually see it.

The reason you need to know about the DOM Tree, even though you can't see it, is because the DOM Tree is what code interacts with. Later, in the JavaScript chapter, we'll use JavaScript to *do* things to the web page. Behind the scenes, the JavaScript is not interacting with the HTML, instead, it's interacting with the browser's DOM Tree. The browser *does not* let us interact with the HTML.

🔑 DOM Tree is an Abstraction of the HTML

I know this is confusing and easily lost in part because you can't see any of it. But remember, the DOM Tree is the browser's abstraction of the HTML. The browser lets us - developers - interact with the DOM Tree.

The significance of the DOM Tree will become more evident in the JavaScript chapter. But, even in this Chapter, during the last Exercises when we were modifying the web page via the Elements panel, we were modifying the DOM tree! We were *not* modifying the HTML document. That is why you can't break anything or save your changes when you're in the Elements panel. You're not playing with the actual HTML; you're playing with an abstraction of it.

Internet Not Required

It may surprise you to know that you don't need the internet to load a web page. The browser can do all the rendering and DOM Tree creation without a connection to the internet.

The reason you are connected to the internet when browsing web pages is that HTML files are generally stored in places on the internet, thus requiring the browser to use the internet to retrieve them.

Exercise 8 of 8: First Web Page without the internet

1. We're going to use our `2-html/1-first-web-page.html`[31] document for this Exercise, the one we've been uncommenting snippets in. Make sure this document is opened in a browser, and that it's loading just fine.

2. Turn the internet connection on your computer off.

---

[31]code/src/2-html/1-first-web-page.html

3. Now refresh the 1-first-web-page.html document in the browser. You should still see it, no problem.

Try out another web page, like say Google[32]; you should not be able to load or use Google. The browser needs HTML documents to load Google, and those HTML documents live somewhere on the internet. The browser can't access the internet, so you can't access Google.

Key Takeaways

- A **web page is an HTML document**.
- **HTML is a markup language**. Markup languages define rules on how to structure and format a document.
- HTML rules use a system of **tags** and **elements**.

```
1    // Tag example:
2    <p>
3    // Element example:
4    <p>hey there!</p>
```

- **Attributes** are a part of the HTML language. They are often optional and go inside an HTML tag. They provide additional information. For example, the href attribute provides the URL for the anchor element.

```
1    // Attribute example:
2    <a href="www.newline.co">Link</a>
```

- **Nesting** is a pattern that gives the HTML file structure.

---

[32]https://www.google.com/

```
1    // Nesting example:
2    <p><b>nested bold word</b></p>
```

- **Parent and Child** are terms used to help clarify the hierarchy of nested elements.

```
1    // Example:
2    <parent><child /></parent>
```

- **Indentations** make HTML human readable.
- You can use the DevTool's Elements panel to make changes to the web page (not to the HTML but to the DOM Tree).
- A **browser renders an HTML document** by parsing and creating a DOM Tree.
- The **DOM Tree** is the browser's model of a parsed HTML file. The DOM Tree is an abstraction of the HTML file, allowing us to modify and play with it via the browser.

Considerations for Further Study

Even though HTML is the foundational language of the web, Web Developers do not spend their days writing HTML. Why this is will become more apparent in later chapters.

Regardless, HTML is a language you will need to understand in much greater detail than we have covered here. I hope this chapter got you excited to learn more about HTML. Maybe it even inspired you to open the Elements panel on other websites and to start poking around.

HTML is a fun language to learn. It's relatively quick to pick up and opens a lot of doors for you to start creating things.

Further Readings

All of HTML Elements are listed online with very clear definitions and helpful examples. The best resource I've found for looking up an HTML element is W3Schools' HTML Element Reference[33]. When you are working through any HTML learning

---
[33]https://www.w3schools.com/tags/default.asp

material, focus on the concepts. If you find yourself trying to memorize which elements mean what, you're wasting your time.

For a deeper dive into HTML, I recommend MDN web docs' on HTML[34]. From here, if any topics continue to evade you, you can dig further either via books or other web resources.

If you want to learn more about how to use the DevTools, focusing on HTML and the DOM, I recommend DevTools for Beginners: Getting Started with HTML and the DOM[35]. This web page lives on the developers.google.com website; a valuable resource for anyone working with the Chrome DevTools. There is a lot here, and any time spent learning about how to use the DevTools is time well spent.

What's Next?

In the next chapter, we'll be learning about CSS, another markup language. But this time, instead of focusing on structure, we'll be focusing on style.

---

[34]https://developer.mozilla.org/en-US/docs/Web/HTML
[35]https://developers.google.com/web/tools/chrome-devtools/beginners/html

Chapter 3: Using CSS to add Style

In the previous chapter, we introduced you to HTML. You learned some basic syntax and walked away with a rough understanding of what a web page is.

Admittedly, all the examples in that chapter didn't look very good. They were rather dull, with no color or unique font. In this chapter, we are going to change that.

Here we are going to introduce you to **CSS**. CSS works hand-in-hand with HTML to give your web page "style."

This chapter is an overview of CSS, covering some of the more essential concepts, and reviewing basic syntax.

What is CSS

Cascading Style Sheets, better known as **CSS**, is a stylesheet language.

You may be asking yourself, why two different languages: HTML *and* CSS? Without getting into the history of it all, the simple answer to that question is: each has a role. Where HTML defines the structure, CSS gives the structure *style*.

Style includes things like **color**, **font**, **size**, **layout**, and **position**. Need to make a paragraph blue? HTML defines the paragraph, and CSS makes the paragraph blue.

Our First Introduction to CSS

The best way to get familiar with CSS is to play around with it. I've created some HTML files we can play with.

Exercise 1 of 6: HTML & CSS in one file

1. In the code that comes with this book, open the following HTML file with your text editor: `3-adding-style/1-html-css.html`[36]

2. Once open, you should see HTML that looks like the following screenshot. I've added the pink circle to show the area where we are going to be adding CSS.

---

[36]code/src/3-adding-style/1-html-css.html

```
HTML                                                        ▼
 1  <!DOCTYPE html>
 2▼ <html>
 3▼   <head>
 4▼     <title>Page Title</title>
 5▼     <style>
 6▼        /* put your css here */
 7        </style>
 8      </head>
 9▼   <body>
10▼     <h1>Teddy the Porcupine likes Corn on the Cob</h1>
11▼     <p>"Teddy Bear" the Porcupine gets a cob of corn for a
    treat.  Try and take it away from him and he complains</p>
12▼     <iframe
13          width="560"
14          height="315"
15          src="https://www.youtube.com/embed/UGz8jcbJjRw"
16          frameborder="0"
17          allow="accelerometer; autoplay; encrypted-media;
    gyroscope; picture-in-picture"
18          allowfullscreen>
19        </iframe>
20      </body>
21  </html>
```

3. Next, open the file in a browser window. Watch the porcupine video; it's well worth it.

4. Right now the file doesn't have any CSS on it. We are going to change that.

We're going to use the CSS code below to add some style. Either copy and paste the following CSS into the area where it says /* put your css here */, or type it in.

You can copy the CSS from the file 3-adding-style/2-html-css-final.html[37] if you'd rather not type it in (row 6-18).

 When you put this code in the HTML file, the code goes **in-between** the opening <style> and closing </style> tags.

In the following screenshot, I have highlighted in a pink box the CSS that we are adding in, replacing the /* put your css here */.

---

[37] code/src/3-adding-style/2-html-css-final.html

```
<style>
    /* put your css here */
</style>

3 ▾   <head>
4 ▾     <title>Page Title</title>
5 ▾       <style>
6 ▾         h1 {
7             color: darkcyan;
8             text-align: center;
9         }
10 ▾        p {
11            color: blueviolet;
12            font-style: italic;
13            text-align: center;
14        }
15 ▾        #video-holder {
16            display: flex;
17            justify-content: center;
18        }
19        </style>
20      </head>
```

5. Once you've added the CSS above to the HTML file, **save the file**, switch to your browser, and refresh the page.

6. Don't be too concerned with the semantics of the CSS itself; focus on what the CSS does. In the screenshot, I added pink boxes around the chunks of CSS to help show what CSS is affecting what HTML element.

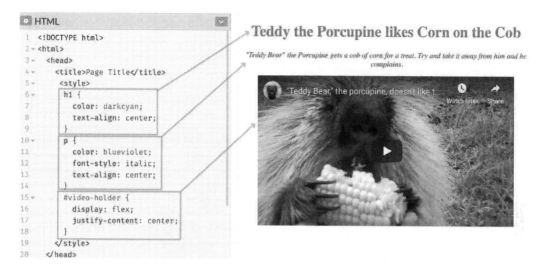

Notice how the header is now a darkcyan, and the paragraph text is now blueviolet? All of the content is also centered. That was all done via CSS. We didn't change the HTML at all.

7. Now let's try modifying some of the CSS. We'll keep it simple.

In your text editor, change the heading color from darkcyan to blue. Also, try changing the paragraph from center to right.

After making the changes, press save in your text editor and refresh your browser window.

Your style changes and web page should now look something like the following:

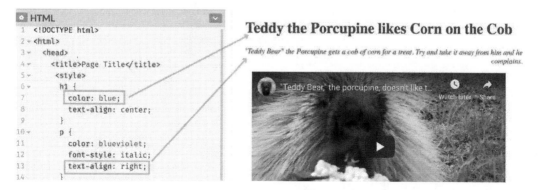

Notice the header color changed to blue and the paragraph text is now aligned right?

We'll learn more about how CSS is doing this and specifics about the syntax, but give yourself a pat on the back, you've just written CSS!

CSS via the DevTools

Next, we are going to look at CSS in the DevTools. The DevTools is an interface to play with CSS and HTML in real-time.

Exercise 2 of 6: Looking at CSS in the DevTools

1. Go back to your "Teddy the Porcupine" page in a browser window. In case you closed the previous file, here it is again: `3-adding-style/1-html-css.html`[38]

> Make sure you're using the previous `1-html-css.html` that you added style information to. If you don't have styles added to that file, go ahead and use the `3-adding-style/2-html-css-final.html`[39] instead.

2. Open the DevTools (`command + alt + j`). By default, you will be taken to the "Console" panel. To the left of the Console, click on the "Elements" panel.

---

[38]code/src/3-adding-style/1-html-css.html
[39]code/src/3-adding-style/2-html-css-final.html

Right away, you'll notice a lot is happening in the Elements panel. For our purposes, we will be focusing only on a couple of elements and styles. Don't get overwhelmed or feel like you need to understand everything you see here.

3. In addition to the Elements panel, you should also see a **Styles pane**[40] - to the right of the Elements panel view.

In the following screenshot, I've highlighted with a pink box where the Styles pane is.

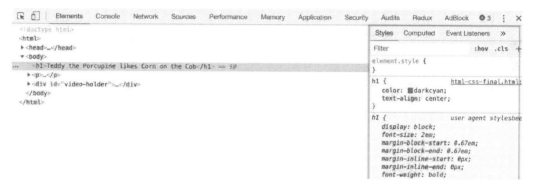

The Styles pane is where you can add CSS to HTML. It is also where you can find any CSS already applied to the HTML.

For example, if I select the heading1 element in the Elements panel, and then look over in the Styles pane, I can see all the CSS being applied to that heading1 element.

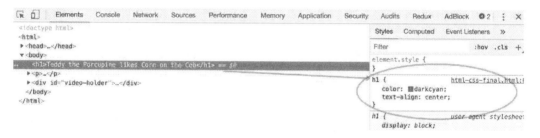

 To select any element in the Elements panel, click on the element with your mouse. The element will become highlighted in blue when you have it selected.

[40]https://developers.google.com/web/tools/chrome-devtools/inspect-styles/edit-styles

4. Go ahead and select the paragraph element. Then find the style being applied to it in the Styles pane.

Your Elements panel should look something like the following:

5. Look over at the Styles Pane. There is a link just to the right of the paragraph's styles. The following screenshot highlights the link in a pink box.

The link highlighted in the screenshot links to a stylesheet. The browser is reading that stylesheet and figuring out what styles should be applied to the web page.

That might sound a little confusing as I haven't explained what a "stylesheet" is. In short, a stylesheet is where the style (a.k.a., CSS) is set.

Let's see what I mean. Click on the link in the Styles pane. Once you click, you'll be taken to the **Sources panel**.

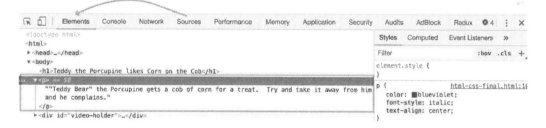

Notice that all the style you had inserted on the HTML file is shown (I've highlighted it with a pink box). Pretty cool right?!

6. The Sources panel is just what the name indicates; it holds the source files for what makes up your web page.

When we clicked on the link to the stylesheet, the DevTools took us to the "source" of that CSS; which in this case is 1-html-file.html on rows 6-18.

7. Next, navigate back to the Elements panel. Select the paragraph element again.

Then in the Styles pane, change the color from blueviolet to orange. Also, change the font-style from italic to normal.

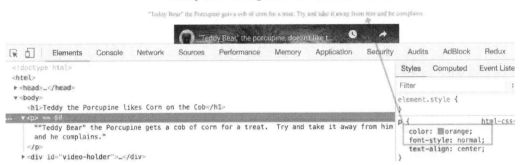

8. How great is that, you changed the style via the Styles pane! The Styles pane is one of my favorite features of the DevTools. The more you play with it, the more fun you'll find you can have with it.

 You haven't modified any of the CSS files, just your preview. In other words, none of these changes are saved.

9. For the last step, let's try *adding* a CSS property.

We are going to add something called **padding**. Padding is a very common CSS property. Padding uses units to add space around an element.

In the following drawing, the porcupine has 10px of padding around it.

We are going to be a bit more dramatic than our porcupine drawing. We are going to add *100px* of padding, and we're going to add it around the porcupine video on our web page.

To do this, in the Elements panel, select the element holding the porcupine video. Look for the `<div>` with the id of "video-holder."

Once selected, double-click in the Styles pane under the `#video-holder` and type to add `padding-top:100px;` as shown in the following screenshot.

Now look back at the porcupine video. Can you see that the space between the paragraph and the video got larger?

It got larger because there is now 100px of padding between the video and the paragraph.

We'll talk later about what `px` means later on, but for now, know that it's a unit that describes space.

CSS Syntax

We have worked through several CSS examples, but I have yet to show you how to write CSS.

CSS syntax is relatively straightforward, and you may have even picked up on the basics through some of the previous examples. The three key components of writing CSS are **Selector**, **Property**, and **Value**.

Selector

A **Selector** is what points to the HTML element. In the previous screenshot, p is the selector. This selector points to *all* paragraph elements on the page. Thus, p { color: blue; } is telling us that all paragraph elements should be the color blue.

Selectors are an important part of CSS Syntax. We will revisit them in more detail later.

Property

A **Property** tells the browser what style you want to add. Is it *color*, *font-style*, or *alignment*?

There are a lot of CSS properties. As you work with CSS, you'll naturally memorize some of them, but there will always be some you have to refer back to documentation about.

A great place to search for information about CSS properties is the Mozilla CSS Reference[41] (a.k.a., MDN web docs).

---

[41]https://developer.mozilla.org/en-US/docs/Web/CSS/Reference

Value

A **Value** tells the browser by *how much*, *what color*, or the *allowed value* you want to apply to that property. In the examples we've seen so far, this would include things like right, orange, and 100px.

Here's an example of a value and property from when we changed the padding around our porcupine video.

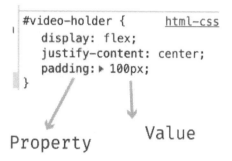

Selector Specificity

A **Selector** is what points to the HTML element, and **Specificity** is just a fancy way of saying *specific*. The more specific a selector is the higher its priority. You use different types of selectors to indicate how specific you want to be.

```
#video-holder {          html-css
    display: flex;
    justify-content: center;
    padding: ▸ 100px;
}
```

Selector that targets the
element holding the video

 What's easier to say, "toy boat" or "selector specificity" three times fast? Try it out. I can say neither.

Different types of Selectors

There are three different types of selectors: Tag, Class, and Id.

We've already seen the Tag and Id Selectors. The third selector - Class - we haven't seen. I've added the Class selector to the following screenshot.

```
<style>
  h1 {
    color: blue;                          →  Tag Selector
    text-align: center;
  }
  p {
    color: blueviolet;
    font-style: italic;
    text-align: right;
  }
  #video-holder {                         →  Id Selector
    display: flex;
    justify-content: center;
  }
  .some-className {                       →  Class Selector
    color: coral;
  }
</style>
```

Specificity comes into play because there is a pecking order between the 3 selectors. The Id selector is the most specific (#1), the Tag selector the least specific (#3), and the Class selector is in-between (#2).

The reason it's important to know what selector is relatively more specific is that the more specific selector trumps the less specific selectors.

Thus, if I set a paragraph to blue using the tag selector, but also set the same paragraph to hotpink using the Id selector, the paragraph will be hotpink, not blue.

```html
<style>
    #paragraph-id {
        color: hotpink;
    }
    p {
        color: blueviolet;
    }
</style>
</head>
    <p id="paragraph-id">What color am I?
</p>
```

To better understand the selector hierarchy, I am going to use an analogy and refer back to it as I walk through each selector's definition.

Analogy

Imagine you have a room full of friends, half identify as female, and one of your female friends is named Max.

Tag Selector

When you assign CSS by a Tag selector, you are assigning CSS to *any* HTML tag of that type. For example, we used the paragraph tag to apply a color to it.

```
⚙ HTML                                                                      ⌄
 9          }
10 ⌄      p {
11            color: blueviolet;
12            font-style: italic;
13            text-align: right;
14          }
15 ⌄      #video-holder {
16            display: flex;
17            justify-content: center;
18          }
19 ⌄      .some-className {
20            color: pink;
21          }
22        </style>
23      </head>
24 ⌄    <body>
25 ⌄      <h1>Teddy the Porcupine likes Corn on the Cob</h1>
26 ⌄      <p>"Teddy Bear" the Porcupine gets a cob of corn for a treat.  Try and take it away
     from him and he complains.</p>
```

> Referring back to the friends' analogy, a Tag selector would be like saying, OK all my "friends," raise your hands. It's not very specific, so everyone in the room raises their hands.

Class Selector

A Class Selector is when you use an HTML element's **class** name to select it.

A class is another type of **attribute**. Remember our attributes discussion in the previous chapter? Attributes live inside the element tag and provide additional information about that element.

The great thing about the class attribute is we can use it to give a class name to multiple elements. Say, for example, we wanted a paragraph *and* header element to both have a coral color. Using the class attribute, we would give both elements the same class name.

In the following example, I have given the heading1 and paragraph elements the same class name: "some-className." I then under styles, assigned the "some-className" a color of coral.

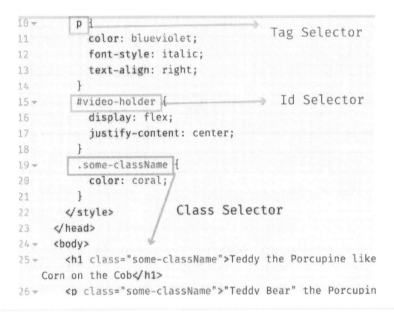

By using the class selector, we avoided having to assign a color value to both the heading1 and paragraph tag. Instead, we were able to do it with one CSS selector.

To use a class selector, you use a dot `.` + `className`.

```
10 ▾          p {                              ————————→   Tag Selector
11              color: blueviolet;
12              font-style: italic;
13              text-align: right;
14            }
15 ▾          #video-holder {   ————————→   Id Selector
16              display: flex;
17              justify-content: center;
18            }
19 ▾          .some-className {
20              color: coral;
21            }
22          </style>                  /   Class Selector
23        </head>                     /
24 ▾      <body>                     /
25 ▾        <h1 class="some-className">Teddy the Porcupine like
          Corn on the Cob</h1>
26 ▾        <p class="some-className">"Teddy Bear" the Porcupin
```

Referring back to the friends' analogy, a class selector is a little more specific than "friends," so it would be like saying, OK everyone who identifies as female jump up and down. Now you have everyone raising their hands, but only the females jumping up and down while also raising their hands.

Id selector

Ids are also another type of HTML attribute. However, Id attributes, unlike class attributes, have to have a unique value.

You can give multiple HTML tags the same class name, but if you use an Id CSS Selector, the Id's value can only be used once on the HTML document.

To select an element by its Id, you use the pound # + idName syntax. See the following example.

```
10 ▾        p {                          ──────────────▸   Tag Selector
11              color: blueviolet;
12              font-style: italic;
13              text-align: right;
14          }
15 ▾        #video-holder {              ──────────────▸   Id Selector
16              display: flex;
17              justify-content: center;
18          }
19 ▾        some-className {             ──────────────▸   Class Selector
20              color: coral;
21          }
22      </style>
23    </head>
24 ▾  <body>
25 ▸      <h1 class="some-className">↔</h1>
26 ▸      <p class="some-className">↔</p>
27 ▾      <div id="video-holder">
```

Referring back to the friends' analogy, an Id selector is the most specific selector, and it has to be unique, much like a person's name is unique. Assigning style based on an Id selector would be like saying, "Hey Max, just *you*, I want you to sing while you jump." Now you have everyone raising their hands, but only the females jumping, and poor Max jumping and singing.

Exercise 3 of 6: Selector Specificity

To get more comfortable with Selector Specificity, let's revisit our Porcupine HTML document, but this time I've added a couple more paragraph elements, along with class names, and an Id.

1. In the code that comes with this book, open the following with your text editor: `3-adding-style/3-html-css-selector.html`[42]

2. Notice that in the HTML document, there are:

- 6 paragraph elements
- 2 paragraph elements with the class name "true"
- 1 paragraph element with the Id of "answer"

The following screenshot shows the HTML next to what the HTML looks like on a browser window. On the left side, I've highlighted in blue the paragraph tags, in pink the class names that equal "true," and the Id in green.

Teddy the Porcupine likes Corn on the Cob

"Teddy Bear" the Porcupine gets a cob of corn for a treat. Try and take it away from him and he complains.

Which one of the following statements is true?

A. Porcupines are excellent swimmers

B. Porcupines can throw their quills

C. Porcupines can climb trees

Answer: A and C

There are two types of Porcupines, New and Old World. Old World Porcupines that live in Southern Europe, Asia, and Africa are good swimmers, but poor climbers. New World Porcupines that live North America are good climbers and poor swimmers.

---

[42]code/src/3-adding-style/3-html-css-selector.html

3. Let's add CSS, focusing on Selector Specificity, to make changes to all six paragraphs, the elements with the class name of "true," and the element with id of "answer."

Add the following CSS inside the style tags where it says /* put your css here */.

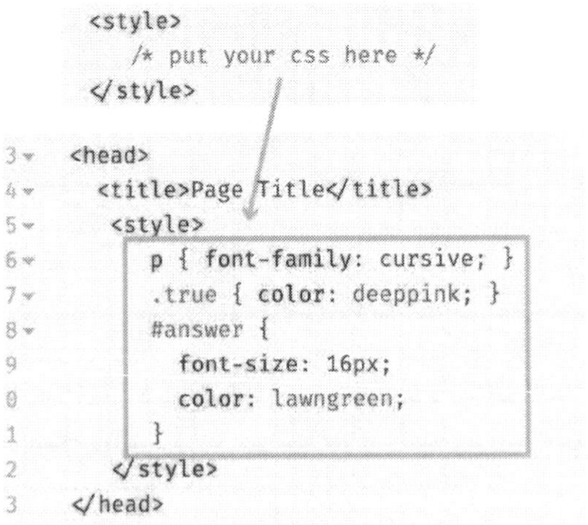

```
<style>
    /* put your css here */
</style>

3 ▾    <head>
4 ▾      <title>Page Title</title>
5 ▾        <style>
6 ▾          p { font-family: cursive; }
7 ▾          .true { color: deeppink; }
8 ▾          #answer {
9              font-size: 16px;
0              color: lawngreen;
1            }
2        </style>
3      </head>
```

If you'd like to copy-paste this CSS, you can copy it from the:

`3-adding-style/4-html-css-selector-final.html` file, rows 6-11.

4. When you put this CSS in the HTML file, press **save** and open the file in a browser. You should see the following rendered HTML (the screenshot shows the HTML next to what it looks like in a web browser).

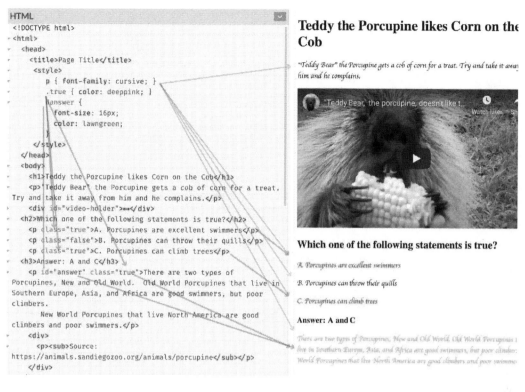

The CSS changed the following:

- All the paragraphs' font changed to cursive. See the blue arrows on the screenshot.
- Any element with the class of true changed to the color deeppink. See the pink arrows on the screenshot.
- The paragraph with the Id of answer did not change to deeppink. The Id is the most specific selector, so it trumps the class selector. It's color changed to lawngreen. See the green arrows on the screenshot.

My screenshot looks a bit like a laser show, but my hope is the arrows help you see how different selectors changed different HTML elements. Additionally, you can see that the Id selector trumped the class selector's color choice.

Color Values

Some CSS properties require a color value. For these CSS properties, we've just been writing out color names, such as deeppink. But naming a color is not the only color value CSS properties can accept. Below are some of the more common color values.

Color Value	Description
blue	**Color Name**. This is what we have been using in our examples. The browser pre defines these.
#0000FF;	**Hexadecimal Colors**. These are specified with #RRGGBB, RR = red, GG = green, and BB = blue. All values are between 00 and FF. #0000FF is blue because the last two digits are set to the highest value, FF.
rgb(0,0,255)	**RGB**. Similar to hex, the values read rgb(red, green, blue). The color's intensity can vary by an integer between 0-255. rgb(0,0,255) is blue because the third value - blue - is set to the highest number.
rgba(0,0,255,0.5)	**RGBA**. Exactly like RGB but with an added alpha42 value that specifies the opacity. rgba(0,0,255,0.5) would be blue set at opacity 50%.

In this table you'll see the color value on the left-hand side, and the color as it appears on the right-hand side.

Color Value	Description
color: blue	Howdy!
color: #0000FF;	Howdy!
color: rgb(0,0,255)	Howdy!
color: rgba(0,0,255,0.5)	Howdy!

Units

The pixel unit type px is one we've used several times. A px is a **Unit** that CSS properties use when describing the size of something. Any CSS property that deals with size takes px. But px is just one of the many units CSS properties accept.

Unit Value	Description
px	Pixels are relative to the view device. In general, pixels measure out to be 1 px = 1/96th of an inch.
pt	Points. Traditionally used in print media. 1 pt = 1/72 of an inch.
em	em is a scalable unit. You define a base, and then use that as a reference point. Say 1em is equal to the current font size then 2em would be double the current font size. They are popular on the web because they are 'mobile friendly.'
%	Percent. An example might be 50%. These are also scalable and relative to a base.

In most cases, these units are set to be equal to each other such that: 16px = 12pt = 1em = 100%. Let's apply these to the following text:

font-size: value	Example
font-size: 16px	Howdy!
font-size: 12pt	Howdy!
font-size: 1em	Howdy!
font-size: 100%	Howdy!

Now let's see what happens when we use the same number for each unit type. Notice how much larger em is than 5%? You can't even see 5%, and 5em is huge.

font-size: value	Example
font-size: 5px	Howdy!
font-size: 5pt	Howdy!
font-size: 5em	# Howdy!
font-size: 5%	

Exercise 4 of 6: Using the DevTools to play with colors and units

To get more familiar with color values and units, we are going to be using the DevTool's Style pane to make changes to our previous Porcupine HTML document.

1. Open the previously complete `3-adding-style/4-html-css-selector-final.html`[43] in a browser window.

2. Open the DevTools. In the Elements Panel, click on the paragraph with `id=answer` to select it.

Notice under the Styles pane, the `font-size: 16px` and the `color: lawngreen`. We are going to change that.

---

[43]code/src/3-adding-style/4-html-css-selector-final.html

3. Double-click on the font size and change it to 1em, and then 2em. Watch the font size change pretty dramatically. Remember em is a scalable unit, so a change from 1 to 2 makes a big difference. Try changing it to something like 50%, or 20pt, and see what happens. Play around.

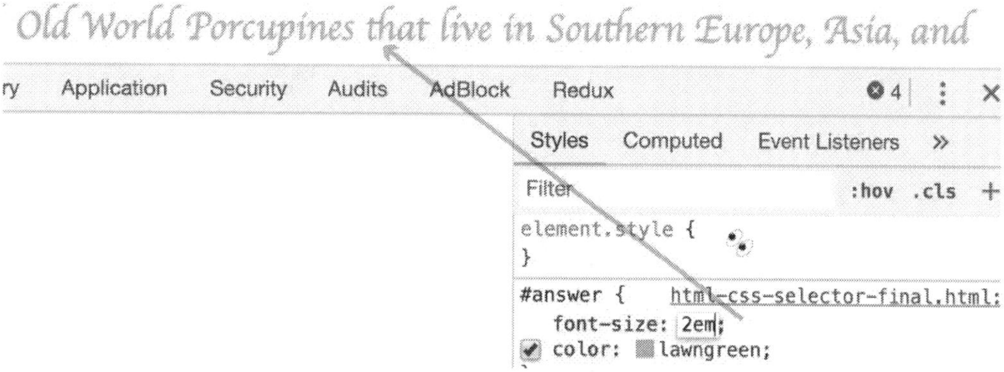

4. Next, double-click on the color lawngreen, and change it from lawngreen to #0000FF. That changes the color to blue.

But what if you wanted to make the blue somewhat transparent? Use the RGBA color unit, and set the last value to the level of transparency you'd like. In the following screenshot, I've changed it to transparency 0.5 or 50% of its regular color rgba(0,0,255,0.5).

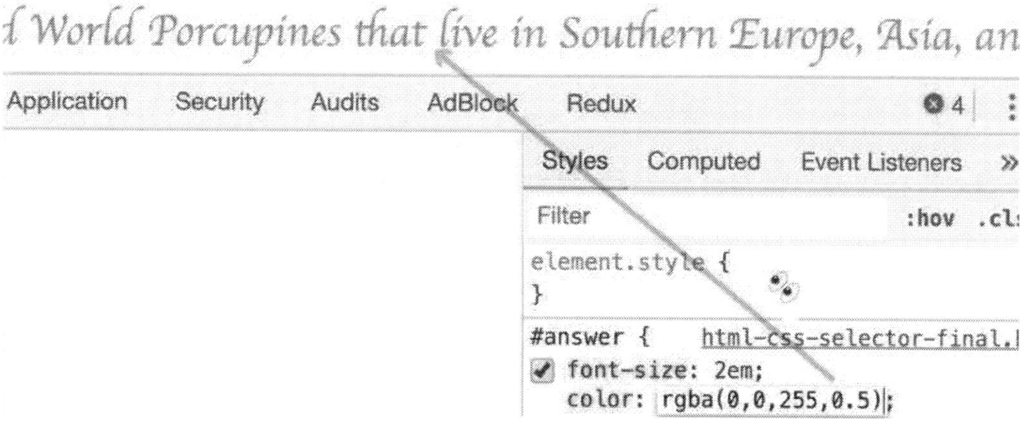

5. Now let's play with the DevTools' Color Picker. Click once on the color in the Styles pane, and the color picker will come up. You can slide the rulers to change

colors or click inside the color palette to choose colors.

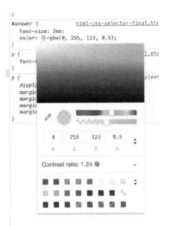

6. If you click on the ↕ you can select any of the color value types. This tool is super handy and fun to play around with.

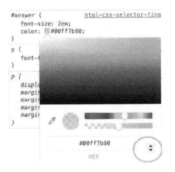

How do you add CSS to a web page?

There are three basic ways of adding CSS to your web page. So far we've only explored one of them. We've been adding CSS directly onto the HTML document, inside a `<style></style>` element.

```
<head>
   <title>Page Title</title>
   <style>
      p { font-family: cursive; }
      .true { color: deeppink; }
      #answer {
         font-size: 16px;
         color: lawngreen;
      }
   </style>        Internal Style
</head>
```

This approach is called **Internal Stylesheet**, but it's just one of the three ways you can add CSS to an HTML document.

We will cover each of these in more detail, but in summary, the three ways to add style to an HTML document are as follows:

1. External stylesheet
2. Internal stylesheet
3. Inline style

1. External stylesheet

If you add CSS via an External stylesheet you are telling the browser to find another file, and use that file to define the styles. You do this by adding a `<link>` element with an `href` attribute pointing to an external CSS file.

The browser looks for external stylesheets inside the `<link>` element[44]. If it comes across the link element with reference to a CSS file, the browser knows to import the CSS file and use it.

In the following example, the `<link>` element is telling the browser: use the file called "external-stylesheet.css" to apply style to this document.

[44]The browser is also expecting that the link element is nested inside the head element. The basic structure of an HTML page can be found here.

```
🔲 HTML
1 ▾ <head>
2      <link rel="stylesheet" type="text/css" href="./external-
    stylesheet.css">
3    </head>
```
link to external stylesheet

Exercise 5 of 6: Make an External CSS file

Our previous Porcupine HTML file has been using an internal stylesheet. In this exercise, we're going to change that to an external stylesheet.

1. Open `3-adding-style/4-html-css-selector-final.html`[45] in your text editor.

2. Copy and remove (`command + x`) all the style between the style tag.

```
<head>
    <title>Page Title</title>
    <style>
        p { font-family: cursive; }
        .true { color: deeppink; }
        #answer {
            font-size: 16px;
            color: lawngreen;
        }
    </style>
</head>                          Copy and remove
<body>
```

3. Now that we have all of our style removed from our HTML document, we are going to make a new file called `external-stylesheet.css`.

Open a new file in your text editor and paste all the previously copied style into it. **Save** the file and name it `external-stylesheet.css`.

Notice the `.css` file ending. That tells the editor and browser that this is a CSS file.

---

[45]code/src/3-adding-style/4-html-css-selector-final.html

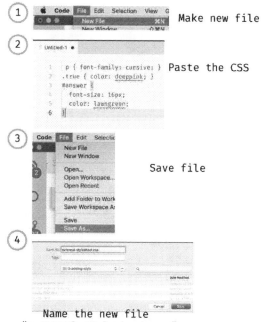

1 Make new file

2 Paste the CSS

3 Save file

4 Name the new file
"external-stylesheet.css"

If you'd like to see an example file, you can here:

3-adding-style/external-stylesheet.css[46]

4. Go back to the HTML file, and inside the `<head></head>` element add a `<link>` element with the following information:

---

[46]code/src/3-adding-style/external-stylesheet.css

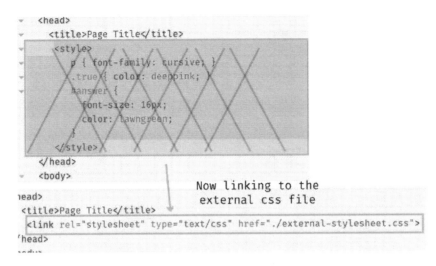

In the previous screenshot, the pink box with the multiple *X*s over it is the style you removed and have now replaced with the `<link>` element below it.

If you'd like to copy-paste the link tag, you can find it on the

`3-adding-style/external-stylesheet-final.html`[47]

5. Save the updated HTML file.

Go back to your Finder, and open the file in a browser window. As long as you've opened the HTML file in the same folder as the `external-stylesheet.css` file, you will see the CSS applied even though we've removed it from the HTML file.

 Summary

To summarize, you removed the previous style on the HTML page and moved it to its own CSS file. You then linked to that new CSS file in the HTML document. Thus, successfully adding style to a web page via an External stylesheet.

2. Internal stylesheet

Another way to add CSS to an HTML file is within the `<style></style>` element. This is an approach we are familiar with as we've been using this for all our earlier

---

[47]code/src/3-adding-style/5-external-stylesheet-final.html

examples.

The following is a refresher from our earlier `4-html-css-selector-final` example.

```
<head>
    <title>Page Title</title>
    <style>
        p { font-family: cursive; }
        .true { color: deeppink; }
        #answer {
            font-size: 16px;
            color: lawngreen;
        }
    </style>          Internal Style
</head>
```

Whether you are adding CSS via an **External stylesheet** or **Internal stylesheet**, the syntax is the same. You wrap the CSS in curly braces {}, i.e., a **declaration block**. And inside the declaration block, you list the **Property** followed by a colon : and then the **Value**. Each property : value statement ends with a semicolon.

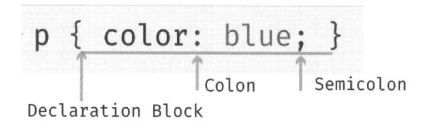

3. Inline style

The third way to add CSS to HTML is via **Inline style**. Inline style adds CSS directly inside any HTML element[48]. To do this, you use the `style` attribute on the HTML element you want to add style to.

---

[48]I say "any" because technically that's true, but you generally only find inline styles added to elements that show content.

```
⚙ HTML                                          ☑    I am a blue paragraph
1 ▾ <body>
2 ▾   <p style="color:blue">I am a blue paragraph</p>
3   </body>
```

There are some small syntax differences between adding Inline style vs. the other methods. Unlike External or Internal stylesheets, Inline styles are surrounded in quotations after the `style` attribute, and there is no declaration block. See the example below.

```
<p style="color:blue">I am a blue paragraph</p>
```
↖ style attribute   ↖ Quotations, no
                           declaration block

Exercise 6 of 6: Playing with Inline style

Let's revisit our Porcupine HTML document that uses an External stylesheet. We'll be adding some Inline style, and looking at what happens when we have conflicting styles.

1. Open `3-adding-style/5-external-stylesheet-final.html`[49] in a text editor.

Right now this file references an External stylesheet, which is making the paragraph with the `id=answer` the color lawngreen. We are going to change that by using Inline styles.

2. In your text editor, add the following Inline style to the `<p id="answer" class="true">`.

```
15 ▾   <p id="answer" class="true" style="color:salmon">There are two
    types of Porcupines, New and Old World.  Old World Porcupines that
    live in  Southern Europe, Asia, and Africa are good swimmers, but poor
    climbers.
16       New World Porcupines that live North America are good climbers
    and poor swimmers </p>
```

There are two types of Porcupines, New and Old World. Old World Porcupines that live in Southern Europe, Asia, and Africa are good swimmers, but poor climbers. New World Porcupines that live North America are good climbers and poor swimmers.

3. Save your file and open it in a browser window. Notice that the paragraph with the `id=answer` is now the color of salmon.

---
[49]code/src/3-adding-style/5-external-stylesheet-final.html

A couple of things to note:

- Inline style trumped the color lawngreen even though that color was being set using the most specific selector, the Id #answer.
- Inline style trumped External and Internally set styles, which is why the paragraph changed colors.

4. To better see what happened, let's investigate our salmon colored paragraph in the Styles pane.

Open the DevTools and select `<p id="answer" class="true" style="color:salmon;">`.

5. Look over at the Styles pane. Notice the `color:lawngreen` and `color:deeppink` are crossed out? That means they were "trumped" by the salmon color.

The order for this particular element's coloring went as follows:

.true {   extern
  ☑ color: ▇deeppin 🚫   Set by class selector on
}   External Stylesheet

#answer {   external-stylesheet
  font-size: 16px;
  color: ▇lawngreen 🚫   Set by ID selector on
}   External Stylesheet

element.style {
  color: ▇salmon;   ☞   Set by an Inline Style
}

If you'd like a final version of the HTML file with the Inline style already added, you can find it here: `3-adding-style/6-html-css-inline-style-final.html`[50]

When should I use External, Internal, or Inline styles?

You may be asking yourself why you *need* three different ways to add CSS to an HTML document, why not just have one?

There are several answers to this question. But, the one I think is most relevant to a beginner is: using an External stylesheet means **all your web pages can use the same stylesheet**. Compare this to a situation where you add the same `p {color: blue; }` to each html file in your website. That's potential for a lot of duplication.

By using External stylesheets, you're able to **reuse** the same CSS file across multiple HTML files.

Key Takeaways

- CSS is a stylesheet language that applies style to HTML elements.
- There are three CSS selectors: **Tag**, **Class**, and **Id**.

```
1    // Tag example:
2    p {color: blue;}
3    // Class example:
4    .className {color: blue;}
5    // Id example:
6    #idName {color: blue;}
```

- All CSS has a **selector**, **property** and a **value**.

---

[50]code/src/3-adding-style/6-html-css-inline-style-final.html

```
1  // Selector example:
2  `p`
3  // Property example:
4  `color`
5  // Value example:
6  `blue`
```

- There are several unit types and color values that CSS properties accept.

```
1  // Unit examples:
2  px, %, em, pt
3  // Color values examples:
4  blue, #0000ff, rgb(0,0,255)
```

- If you write CSS on an External or Internal stylesheet, you need to use a declaration box.

```
1  { padding-top: 10px }
```

- When writing Inline styles, you need to use the `style` attribute. Additionally, you surround the property and value with quotation marks.

```
1  <p style="padding-top:10px"></p>
```

- There are **3 ways to add CSS** to a web page.

```
1  // 1. External stylesheet by linking to the file via the link tag:
2  <link href="./external-stylesheet.css">
3  // 2. Internal stylesheet in the HTML style element:
4  <style></style>
5  // 3. Inline style using the style attribute inside an HTML tag.
6  <p style="color: blue">I am blue paragraph</p>
```

- You can use the DevTools to manipulate styles on a web page.

Considerations for Further Study

CSS cannot adequately be covered in one chapter of a book. I have done my best to summarize key concepts and ideas. If you continue in Web Development, regardless of which path you choose, CSS is a foundational language and one with which you should be reasonably familiar.

In addition to CSS syntax, which was what we mostly focused on in this chapter, you'll want to get familiar with *how* CSS is applied. The browser works through a series of steps when reading CSS, and it does this via the Cascading Mechanism (the "C" is CSS). Understanding, even broadly, how the Cascading Mechanism works will help you later down the road problem solve any CSS conflicts or bugs.

No matter what article or tutorial you choose to learn more about CSS, make sure to **stay in the DevTools!** A lot of CSS tutorials do all their exercises in a controlled, simple environment where you work with one HTML file and one CSS file. The real world, however, couldn't be farther from that 1-2-page truth. The reason we spent time in the DevTools is that when you are working with CSS - in the real world - you'll spend a lot of time there.

Further Readings

A great starting place to refresh some of the content learned here and get a little deeper into CSS syntax is MDN web docs' on CSS[51].

MDN's Web Docs[52] have an excellent overview of the Cascading Mechanism. If you'd like to get more in-depth, and subsequently be more challenged, I recommend both the article and video on How Browsers Works[53] by HTML5rocks. I wouldn't expect even experienced Web Developers to understand all the concepts in this article, but they are very interesting and enlightening.

I did not talk about the CSS Box Model, even though it's a topic often discussed in introductions to CSS. MDN Web Docs have a section on the Box Model[54], but I also like this article about the Box Model in the web series "HTML & CSS IS HARD."[55]

I did not spend any time discussing how CSS manages layout, but it's a central CSS concept. One website I still use often to learn about the various CSS tricks, specifically those involved in layout, is a website aptly named CSS-TRICKS[56].

---

[51]https://developer.mozilla.org/en-US/docs/Web/CSS
[52]https://developer.mozilla.org/en-US/docs/Learn/CSS/Introduction_to_CSS/Cascade_and_inheritance
[53]https://www.html5rocks.com/en/tutorials/internals/howbrowserswork/
[54]https://developer.mozilla.org/en-US/docs/Web/CSS/CSS_Box_Model/Introduction_to_the_CSS_box_model
[55]https://internetingishard.com/html-and-css/css-box-model/
[56]https://css-tricks.com/

In addition to the websites I've listed above, I would suggest taking an online course or reading a book on CSS. It doesn't have to be anything too intensive, just something that walks you through some of the more critical properties, and applications.

What's Next?

In the next chapter, we'll move away from Markup languages, and cover our first Programming Language, JavaScript.

As you'll come to learn, JavaScript is everywhere. JavaScript completes the trio of core Web Development Languages: HTML, CSS, and JavaScript.

Chapter 4: JavaScript

HTML gives the web structure. CSS provides that structure with style. **JavaScript makes that structure _interactive_**.

To give you a better sense of what I mean by "interactive," we are going to play with JavaScript using HTML examples that have JavaScript already on them.

 JavaScript is a Programming Language

JavaScript is a Programming Language, unlike HTML and CSS, which are markup languages. We will learn more about Programming Languages in the Programming Languages Chapter.

Exercise 1 of 12: What does "interactive" look like?

1. In the code that comes with this book, open the following HTML file in a web browser: `4-javascript/js-example-1.html`[57].

Once open you should see a web page that looks something like the following:

---

[57]code/src/4-javascript/js-example-1.html

Go turtle Go!

JavaScript is causing the following two images to race each other.

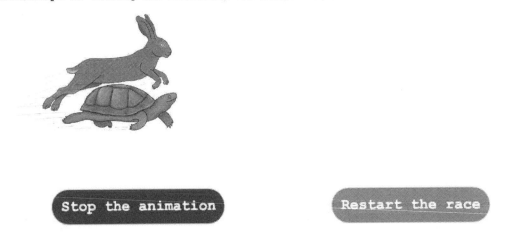

Stop the animation   Restart the race

2. The rabbit and turtle will start racing right away. Play around with stopping and restarting the animation.

3. The "racing," "stopping" and "restarting" the race, is done through JavaScript. This is an example of what interactivity looks like.

If you are curious and would like to look at the JavaScript causing this interactivity, in your text editor, navigate to row 61 on the js-example-1.html file. Row 61 is where the JavaScript code starts.

 Don't let the code overwhelm you. I simply want to point out where it lives on the HTML file. By no means do I expect you to understand it.

In this chapter, I will introduce you to some core JavaScript concepts. During this process, you should start to understand - even if only generally - how JavaScript affects your interactions/experience with web pages.

Why are we Focusing on JavaScript?

No matter what kind of programmer you decide to become, JavaScript is a language that you will need to know. The most recent statistics show that JavaScript is used by about **95% of all websites**[58].

JavaScript is *everywhere* and because your browser can read and process the JavaScript language, anyone with access to a web browser can, in theory, program in JavaScript.

Sometimes to appreciate something, you have to lose it. We're going to take that approach with JavaScript; we're going to interact with the web *without* JavaScript. Hopefully, this Exercise will show you just how much of your day-to-day interactions with the web rely on JavaScript.

Exercise 2 of 12: The Web without JavaScript

1. In your Chrome settings there is an option to disable JavaScript, here is a quick link[59] to get there.

2. Toggle off JavaScript.

3. Get ready to miss JavaScript.

Toggle the JavaScript option in Chrome on and off. Then, compare before and after versions of various websites. Try Twitter, YouTube, or try searching for something on Google.

---

[58]https://en.wikipedia.org/wiki/JavaScript
[59]chrome://settings/content/javascript?search=javaScript

Here is what Twitter looks like without JavaScript enabled; ugly and hard to use.

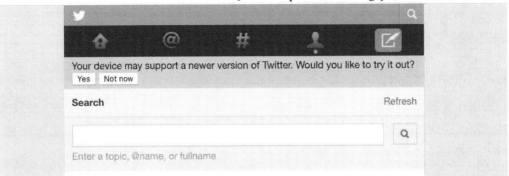

4. Don't forget to turn JavaScript back on. You may need to close and open your browser again for JavaScript to be reapplied.

Did you miss it? I sure did. The web isn't the same without JavaScript.

JavaScript Basics

There is no way we could reasonably teach you all you need to know about JavaScript in just one chapter. Instead, I am using this chapter to introduce you to some core JavaScript concepts.

We will cover the following topics:

- JavaScript in the Console
- JavaScript Comments
- HTML Element Selectors
- Event listeners
- Arrays
- Objects

JavaScript in the Console

All major web browsers come shipped with JavaScript[60]. Without getting into too many details, what this means is that the browser can *read* and *run* the JavaScript language[61].

For us, this also means that we can type JavaScript directly into the browser's DevTools Console and it will read and run JavaScript on the fly.

Exercise 3 of 12: JavaScript in the Console

1. In a browser, open the `4-javascript/js-example-1.html`[62] file we used Exercise #1.

Next, open the DevTools.

2. Navigate to the **Console**. You'll find this panel just to the **right** of the Elements panel.

3. The **Console** is a panel in the DevTools where Chrome executes commands that you type there. The Console is not unique to Chrome. All major browsers have one.

4. Go ahead and type or copy-paste the following commands into the Console. Once added, press **enter** to execute the command.

---

[60]https://www.enable-javascript.com/
[61]https://en.wikipedia.org/wiki/JavaScript_engine
[62]code/src/4-javascript/js-example-1.html

Type what follows ›

In the following screenshots, you will see the word undefined. This is what the browser returns after declaring a variable. You should be typing what follows the greater than › symbol. The browser's response will come after the follows the less than ‹ symbol.

For the following command, go ahead and replace Angel with your name.

```
> var name = "Angel"
‹ undefined
> name
‹ "Angel"
> |
```

5. The next couple of commands perform simple calculations. Go ahead and type these in the Console as well.

```
> var number = 2+2
‹ undefined
> number
‹ 4
> number * 100
‹ 400
> var smallerNumber = number / 2;
‹ undefined
> smallerNumber
‹ 2
> |
```

6. Next, we'll trigger a prompt message (a window that opens up asking you to fill something in). To do this, type the prompt command into the Console with a message.

```
> prompt("this is fun")
```

Now enter a response in the prompt that pops up and click "OK." Look back in the Console. You should see your response.

Go turtle Go!

JavaScript is causing the following two images to ra

This page says

this is fun

Sure is!

Cancel   OK

| Elements | Console | Network | Sources |

top   ▼   ◉   Filter   Default levels ▼

☐ Hide network   ☐ Log XMLHttpRequests
☐ Preserve log   ☑ Eager evaluation
☐ Selected context only   ☑ Autocomplete from history
☑ Group similar

Console was cleared
← undefined
> prompt("this is fun")
>

The above Exercises are designed to get you familiar with playing with JavaScript in the Console. Don't get caught up on the syntax; get comfortable with executing JavaScript in the Console.

Console command: console.log()

We will be using the command `console.log()`. It is a command provided by the browser, and prints messages inside of the Console panel (this is how error and warning messages find their way into the Console).

The console.log() command is very helpful and often used by developers when they are trying to figure out how to debug something. We will use this command later in the book, so I want to introduce you to it here.

Exercise 4 of 12: console.log()

1. In the Console, type `console.log("howdy")` and then hit **enter**. The `console.log()` command printed whatever you put inside the parentheses following it.

```
>  console.log("howdy!")
   howdy!
<- undefined
```

2. Now let's use the `console.log()` command inside the JavaScript code on our HTML file. Open the `4-javascript/js-example-1.html`[63] file in your text editor (if you don't already have it open).

3. On row 62, below the `<script>` tag, hit enter to add a new line. On the new line, add `console.log("howdy!");`. Your HTML file should now look like this:

```
61        <script>
62            console.log("howdy!");
63            // Everything Between the Scrip
64            // You do not need to understan
```

4. Press save in your text editor, switch back to your browser, and refresh the browser window showing that file. Look at the Console. You should see the "howdy!" message printed there.

```
  howdy!                                           js-example-1.html:62
>
```

Pretty cool right? We typed a message in our HTML file - written between the opening and closing `<script>` tags - that then printed to the Console. It may not seem like it right now, but the `console.log()` method is very handy.

---

[63]code/src/4-javascript/js-example-1.html

Console command: clear()

Another useful Console command is `clear()`. This command *clears* out whatever may already be in the Console. Sometimes when you open the Console on a website, there are messages already in there. This clears the messages out.

In the following screenshot, I've cleared out Console error messages that showed up when I opened the Console on the Google web page.

Before executing clear()

```
⊘ GET https://clients5.google.com/pagead/drt/dn/dn.js net::ERR_BLOCKED_BY_CLIENT            clients5.google.com/:4
⊘ ▶Uncaught ReferenceError: gbar is not defined                                                      (index):6
    at onload ((index):6)
⊘ ▶GET https://adservice.google.com/adsid/google/ui net::ERR_BLOCKED_BY_CLIENT         adservice.google.com/adsid/google/ui:1
› clear()
```

After executing clear()

```
  Console was cleared                                                                                  VM389:1
‹ undefined
›
```

Exercise 5 of 12: clear()

1. Type some commands into the Console. You can take anything from the previous example, such as our `console.log("howdy!")`.

Once typed, go ahead and clear the console using the `clear()` command.

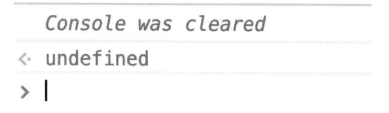

There is no harm in using the `clear()` command. Clearing messages do not affect the website or code.

Warning messages in the Console

Heads up! Sometimes you'll see warning messages. For example, Facebook's Console looks like the following screenshot. This is a good reminder that JavaScript *can be executed* from the Console, and some hackers use this to their advantage. Executing unknown or untrusted code inside the Console can be malicious. Use common sense.

JavaScript Comments

Most programming languages allow programmers to write **comments**. JavaScript is no different.

Comments are used by programmers to write helpful notes about the code. Comments are there to help the programmer writing or reading the code.

You removed HTML comments in the HTML chapter. JavaScript comments provide a similar function but are written differently.

In JavaScript, you can write **single line** or **multiline comments**.

To write a single line comment in JavaScript, you use a double forward slash `//` followed by your comment.

```
// single line comment
```

To write a multiline comment in JavaScript, you use an open and closing forward-slash (/) + asterisk (*) combination. You can add as many lines of comments as you'd like in-between.

```
/*
multiline comment
See, multiple lines of comments
Woot!
*/
```

Exercise: 6 of 12 Comments

1. Open the Console again.

2. Type or copy-paste the single line and multiline comments shown earlier into the Console.

```
> // single line comment
< undefined
> /*
  multi-line comment
  See, multiple lines of comments
  Woot!
  */
< undefined
```

3. Notice that nothing happens, but you also don't get an error. If you typed in the following - without the // you'd get an error. Without the // or /**/, the browser doesn't know that you're trying to make a comment, so it throws an error.

```
>  // single line comment
<  undefined
>  /*
   multi-line comment
   See, multiple lines of comments
   Woot!
   */
<  undefined
>  single line Comment
⊗  Uncaught SyntaxError: Unexpected identifier
```

HTML Element Selectors

For JavaScript to interact - *do* something - to HTML elements (like make our rabbit and turtle image "race"), JavaScript must first **select** the HTML element(s).

 Remember our DOM Tree discussion in the HTML chapter; The gist of which is that the DOM Tree is the browser's abstraction of the HTML. When JavaScript **selects HTML elements** it is selecting DOM Tree nodes. The browser gives us access to these DOM Tree nodes, but it does not give us access to the actual HTML.

What do I mean by select?

CSS Selectors: a refresher

Remember in the CSS Chapter, when we wanted to apply style to specific elements, we specified the element by its Tag, Class, or Id? Or what about when we wanted to tell all of our friends to raise their hands, just the females to jump, and Max to sing?

Here's a quick example refresher of CSS selectors. In the following screenshot, I am using the Tag selector `<h1>`, the Class selector `.someClassName` and the Id selector `#someUniqueId` to apply different text colors to the elements.

```
HTML
1 <h1>I am a Heading Element</h1>
2 <h3 class="someClassName">I am a Heading Element with a class name</h3>
3 <p id="someUniqueId">I am a Paragraph Element with an ID</p>

CSS
1 h1 {color: orange}        Tag Selector
2 .someClassName { color: purple }   Class Selector
3 #someUniqueId { color: red }   ID Selector
```

I am a Heading Element

I am a Heading Element with a class name

I am a Paragraph Element with an ID

JavaScript Selectors

The reason I am referring back to the CSS Selector discussion is that JavaScript selects elements in much the same way, but it uses a different syntax.

In JavaScript, you also select elements by their Tag, Class, or Id. Here is a screenshot of the same elements being selected by their Tag, Class, and Id but this time by JavaScript. I added pink arrows to show the connection of the JavaScript Selector and the HTML element.

Here CSS is changing the text color, and JavaScript is changing the background color[64].

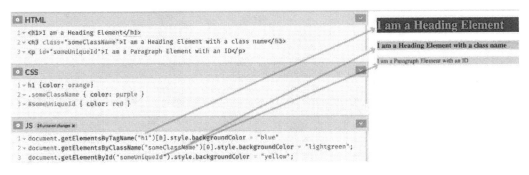

 I realize in the above example we are using JavaScript to change the *style* of an element. A job that is generally better suited for CSS. I did this to keep the example simple and visual.

Now that we've previewed JavaScript HTML Element Selectors in action, let's take a closer look at each selector type.

By Tag

The following code snippet finds all the header1 elements on the page.

To select a Tag in JavaScript, you use getElementsByTagName().

```
document.getElementsByTagName("h1");
```

By Class Name

The following code snippet finds all the elements by their class name.

```
document.getElementsByClassName("someClassName");
```

By Id

This code snippet finds the element with the Id = "someUniqueId".

---

[64]For both the .getElementsByTagName and .getElementsByClassName I had to include the index number right after the selector [0]. The reason is that this selection returns an array, and to do something to a value in that array, you have to define which item you want - in this case, it's the first item, and thus index = 0 or [0]. Don't worry yourself too much with this now, but if you caught this, I wanted to explain the reason why.

```
document.getElementById("someUniqueId");
```

Remember Ids should be unique, which is why instead of `elements` that we've seen in the two previous selectors, `element` for this selector is singular.

```
document.getElementsByTagName("h1").
document.getElementsByClassName("som
document.getElementById("someUnique]
```

JavaScript makes it pretty easy to guess what selector type to use; Wanna grab the element by its Id? Then `.getElementById()` makes sense.

- **Tag**: document.getElementsBy**TagName**();
- **Class**: document.getElementsBy**ClassName**();
- **Id**: document.getElementBy**Id**();

Don't worry yourself too much here with syntax. The point I want to stress is that **JavaScript selects HTML elements** using Tags, Class Names, and Ids.

Exercise 7 of 12: Playing with JavaScript Selectors

1. In the code that comes with this book, open the following HTML file in a web browser: 4-javascript/js-example-selector.html[65]

2. Open the same file in your text editor.

3. In your text editor, look at line 46 and 50. There are two `div` elements, both with `class="racing"`. One of the `div` elements has an `id="rabbit"` the other `div` an `id="turtle"`.

---

[65]code/src/4-javascript/js-example-selector.html

```
46     <div class="racing" id="rabbit">
47       <img src='./rabbit-change-to-svg.png' width="200px">
48     </div>
49     <!-- Adding in the turtle image.  It's an image element inside a di
50     <div class="racing" id="turtle">
51       <img src='./turtle-change-to-svg.png' width="200px">
52     </div>
```

 The id HTML attribute is lower case, which is why you see id="rabbit". When we talk about the Id Selector, we use an uppercase "I". However, when we declare and "id" as an attribute in the HTML, it needs to be all lowercase. All HTML attributes are written in lowercase.

4. Next, look at lines 70 and 71 on that same file. You'll see that I'm using the document.getElementById() selector to select both the turtle and rabbit[66].

```
69     // the style left = 0px means they are starting at (
70     document.getElementById("rabbit").style.left = "0px";
71     document.getElementById("turtle").style.left = "0px";
72
```

5. The .style.left = "0px" tells the browser to set elements to the very left of the screen. Go ahead and on line 71 (the line where I'm setting the "turtle" element to style.left), change the "0px" to "200px". This change will only affect the turtle image. Press save and refresh the browser displaying the js-example-selector.html file.

We're giving the turtle a 200px head start. Hopefully, that provides the turtle with a chance to win the race. The change in your text editor should look like this.

```
70     document.getElementById("rabbit").style.left = "0px";
71     document.getElementById("turtle").style.left = "200px";
```

If you'd like to see a final version of this file with the changes made for you, open 4-javascript/js-example-selector-final.html[67].

---

[66]I am selecting the "rabbit" and "turtle" by selecting the Ids associated with those <img /> elements.
[67]code/src/4-javascript/js-example-selector-final.html

6. Navigate back to the Console. Now, let's use the Console to select an element by its Id, then by Class, and lastly by a Tag.

Go ahead and stop the animation by clicking on the "Stop the animation" button. Then, in the Console type the following:

```
document.getElementById('rabbit')
```

After typing in the command and pressing enter, you should see:

```
> document.getElementById('rabbit')
<  ▼<div class="racing" id="rabbit" style="left: 0px;">
        <img src="./rabbit-change-to-svg.png" width="200px">
      </div>
```

The output is the return of the id='rabbit' element. The HTML element and the output in the Console are almost identical.

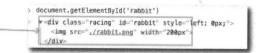

You just used JavaScript to select an element off of a web page. Pretty cool, right?

7. Now let's select all the elements with the class name of "racing."

If you look back at your text editor, you'll see two elements with class="racing". These are on rows 47 and 51. Yes, these elements also have Ids, but we can select them by their class name as well.

```
47        <div class="racing" id="rabbit">
48          <img src='./rabbit-change-to-svg.png' width="200px">
49        </div>
50        <!--div element with className of "racing"-->
51        <div class="racing" id="turtle">
52          <img src='./turtle-change-to-svg.png' width="200px">
53        </div>
54      </div>
```

In the Console type or copy-paste the following to return the elements with class="racing".

```
document.getElementsByClassName('racing')
```

Once you've entered the code snippet into the Console, you should see something like the following:

You may need to click on the sideways triangle icon in the Console to expand the output.

```
> document.getElementsByClassName('racing')
< ▾ HTMLCollection(2) [div#rabbit.racing, div#turtle.racing, rabbit: div#rabbit.racing, turtle:
    div#turtle.racing]
    ▸ 0: div#rabbit.racing
    ▸ 1: div#turtle.racing
      length: 2
    ▸ rabbit: div#rabbit.racing
    ▸ turtle: div#turtle.racing
    ▸ __proto__: HTMLCollection
```

8. Our last selector is our **Tag Selector**. As you likely already know from the HTML chapter, a div is a kind of HTML tag. We have 4 <div></div> elements in this HTML document. If you look back in your text editor, you can see all 4 div elements on lines 45-62.

I have highlighted the 4 <div></div> elements in pink in the following screenshot taken from lines 45-62 of my text editor:

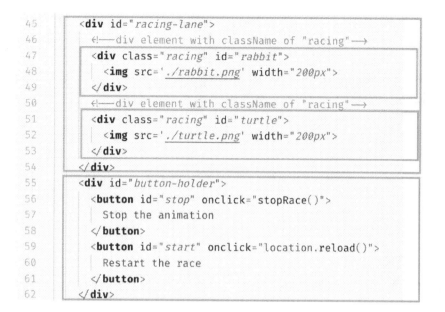

```
45   <div id="racing-lane">
46      <!--div element with className of "racing"-->
47      <div class="racing" id="rabbit">
48         <img src='./rabbit.png' width="200px">
49      </div>
50      <!--div element with className of "racing"-->
51      <div class="racing" id="turtle">
52         <img src='./turtle.png' width="200px">
53      </div>
54   </div>
55   <div id="button-holder">
56      <button id="stop" onclick="stopRace()">
57         Stop the animation
58      </button>
59      <button id="start" onclick="location.reload()">
60         Restart the race
61      </button>
62   </div>
```

Flashback to the HTML chapter: The first div element is a parent to two sibling div elements. The two sibling divs are *nested* inside this parent div. We've used *indentation* to help make the structure easier to read.

In the Console, type or copy-paste the following to grab all the div elements on the HTML document.

```
document.getElementsByTagName('div')
```

Once entered, you should see the following output:

```
>   document.getElementsByTagName('div')
<   HTMLCollection(4) [div#racing-lane, div#rabbit.racing, div#turtle.racing, div#button-holder
    ▶, racing-lane: div#racing-lane, rabbit: div#rabbit.racing, turtle: div#turtle.racing, butto
    n-holder: div#button-holder]
```

See the number 4 right after "HTMLCollection(4)"? That number is saying there are 4 elements returned. If you expand the output by clicking on the sideways triangle icon, you'll see all 4 div elements.

9. Let's do one last step before we wrap up this Exercise. **Let's return a CSS style** that is being applied to one of the elements.

As mentioned earlier, the way JavaScript is making the rabbit and turtle "race" is by changing a CSS property called left. The higher the left value, the more the image moves to the right. This is because the image is being *pushed* away from the left-side. In the following image, the rabbit is *pushed* 100px away from the left side. Thus, moving it *right*.

left: 100px

10. In the Console, type or copy-paste the following code snippet:

```
document.getElementById('rabbit').style.left
// "0px"
```

Once you hit enter, the Console will return the value of whatever the left property value is for the element with the id="rabbit".

The value returned for me is 0px. The value returned for you is likely different than mine. It all depends on how far along in the race your rabbit was when you entered the command.

If you start back up the animation and repeat that last line of JavaScript, the number returned will increase as the rabbit moves across the screen.

```
> document.getElementById('rabbit').style.left
< "40px"
> document.getElementById('rabbit').style.left
< "114px"
> document.getElementById('rabbit').style.left
< "205px"
```

The point of this last step is to show you that you can return a CSS property value using JavaScript.

Event Listeners

Another very powerful thing JavaScript allows us to do is "listen" and respond to events. In our `4-javascript/js-example-selector.html`[68] we have 2 listeners setup.

If you look at the HTML file in the browser, try and identify 2 different elements on the page that "respond" or "react" to an action, for example clicking something. Cough, cough, look at the buttons.

When you *click* on any of the 2 buttons, JavaScript responds to those clicks. JavaScript can respond because each of those buttons is set up to *listen* for a click event.

The browser is always listening to things you do on it. A little creepy, I know. But let me explain, and hopefully, you'll be more impressed than creeped out.

The browser is listening to things like mouse clicks, or whether or not you're scrolling down the page. Because the browser is listening for these types of things, when you click on something, stuff happens, and when you scroll down, the page moves. If the browser were *not* listening, your experience with the web would be rather dull and unresponsive.

JavaScript knows the browser is always listening. So JavaScript takes advantage of this and tells the browser something like,

> "Hey browser, I want to know when someone has clicked on this button. Would you let me know when that happens?"

And the browser does.

There are two main ways to set up listeners with JavaScript. The first is to utilize HTML Event Attributes, and the second is to use JavaScript Event Listeners. It's not super important you understand the specific differences between the two, but we will play with both so you can get experience using them.

---

[68]code/src/4-javascript/js-example-selector.html

Exercise 8 of 12: Event Listeners

1. Let's go back to our text editor with the previous file open. Navigate to line 56.

```
56    <button id="stop" onclick="stopRace()">
57      Stop the animation
58    </button>                          JavaScript Function
```
                 Event Attribute

This is the HTML for the "Stop the animation" button. Inside the HTML `<button></button>` element, there is an attribute called `onclick`.

The `onclick` attribute is different than other HTML attributes that we've already discussed (e.g., `style` or `src` attributes) because it is an **Event Attribute**[69]. As the name suggests, an Event Attribute is setup to *listen* to an event.

When the button is clicked, the browser knows that event happened - remember it's always listening - and it tells the `onclick` attribute about it. Once the `onclick` attribute gets word that a click event happened on its element, it fires off whatever is after `onclick` = . In this case, it fires off a JavaScript function called `stopRace`.

2. On line 56, let's add another Event Attribute. You can find a list of available Event Attributes on the W3Schools' web page[70].

Let's add the one called `onwheel`. This attribute listens for your finger moving up and down on the trackpad, or when you move your mouse wheel up or down.

Let's revisit our handy `console.log()`. On line 56 add an `onwheel` Event Attribute and have it console.log anything you want. Here I have it console logging "meep". I also have the code written in the `4-javascript/js-example-selector-final.html`[71] if you'd like to look at it already written out.

---

[69] `onclick` is an HTML attribute and not JavaScript. It is considered a best practice to avoid `onclick` or similar Event Attributes and use JavaScript Event Listeners for performance purposes. I have avoided this conversation because of this book's audience, but if you're curious, there is a good Stack Overflow discussion on the topic here.

[70] https://www.w3schools.com/tags/ref_eventattributes.asp

[71] code/src/4-javascript/js-example-selector-final.html

```
56    <button id="stop" onclick="stopRace()" onwheel="console.log('meep')">
57      Stop the animation
58    </button>
```

 You'll need to use single quotations around the item inside of the `console.log()` function. The reason is that you've already used double quotation marks, and the browser won't know which set you intend to close.

3. Save your changes and refresh your browser window - make sure you have the Console panel visible. Now, instead of clicking on the "Stop the animation" button, use either your trackpad or mouse wheel and roll it up or down over the button. Ta-da, that action console logs whatever you put inside your `console.log()` - in my example that is "meep".

The functionality will feel a bit strange; you usually don't use your mouse wheel to trigger buttons. The point is that by adding the `onwheel` Event Attribute, you just connected the action of moving your mouse wheel up or down with the JavaScript `console.log()` function. Neat!

4. Next, let's look at the second way to add Event Listeners. The second way explicitly attaches the Event Listener with JavaScript.

Again, don't worry too much about the details of *how* this works. Just focus on the interaction between the browser and JavaScript.

On the same 'js-example-selector.html' file we were looking at before, in the Console, type or copy-paste the following JavaScript:

```
function message(){ console.log("wow this is cool!") }
```

That code defines a function called **message**, which when called will print in the Console: "wow this is cool!".

After you enter this function, the message will not show in the Console because we haven't *called* on the function yet. We'll set that up in the next step.

5. Now in the same Console, right after you defined the function **message**, type or copy-paste the following:

```
document.getElementById("start").addEventListener("mousemove", message);
```

What this code snippet does is attach an **Event Listener** called **mousemove** to the Start button. The mousemove Event Listener listens for any mouse movement over the element you attach it to. The second part of this snippet, the message part, is saying,

> OK browser, *when* you detect mouse movement over the "Restart the race" button, fire off this javaScript function called **message**.

The **message** function is what we defined in the step just before this step: step 4.

6. Now move your computer mouse over the "Restart the race" button, and look at the Console when you do.

Every time you move your mouse over the button, the function **message** is fired, printing the "wow this is cool!" message to the Console. Any movement of your mouse is picked up in this listener so that message will fire a lot.

```
> function message(){ console.log("wow this is cool!") }
< undefined
> document.getElementById("start").addEventListener("mousemove", message)
< undefined
78 wow this is cool!
>
```

Refresh the page if you'd like to remove the listener.

Again, don't worry about being able to write or even fully understand these code snippets. The purpose of this Exercise is to introduce you to the concept of Event Listeners and give you a better understanding of *how* JavaScript adds functionality using them.

Arrays & Variables

I casually introduced the concept of variables; we used them in the very beginning of this chapter when we talked about JavaScript in the Console. See the following example from our earlier discussion.

```
> var name = "Angel"
< undefined
> name
< "Angel"
> |
```

Variables are a way to store information. You give the variable a name, assign it a value, and that value is stored there.

Storing one value like "Angel" as a person's name is useful, but a common need is to store *more than one* value in a variable.

In comes the concept of **Arrays**. In short, **Arrays are a variable that let you store a *list* of data**. The syntax for creating an Array is very similar to a regular variable, but you wrap the *list* in an opening and closing brackets [ ], and separate the list items by commas.

Example of an Array

```
var groceryList = ["eggs","butter","carrots","flour"];
```

To get more familiar with Arrays, and *why* and *when* you might use them, we are going to explore Arrays in a simple Console Exercise. We will then do a second Exercise using an HTML document with JavaScript added to it.

Exercise 9 of 12: Playing with Arrays Part I

1. Open up a browser window - it does not matter which web page you are on. Open the DevTools and navigate to the Console.

2. To get comfortable with Arrays, we are going to start with a very simple Array that holds a list of numbers. In the Console type, or copy-paste the following:

```
var arrayOfNumbers = [0,1,2,3,4,5];
```

Ta-da you just created an Array! All you had to do was declare a variable. Then put a *list* of things inside an opening and closing bracket. Now let's call our Array.

 I want to clarify what I mean by "call." Programmers often use the word "call" to indicate that you are executing something. You'll learn more about executing and invoking as you progress in JavaScript, but for now, think of it like when you "call" your friend. You ring them and expect that they answer. When I say "call our Array" I mean, I expect the array to answer (i.e., return).

3. In the same Console window, type arrayOfNumbers and your Array will return.

```
> var arrayOfNumbers =[0,1,2,3,4,5]
< undefined
> arrayOfNumbers
< ▶ (6) [0, 1, 2, 3, 4, 5]
```

The (6) in front of the returned Array is letting you know there are 6 list items in the Array.

4. Arrays take more than just numbers; they also take words (a.k.a., **strings**[72]). Let's make another Array, this time of strings, and numbers.

---

[72]Technically, that is not a complete definition of a **string**. To avoid introducing more terminology, I have avoided going into what a String is. If you are curious, W3Schools provides a good definition with examples.

Strings are a series of characters

Examples include "Angel," "Angel Garbarino," "enter your name here." You'll get more familiar with them, and their significance as you progress in JavaScript.

In the same Console window type or copy-paste the following:

```
var arrayOfThings = [1,"Angel",arrayOfNumbers]
```

Notice how I snuck in **arrayOfNumbers** into the list? Arrays accept Strings, numbers and even other Arrays![73]

```
> var arrayOfNumbers =[0,1,2,3,4,5]
< undefined
> arrayOfNumbers
< ▶ (6) [0, 1, 2, 3, 4, 5]
> var arrayOfThings = [1,"Angel",arrayOfNumbers]
< undefined
> arrayOfThings
< (3) [1, "Angel", Array(6)]
```

Hopefully, this short Exercise clarified that **an Array is a variable that holds a *list* of "things"**. We'll get more familiar with what we can do with Arrays in the next Exercise.

Exercise 10 of 12: Playing with Arrays Part II

1. In the code that comes with this book, open the following HTML file in a web browser: 4-javascript/js-arrays.html[74].

---

[73]Arrays accept functions as well, but because we are not covering functions here, I did not mention them. To learn more see the Mozilla Docs on Arrays

[74]code/src/4-javascript/js-arrays.html

An Array of Donuts!

The index of the selected donut

2. Play around by clicking on the buttons to add a donut, and remove a donut. All the adding and removing is done via JavaScript.

If you'd like to look at the code, I have created a simplified version of the file that should make it easier to read. Open the 4-javascript/js-arrays-simplified.html[75] in your text editor.

On lines 53-82 you'll see all the JavaScript code. We're going to use the code to help us understand Arrays. I have added comments in the code to help you *read* what it's doing. I don't expect you to understand what is happening or how you might write this yourself. Just look at the code, and read through the comments.

---

[75]code/src/4-javascript/js-arrays-simplified.html

```
53    <script>
54      // Define a donut image tag
55      var donut = '<img src="./donut1.png"/>';
56
57      // Create our initial donutArray, which will be changed by later functions
58      // and holds all of our donut img tags
59      var donutArray = [donut];
60
61      // Add a donut to our array and update our view
62      function addDonut() {
63        donutArray.push(donut);
64        updateView();
65      }
66
67      // Remove a donut from our array and update our view
68      function removeDonut() {
69        donutArray.pop();
70        updateView();
71      }
72
73      // Updates the view
74      function updateView() {
75        // This gets the "donut-holder" element and sets the HTML to our
76        // donutArray
77        document.getElementById("donut-holder").innerHTML = donutArray;
78      }
79
80      // Update our view for the first time
81      updateView();
82    </script>
```

3. The donuts you see are apart of an Array. There is a variable called "donutArray" and it is holding a "list" of donuts. See line 59.

```
57      // Create our initial donutArray, which will be changed by later functions
58      // and holds all of our donut img tags
59      var donutArray = [donut];
```

On the browser window that is displaying the "js-arrays.html" we opened in step 1, open the Console and type or copy-paste the following:

donutArray // returns the array

The Array's variable name is **donutArray**. So when we type **donutArray** and press

enter in the Console, the Array comes back. This Array's list of values are `<img />` elements. See the following screenshot:

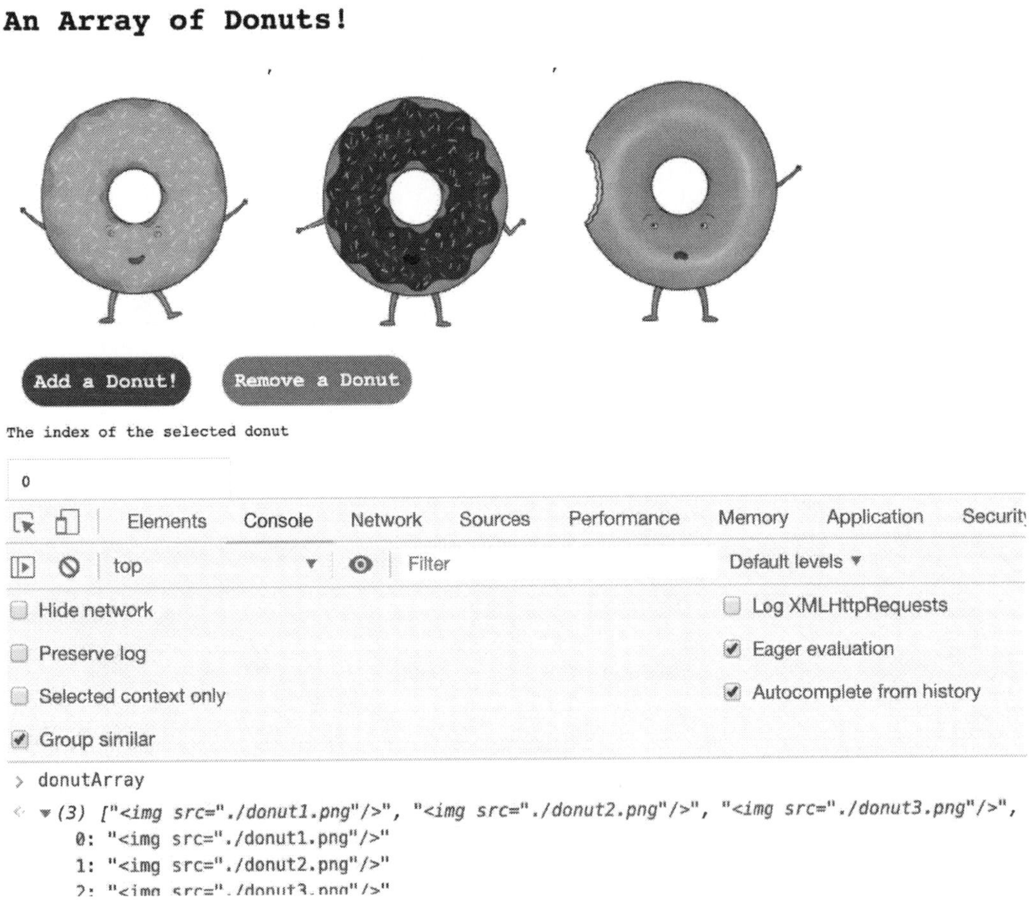

An Array of Donuts!

The index of the selected donut

```
0
```

```
>  donutArray
<  ▼ (3) ["<img src="./donut1.png"/>", "<img src="./donut2.png"/>", "<img src="./donut3.png"/>",
      0: "<img src="./donut1.png"/>"
      1: "<img src="./donut2.png"/>"
      2: "<img src="./donut3.png"/>"
```

To help you visualize this more clearly, here is what the Array would look like written in JavaScript instead of as output in the Console.

```
var donutArray = [
  '<img src="./donut1.png"/>',
  '<img src="./donut2.png"/>',
  '<img src="./donut3.png"/>'
];
```

Now, go ahead and in the same Console type the following:

```
donutArray.length
```

Adding **.length** onto the end of the Array will return the number of list items in the Array. If you type this command with just two donuts showing your result should look like the following screenshot:

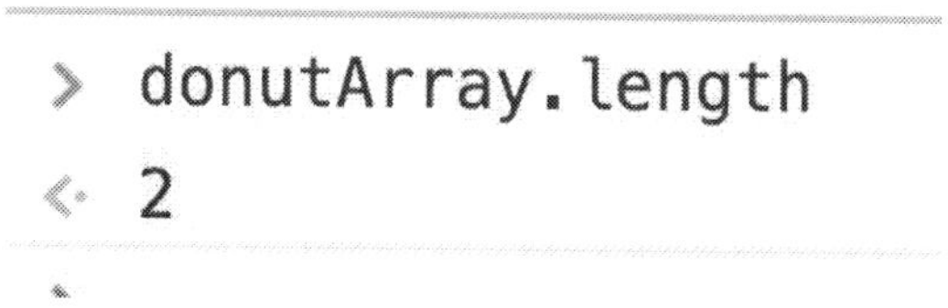

```
>  donutArray.length
<  2
```

Go ahead and add more donuts. Then type the `donutArray.length` command again in the Console. The number returned should match the number of donuts you see.

Push(): Adding a list item to an Array

When you click the "Add a Donut!" button, another donut is being added to the Array. This is done by using the JavaScript **push()** method.

4. The `push()` method is fairly simple to use. In the Console type or copy-paste the following:

```
// pushing another donut onto the donutArray
donutArray.push('<img src="./donut1.png"/>');

// returns new length of the array.
document.getElementById("donut-holder").innerHTML = donutArray;
```

The first command pushes another image onto the Array.

The second command updates the HTML element holding the `donutArray` with the newly updated Array. Once you hit enter after the second command, your extra donut will get added.

What you just did using the **push()** method is the same thing that the "Add a Donut!" button is doing.

Pop(): Removing a list item from an Array

Now let's *remove* a donut. To do this, we are going to use the JavaScript **pop()** method. The pop method *pops*-off the last item in an Array's list.

5. In your Console type or copy-paste the following:

```
// pop-off the last item in the Array
donutArray.pop();


// update the array element with one less donut
document.getElementById("donut-holder").innerHTML = donutArray;
```

The first command pops off the last element of the Array. We don't need to put anything inside pop's parenthesis () because we aren't adding anything, just saying, "pop it off".

The second command updates the HTML element holding the `donutArray` with the newly updated Array, just like we had to do with the push() method.

What you just did using the **pop()** method is the same thing that the "Remove a Donut!" button is doing.

Index

Let's say you want to remove a specific list item, not just the last list item in an Array. To do this, you need to know the item's index.

Index is a special way that Arrays keep track of items in their list. **Each item in an Array has an index.** We saw this when we typed `donutArray` in the Console. You probably didn't notice it at first, but the following screenshot should show you where the index values are.

```
> donutArray
<  ▼ (2) ["<img src="./donut1.png"/>", "<img src="./donut2.png"/>", onclick: undefined]
      0: "<img src="./donut1.png"/>"
      1: "<img src="./donut2.png"/>"
      onclick: undefined                     These are the index values
      length: 2                              of each list item in the
    ▶ __proto__: Array(0)                              array
```

The index count of an Array always starts at zero. I'm guessing that when you start counting something you start the count at 1. That is not the case for Arrays.

In fact, starting at zero is common in programming. When we typed donutArray in the Console, the first value that came back had an index of 0, and the next an index of 1. If you had 10 items in an Array, the index numbers would go from 0-9. And in our case, when we have two donuts in our Array, our index count is from 0-1.

 Why start at Zero?

Because it's more efficient, saving the work of having to add 1. If you'd like to get more mathy about it, I recommend this Stack Overflow thread[76].

Going back to our HTML file in the browser, **refresh the page first**[77]. Then, add some donuts and click on any of the donuts in the Array. As you click on the donuts, look at the value in the input field underneath: "The index of the selected donut." Whatever donut you click on, its index will show.

If I have 3 donuts, and I click on the third one in the list, the index value of 2 will show.

---

[76]https://stackoverflow.com/questions/9174533/why-do-prevailing-programming-languages-like-c-use-array-starting-from-0

[77]We have to refresh the page because we manipulated the donutArray in the Console in the previous Exercise and the code in the HTML file isn't aware of those changes. Essentially, manipulating the donutArray in the Console brakes the Index functionality we are going to play with.

An Array of Donuts!

Let's play with indexes to see how they can be helpful.

Exercise 11 of 12: Playing with Indexes

1. On the HTML file in the browser - the one we've been using with donuts on it - have a least 4 donuts showing.

 If the index functionality is not working, try refreshing js-arrays.html file in the browser window.

2. Let's use the index to remove the third donut in the Array. Because the donut is the third in the Array, it should have an index of 2.

Let's confirm this by clicking on the third donut. Then look at the value returned under "The index of the selected donut."

An Array of Donuts!

The index of the selected donut

2

3. To **remove** an item by its index, you can use the JavaScript **splice()** method. To use the splice() method, you need to tell it what index you want to start at and how many items you want to remove.

We want to start at index 2 and only remove 1 item. Type or copy-paste the following into the Console:

```
// start at index 2, and remove 1 item
donutArray.splice(2,1);


// update the Array element with one less donut
document.getElementById("donut-holder").innerHTML = donutArray;
```

The first command starts at index 2 and removes 1 item.

The second command updates the HTML element holding the Array.

4. And just like that, you've removed an Array's list item by its index! Feel free to play around. Add more donuts using the push method, and slice away more than just one donut. If you need to start over, refresh the page.

Arrays are very common and powerful in JavaScript. I have only covered a couple of the Array methods (push, pop, slice), but there are many more[78].

---

[78]https://www.w3schools.com/js/js_array_methods.asp

Objects

Objects are similar to Arrays. Technically Arrays *are* a type of Object. The main difference between Objects and Arrays is that Arrays are meant for lists that are numerically indexed.

Objects, on the other hand, are indexed with non-numeric keys. Keys are just helpful assignments to the list item; it's better to call your friend by saying, "Hey Max" instead of saying, "Hey 2nd person in the room."

To help explain this better, let's quickly look at the following list written as an Array and then written as an Object.

```
1   // AS AN ARRAY
2   var thingsInFrontOfMe = [
3     "dog sniffing something", index 0
4     "dude standing next to Max", index 1
5     "your friend Max", index 2
6   ];
7
8   // Calling on Max from the Array
9   // by the index value, which is 2
10  thingsInFrontOfMe[2]
11  // returns "your friend Max"
12
```

In this Array, we have 3 list items: a dog, a dude, and your friend Max. If you wanted to call on your friend Max, you'd have to say "Hey 2nd person in the room."

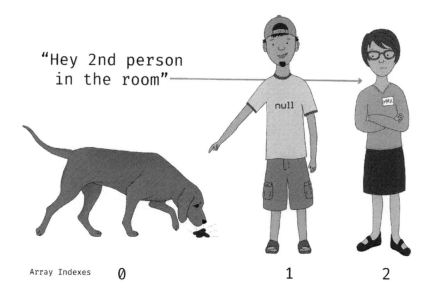

"Hey 2nd person in the room"

null

Array Indexes   0   1   2

If we wrote this same list as an Object, we'd add keys. It would look something like the following:

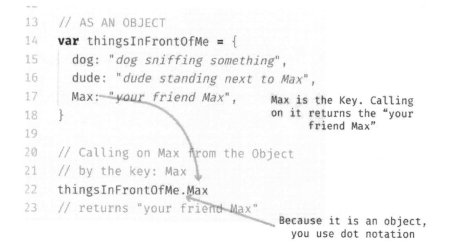

```
13    // AS AN OBJECT
14    var thingsInFrontOfMe = {
15      dog: "dog sniffing something",
16      dude: "dude standing next to Max",
17      Max: "your friend Max",              Max is the Key. Calling
18    }                                       on it returns the "your
19                                                   friend Max"
20    // Calling on Max from the Object
21    // by the key: Max
22    thingsInFrontOfMe.Max
23    // returns "your friend Max"
                                         Because it is an object,
                                          you use dot notation
```

Now, instead of calling our friend by her position in the room, we could just say "Hey Max."

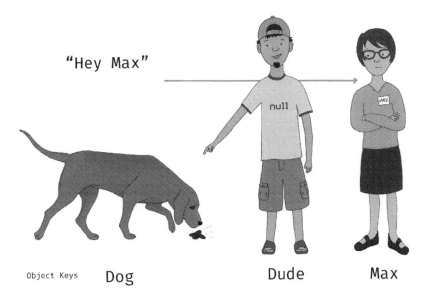

"Hey Max"

Object Keys   **Dog**   **Dude**   **Max**

Here, when we're trying to single out our friend Max, it makes sense that we want to assign a **key**. We are giving "Max" a name (a.k.a. a Key), and we use that key to call on them.

The indexes assigned to the list items in Arrays are automatically applied. The indexes are just there. You don't have to do anything to get them there.

Whereas with Objects, you get to *choose* what that assignment is. We call that assignment a **key**, and the key is assigned to a **value**. Hence the term **key: value** pair, a term often used when talking about Objects.

```
// The Key is Max
// The Value is "our friend Max"

{ Max: "our friend Max"}

// We wrapped this pair in curly braces indicating it's an Object.
```

To write an Object in JavaScript, you use a pair of curly braces { } (for an Array it was a pair of brackets [ ]).

To separate keys from values you use a colon :

To get more familiar with Objects, we are going to play with them using a similar donut example that we used for Arrays. This time, however, we will give our donuts keys.

Exercise 12 of 12: Playing with Objects

1. In the code that comes with this book, open the following HTML file in a web browser: `4-javascript/js-objects.html`[79]. Once open, open the DevTools and navigate to the Console.

2. The web page, "An Object of Donuts!" is slightly different than our Array HTML document. In this HTML document, instead of adding donuts to an Array, we are adding donuts *with names* to an Object.

To add a donut, type in a name, and then select the donut type via a dropdown. Once you click "Add Donut," your donut and name will appear.

The name represents the key, and the donut represents the value (key: value).

Imagine that you added a Strawberry donut and gave it the name "Angel," and a Chocolate donut with the name "Max," you would see something that looks like the following screenshot.

---

[79] code/src/4-javascript/js-objects.html

An Object of Donuts!

Angel   Max

Give a Name (a.k.a. KEY) to the donut

Max

Select a Donut Type

Chocolate Donut

Add Donut

This donutObject behind the scenes looks something like:

```
var donutObject = {
  Angel: "Strawberry donut image",
  Max: "Chocolate donut image",
}
```

3. We are going to return a donut using the donuts name (a.k.a., key).

After adding a couple of donuts to the Object via the "Add Donut" button, type the following in the Console to return the Object.

```
donutObject
```

The donut Object will be returned, and you should see something like the following screenshot. You will likely have to expand the Object by clicking on the sideways triangle icon (caret right icon).

```
>  donutObject
<  ▼ {Angel: "<img src="./donut1.png"/>",
      png"/>"} ℹ
         Angel: "<img src="./donut1.png"/>"
         Ivan: "<img src="./donut2.png"/>"
         Max: "<img src="./donut3.png"/>"
       ▶ __proto__: Object
```

4. The returned `donutObject` should reflect whatever type of donuts and names you assigned them.

Now, let's return a specific donut by calling on its name (a.k.a., key).

In the following, I'm calling on the key "Angel". You will replace "Angel" with whatever key you assigned one of your donuts.

`donutObject.Angel`

You should see something like the following:

```
>  donutObject.Angel
<  "<img src="./donut1.png"/>"
>
```

The practical use of Objects and "key: value" pairs may not be super obvious in our donut example. But imagine a situation where you have a large Object of peoples' contact information. You have assigned peoples name as the key, and the value is all the information about that person. It might look something like this:

```
var contactInformation = {
  Angel: {
    email: "nope@gmail.com",
    address: "north pole",
    twitter: "@angelgarbarino",
  },
  Max: {
    email: "max@gmail.com",
    address: "south pole",
    twitter: "@fullstackio",
  }
}

contactInformation.Angel.twitter;

// returns "@angelgarbarino"
```

The syntax here is a bit new, but it should start to clarify how Objects help organize data. In this example, I essentially *drilled down* into the Object, pulling the data I wanted.

There is a lot more you can do with Objects and Arrays. We've only scratched the surface.

Key Takeaways

- JavaScript adds **interactivity** to web pages.
- **JavaScript is the most popular Programming Language**, in large part because every major web browser can read and process JavaScript.
- You can execute JavaScript in the Console.
- JavaScript **Comments** allow you to annotate code to help the writer or reader. Comments only show on the code file. They do not get processed.

  // I am single line comment

  /* I am a multiline comment */

- JavaScript grabs HTML elements by using HTML Element Selectors.

  // Id selector: document.getElementById('id');

  // Class selector: document.getElementByClassName('class');

  // Tag selector: document.getElementByTagName('p');
- You can use **Event Listeners** in JavaScript to *attach* onto certain events such as a mouse click, and then run code once that event has happened.

  // Event Listener: document.getElementById("start").addEventListener("mouseclick", message));
- **Arrays** are used to store a list of data. You can access an item in the list by calling on its **index**.

  // adds another item onto the end of an Array push()

  // removes the last item of an Array pop()

  // lets you remove specific item(s) from an Array slice()
- **Objects** are also used to store data using a system of **key: value** pairs.

  // Object {Max: "my friend max"}

Considerations for Further Study

Regardless of what path you take in Web Development, you will need to know JavaScript.

There are lots of different JavaScript learning resources out there. As you're looking for more learning opportunities, make sure to get plenty of hands-on practice. You can read all day long about *how* to write JavaScript, but it won't click until you start writing it.

When first learning JavaScript, you may be lured into learning "languages" that are built off of Javascript (e.g., jQuery, React, Angular, Node, etc.). I would strongly suggest you avoid wandering at first. Stay focused on pure JavaScript. Get comfortable with JavaScript, then go out exploring.

Further Readings

My all-time favorite book(s) on JavaScript, is Kyle Simpson's "You Don't Know JS" (YDKJS) book series. There is a free PDF version online[80], but if you're a book person

---

[80]https://github.com/getify/You-Dont-Know-JS

like me, the printed versions are reasonably priced.

The YDKJS book series is more theoretical than it is practical, so that series alone will not be enough to teach you how to read and write JavaScript. Thus, in addition to the YDKJS series, I would add an online course focused on just JavaScript. There are *lots* of JavaScript learning resources out there. I am personally a fan of Frontend Master's courses[81].

To switch up the medium of reading and screen time, I would also encourage you to throw on a JavaScript podcast. It will help you get familiar with the lingo, and be involved in new trends or concerns. There are several JavaScript Podcast out there, but one of my favorites is "Js-Jabber"[82].

What's Next?

The last three chapters - HTML, CSS, and JavaScript - were dense. I fire-hosed you a little, and I apologize if you feel a bit wobbly on your feet.

The next chapter on Programming Languages is less Exercise heavy and should be a more casual read. HTML, CSS, and JavaScript are the core trio of Web Development languages. The language(s) you choose to study after mastering this trio will depend a lot on where in Web Development you want to go.

The Programming Languages chapter will focus on this discussion; introducing you to the top ten Programming Languages.

In all honesty, the Programming Languages chapter is my favorite. But, I am also a touch of a motorhead. Which, as you'll come to see why, may have influenced my penchant for the chapter.

---

[81]https://frontendmasters.com/courses/
[82]https://devchat.tv/js-jabber/124-jsj-the-origin-of-javascript-with-brendan-eich/?utm_medium=email&utm_source=javascriptweekly

Chapter 5: Intro to Programming Languages

How do you know what Programming Language to learn? Do you need to learn more than one Programming Language, and if so in what order should you learn them?

While I can't answer these questions for you, I *can* give you the resources and some guidance so you can answer those questions for yourself.

In this chapter, we will discuss the **state of Programming Languages**, which ones are the most heavily used, and what they are used for. We will look at **recent job postings for programmers**, going through the requirements to decipher what Programming Languages the job might require.

 All of the Exercises in this chapter use different websites to glean more information. Unlike the Exercises in the previous chapters, which have asked you to open HTML files or the DevTools, the Exercises in this chapter are more about introducing you to online tools. I hope to show you how to use these tools. Then, depending on your level of curiosity on the subject, you can use these tools to answer questions specific to your interests or needs.

What is a Programming Language?

Before we begin, I want to define what a Programming Language is. So far the only Programming Language we've introduced is JavaScript; HTML and CSS are both markup languages.

Put very simply, a **Programming Language is a language that is used to write a set of instructions**. These instructions are written to produce some output. A **programmer** is someone who writes these instructions[83].

---

[83]I wrote a blog article that goes into more detail on this subject. In fact, the article comes from a section I had written for this book and for the sake of brevity decided to take out. You can read it here.

You might be wondering, but aren't HTML and CSS just a set of instructions telling the browser how to build a web page? This is a natural point of confusion, while there might be some theoretical debate here; HTML and CSS are not considered "Programming Languages."

How do I know what Programming Language to learn?

You can approach this question a couple of different ways. One is to look at the most popular Programming Languages. Several helpful resources collect information about Programming Language popularity[84]. We will look at two: Stack Overflow's Developer Survey Results[85], and GitHub's Octoverse survey[86].

Most Popular Technologies

Programming, Scripting, and Markup Languages

All Respondents   Professional Developers

JavaScript	67.8%
HTML/CSS	63.5%
SQL	54.4%
Python	41.7%
Java	41.1%
Bash/Shell/PowerShell	36.6%
C#	31.0%
PHP	26.4%
C++	23.5%
TypeScript	21.2%
C	20.6%
Ruby	8.4%

Stack Overflow's Developer Survey Results: Popular Technologies

---

[84]One could also look at the TIOBE Index
[85]https://insights.stackoverflow.com/survey/2019/#technology-programming-scripting-and-markup-languages
[86]https://octoverse.github.com/projects#languages

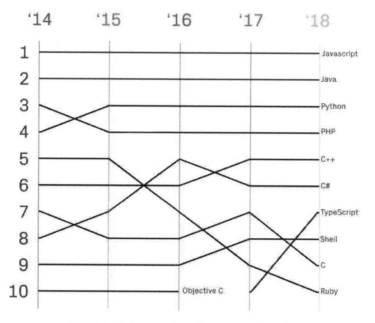

'14   '15   '16   '17   '18

1 — Javascript
2 — Java
3 — Python
4 — PHP
5 — C++
6 — C#
7 — TypeScript
8 — Shell
9 — C
10 — Objective C — Ruby

GitHub's Octoverse: Top Languages Overtime

Stack Overflow includes non-programming languages, like HTML, CSS, and SQL. Also, Stack Overflow looks at the last year, 2019 at the time of writing. GitHub looks at the last 4 years and *only* includes Programming Languages.

You can see some patterns between the Stack Overflow and Octoverse charts. The most obvious is that JavaScript is at the top of each list. This shouldn't be a surprise after learning about JavaScript in the previous chapter.

Java and **Python** are also growing in popularity. Python, in particular, has gotten lots of buzz recently[87].

Ruby's popularity seems to be going down, and the new kid on the block is something called **TypeScript**.

To get an even better picture of what's happening, let's use Google Trends, which tracks Google searches. In Google Trends, you can define the search term, period, and location. We will play around with these options, investigating and comparing different programming languages in the next exercise.

---

[87]https://stackoverflow.blog/2017/09/06/incredible-growth-python/?_ga=2.115552772.385778221.1545856706-1543252599.1522951358

Exercise 1 of 3: Looking at Programming Languages on Google Trends

1. Open the Google Trends website[88].

2. If you haven't played with Google Trends, get ready to have some fun. For someone who likes data, Google Trends is one of my favorite websites.

Let's start by comparing Python on a US level - see chart here[89].

You can either click the link I've included or if you'd like, type JavaScript and compare it with Python. Make sure you select the "Programming Language" term though and not just the word "Python." Otherwise, you'd be comparing JavaScript to the snake.

I am using the default search settings, which has me looking at the US in the last 12 months.

JavaScript vs. Python, US, last 12 months

---

[88]https://trends.google.com/trends/
[89]https://trends.google.com/trends/explore?geo=US&q=%2Fm%2F02p97,%2Fm%2F05z1_

Notice that even though JavaScript is the more "popular" Programming Language, Google Trends shows that Python is searched more often. Stack Overflow uses a survey of developers[90] to gather its data, and GitHub bases[91] its data on the "amount of code written" type measurements. This upturn in Python searches *may* support the buzz that Python is on the up-and-up.

3. Let's switch it up and look at JavaScript vs. Python, but this time **worldwide**, and over the **last 5 years** - see chart here.[92]

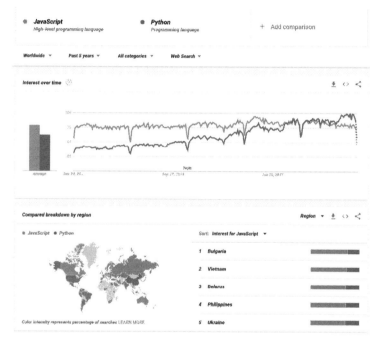

JavaScript vs. Python, Worldwide, last 5 years

Looks like not long ago, JavaScript used to be *more* searched than Python! Additionally, there are still lots of countries where folks search more for JavaScript than they do Python.

It's impossible to explain these differences completely. But it's a good guess that Python is "growing" in popularity, and the rate at which it's growing varies depending on where in the World you are.

---

[90]https://insights.stackoverflow.com/survey/2018/#methodology
[91]https://octoverse.github.com/projects#languages
[92]https://trends.google.com/trends/explore?date=today%205-y&q=%2Fm%2F02p97,%2Fm%2F05z1_

5. Now let's look at **PHP**, **in the US**, over the **last 5 years** - see chart here[93]. GitHub and Stack Overflow show that PHP isn't growing, but it is not obvious if PHP's "popularity" is decreasing.

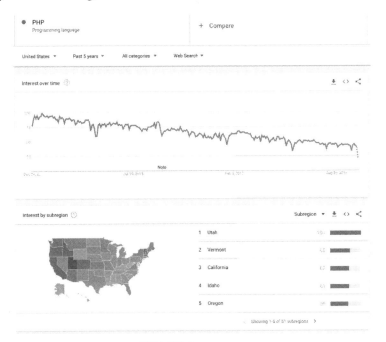

PHP, US, last 5 years

Google Trends gives a little more insight into what's going on with PHP. Depending on how much weight you give searches of the term "PHP," it might be a reasonable guess that PHP's popularity *is decreasing*. Or, at least there's some evidence that suggests it is.

Another interesting tidbit is the popularity of PHP in Utah. I can't explain this entirely, other than to say that Utah has become somewhat of a Silicon Valley of the Rocky Mountains. Utah has a large population, with Universities and a relatively low cost of living. Companies like eBay and Adobe have all recently opened large branches in the state[94].

Feel free to do more Google Trend searches. Play around with other mentioned Programming Languages from the GitHub and Stack Overflow reports. Google

[93]https://trends.google.com/trends/explore?date=today%205-y&geo=US&q=%2Fm%2F060kv
[94]https://www.cnbc.com/2016/07/13/a-high-tech-mecca-rises-to-rival-silicon-valley.html

Trends allows you to get more specific based on region, so it might be worth trying to narrow down trends closer to your home base. Also, try searching for things like "PHP web developer jobs," etc.

A closer look at the Top Programming Languages

OK, now we have a sense of what Programming Languages are popular. But popularity still isn't enough to decide what language(s) to learn. Being an Alaskan Crabber could be super *popular*, but that doesn't mean you want to live your days cold and on a boat.

Our next step is to look at what these top Programming Languages are used for. And hopefully, through this investigation, I can give you a better sense of what language(s) you'd need based on your interest, future or otherwise.

In this investigation, I will cover 10 of the most popular Programming Languages (according to GitHub's Octoverse). For each language, I will look at what type of things the language is used for, include a code snippet of the language, and examples of companies using the language.

Disclaimer

In the following sections, I'll be speaking in very broad terms to try and give you a sense of the space as a beginner – each of these languages are versatile, and you'll see them being used in lots of ways. Consider what I'm describing as a stereotype, with all of the benefits and drawbacks that come from generalizing.

Car Analogy

To help relate these languages to something you are more familiar with, at the end of each discussion, I'll relate the language back to a car[a].

---

[a]I'm taking the concept from Rory MacDonald and his article on the Pros and Cons of Ruby on Rails, but I'll be making some tweaks to fit our discussion

JavaScript: The Language of the Web

As we learned in the previous chapter, JavaScript is seemingly everywhere on the web. It's in every web browser, every smartphone, and billions - literally billions - of other devices.

JavaScript is a great first Programming Language to learn. I would suggest that anyone going into programming should learn JavaScript to an intermediate level. Anyone going into Web Development, focusing on what is called the "client-side" (think anything you and I as users interact with), should master JavaScript to an advanced level.

We've seen JavaScript already in this book, but for reference, here's what JavaScript code looks like:

Example of JavaScript

```
function howdyFolks(){ // define the function
  return "howdy folks!"; // function returns statement "howdy!"
}
howdyFolks(); // call the function
```

Well known companies that use JavaScript[95]:

- Google
- Facebook
- Microsoft
- Twitter
- Uber
- Slack

---

[95]https://siftery.com/javascript

JavaScript = Honda Civic

If JavaScript were a car, it would be a Honda Civic. It's everywhere, affordable, only needs an oil change to keep it going, and dang do people like to trick them out! React - the Library that enhances JavaScript - is a lot like your cousin's tricked-out Civic.

Java: An Industry Workhorse

Not in any way related to JavaScript, Java is an extremely mature language. It is well supported and used in lots of applications, including very large services.

While some may consider Java "verbose", Java is also considered a relatively easy Programming Language to learn. It has a large class library, and a robust open-source community - meaning that a lot of functionality is already written for you.

Java is used for both web applications, like Google Docs, and also for applications on your computer. For example, any Open Office[96] application - think applications like Microsoft Word or Excel - are written in Java.

Java is owned by Oracle[97], so if you are using Oracle products, then it's a safe bet that Java is involved.

Java is also a popular language for use in Android Smartphone applications, and the Internet of Things (IoT).

---

[96]https://en.wikipedia.org/wiki/OpenOffice.org
[97]https://www.oracle.com/sun/

The term IoT[98] will come up in other Programming Languages. It essentially means anything that provides a system of related computer devices that talk to each other over a network. Examples include home security systems (e.g., Nest), or Amazon Alexa and Google Assistant.

A downside of Java is that historically it tends to use up a lot of memory (though this has improved in recent years). It is powerful, but that power comes at a cost.

Example of Java

```
class HowdyFolks {
  public static void main(String[] args) { // "main" where to begin
    int myInt = 10; // int to say use a number
    System.out.println("Howdy Folks!");
  }
}
```

Well known companies using Java[99]

- Google
- Netflix
- Target
- eBay
- T-Mobile
- Accenture

Java = Sprinter Van

If Java were a car, it would be a Sprinter Van. It's practical, strong, easy to adapt to whatever utility. But it's a little slow and forget about getting under its hood.

---

[98]https://en.wikipedia.org/wiki/Internet_of_things
[99]https://siftery.com/java

Python: Bring on the Data

Python has grown into a very popular language used for software development, infrastructure management, and data science. It is also a key driver in big data analytics and artificial intelligence (AI).

Python can be used for desktop General User Interface (a.k.a., GUI) applications; think of any application you download and put on your computer. For example, Dropbox's Desktop interface - as seen in the next screenshot - is built using Python.

Python shines in **data science**. The libraries for scientific and mathematical computing in Python are mature and widely used in both industry and academia.

Nearly all of the popular open-source libraries for *Deep Learning* (such as Tensorflow or PyTorch) are based on Python. If you are interested in machine learning or artificial intelligence, then Python is a mandatory language to learn.

Example of Python

```
# this is a comment
def sayHowdy(name): # def to start function
  print 'howdy',name # uses indentation to figure out end of function

sayHowdy('folks!')
```

Well known companies using Python[100]

- Google
- Facebook
- Spotify
- Instagram
- Dropbox
- Netflix

Python = BMW 3 Series

If Python were a car, it would be the BMW 3 Series. The BMW 3 Series has long been acknowledged as the best of luxury sedans for many years. It's reliable and still offers high performance.

---
[100]https://realpython.com/world-class-companies-using-python/

PHP: One of the Web's Original Languages

PHP, though on a mild downward trend, is not going away anytime soon. WordPress is built on PHP. If you are not already familiar with WordPress, it is a website creation tool. WordPress *is the largest* Website Creation tool, and it is estimated that 27% of the websites on the internet are powered using WordPress[101]. If you want to build WordPress websites, you'll need to know PHP.

Facebook also uses PHP. However, Facebook is somewhat "old," and it is generally thought that if Facebook were to be started today, they would use something other than PHP.

That said, PHP is very powerful, which is why Facebook can still use it. But you'll find that most Silicon Valley companies don't choose PHP for new projects anymore. Instead, they tend to favor other technologies like Node.js[102], Ruby on Rails[103] or other languages like Java/Python for this role.

PHP used to be the de facto Programming Language to learn after JavaScript, but with the rise of Node.js, Java, and Python, this is not the case anymore. While PHP still has its advocates, I would only recommend learning PHP if you want to work on WordPress sites. Or, if the job you want is looking for PHP developers.

Example of PHP

---

[101]https://www.whoishostingthis.com/compare/wordpress/stats/

[102]Node.js is not a Programming Language, Framework or Library. It is a run-time environment built on the Chrome JavaScript engine. https://en.wikipedia.org/wiki/Node.js

[103]https://rubyonrails.org/

```php
<?php // indicate you are using php
function howdyFolks() { // function
    echo "Hello Folks!"; // say "Hello Folks!"
}

writeMsg(); // call the function
?>
```

Well known companies using PHP

- WordPress
- Facebook
- Formstack[104]
- Wikipedia
- Yahoo

PHP = Toyota Camry

If PHP were a car, it would be the Toyota Camry. The Toyota Camry is better today than it has ever been (just like the new PHP 7). The Camry was one of Toyota's best selling vehicles for many years. But times are changing, and everyone wants SUVs.

---

[104]In full disclosure, I work at Formstack. It is not a company the size of say Facebook, but it does use PHP, and I am proud to name drop it; it's a great company.

C: Everyone's Relative

C has been around a long time and influenced a lot of other Programming Languages (ex: Java, PHP, JavaScript, C++). Bell Labs invented C in the early 1970s, and it is still used in many applications today.

The C language is used in companies where performance is a big concern. For example, the video game industry. Today's games are insanely complex and fast-paced. The engines responsible for powering those games are largely written in C.

The Robotics industry[105] - if you were thinking robots you're spot on - relies on C and C's immediate relatives like C++ to help manage large and complex systems.

Because C has been around a long time, some of our "core" technologies are written in C. For example, your computer's Operating System is very likely written in C. Databases as well. Popular databases like MySQL and Postgres are also written in C.

Well known companies/hardware using C

- Operating Systems: Linux, Microsoft Windows, macOs, iOS, Android
- Databases: MySQL, Oracle Database, etc.

Ex:

```
# include <stdio.h>
int main (){
    int x;

    x = returnSomeValue();
    printf("Howdy Folks!");
}
```

C = Ford F Series

If C were a car, it would be the original Ford F-series. The Ford F-Series has been around well over 50 years and continually outperforms the new kids on the block. Its legacy has produced many other spin-off models, but it continues to stand on

---

[105]https://blog.robotiq.com/what-is-the-best-programming-language-for-robotics

its own and up to the test of time.

C++: The C Legacy Continues

C++ (pronounced C plus plus) is from the same family of the C language. C++ introduced in the 1980s. It's newer than C, but it is still considered a mature language.

C++ can be used for web and desktop applications. However, it's more likely used when a programmer needs to communicate directly with computer hardware (e.g., talking with your computer's Operating System). It is also commonly used in database and spreadsheet applications.

C++'s[106] key strengths are in software infrastructure, desktop applications, and servers. C++'s key weakness is that it doesn't provide a lot of guard rails to prevent bugs.

Example of C++

---

[106]https://en.wikipedia.org/wiki/C%2B%2B

```
# include <iostream>
using namespace std;

int main()
{
    cout << "Howdy Folks!";
    return 0;
}
```

Well known companies using C++

- Microsoft
- Oracle
- PayPal
- LinkedIn

C++ = Toyota Tacoma

If C++ were a car, it would be a Toyota Tacoma. It's reliable, robust, but notoriously compromised. The Tacoma feels like a truck, and its makers are just fine with that, stiff handling, uncomfortable seating and all. It's a truck-guy's truck; it's reliable, but it's got a bounce to it.

C#: The Millennial of the C legacy

C# (pronounced C sharp) is the newest of the C legacy. Microsoft introduced C# in 2000.

C#[107] is considered a .NET language because it is used to develop on the .NET framework, which all Microsoft platforms use. Thus, if you want to work on a Microsoft platform, you'll need to know C#.

ink of C# like "Microsoft's Java." It's a lot like Java in that the language syntax is similar, and, like Java, it can run on many platforms. In many ways, C# is like a more "modern" Java.

Example of C#

public class Howdy // class to surround the block of code { // curly braces to define the block of code public static void Main() // tell where the program begins. { System.Console.WriteLine("Howdy Folks!"); // write to Console. } }

Well known companies using C#

- StackOverflow
- Microsoft
- Intel
- GoDaddy
- Unity

C# = Porsche 911

If C# were a car, it would be a Porsche 911. The Porsche 911 has been the long-time steward of sports cars. It is trusted and well known, but its German makers have been reserved and surgical, slowly iterating over its design. So much so that its design hasn't changed much. Rivals have come along with flashier designs, effectively distracting away from the hobbyist. What's left are the true Porsche enthusiasts.

---

[107]https://en.wikipedia.org/wiki/C_Sharp_programming_language

TypeScript: The Hipster

TypeScript is the popular new kid in town. It is a superset of JavaScript and adds static typing to the JavaScript language. For right now, you don't need to know what that means. Other than to say, TypeScript builds off of JavaScript and was developed in large part to overcome some of JavaScript's shortcomings.

Though built by Microsoft, it is used for all sorts of applications. TypeScript is best suited for the development of large applications that would otherwise be written in JavaScript[108].

Well known using TypeScript[109]

- Google
- Microsoft
- Jet.com
- Lyft
- Asana
- 99 Designs

Example of TypeScript

---

[108]https://en.wikipedia.org/wiki/TypeScript
[109]https://stackshare.io/typescript/in-stacks

```
function howdyFolks(person: string) {
  return "howdy " + person;
}
let name = "Folks!";

howdyFolks(name);
```

TypeScript = Tesla Model 3

If TypeScript were a car, it would be Tesla Model 3. Enough people have them now that you would consider getting one if the time, $ made sense. You already have a car and don't *need* a new one yet, but dang, they sound appealing.

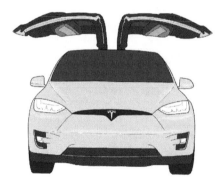

Shell Scripts: Your Computer's Love Language

Shell scripts are a bit different than the Programming Languages we've covered so far. It's not a language you typically use to *write* an application per se, but more of a language to interact with a computer.

Shell scripts are technically different dialects that your *Shell program* can read. Every modern computer comes with a Shell (program). I will avoid details now, as we will cover shells in much greater detail in the Terminal Chapter.

Without getting too much into the weeds, "shell scripting" isn't a language - there are different shells, and each has its own language. For example, Bash would be the most popular shell and "Bash script" would be its language.

Someone pursuing a career as a Systems Administrator (think the IT person) is likely to know Bash scripting. Another role that uses Bash scripting is Developer Operations, or "DevOps" for short. A DevOps person, roughly speaking, is someone who manages a fleet of servers in a data center or in the cloud.

Learning Bash scripting is not *just* for the Systems Administrators or DevOps Engineer. If you become comfortable with Bash scripting, you'll find that it is a powerful tool for automating tasks. And in all honesty, being able to write in a Shell script kicks your cool factor up a notch.

Example of Shell Script

```
echo Hello Folks!
```

Common Developer Positions where Shell Script is a requirement:

- Linux/Unix Administrator
- SQL Developer
- DevOps
- System Administrator
- Hackers as portrayed in movies

Shell Script = Corvette

If Shell Script were a car, it would be the Corvette. It is the quintessential Hollywood car, everyone knows what it is, but only the well trained can drive it. It is a rear-wheel drive, trying to kill you, kind of sports car. Once mastered, it can go around a race track faster than most, but it's intimidating and requires years of practice.

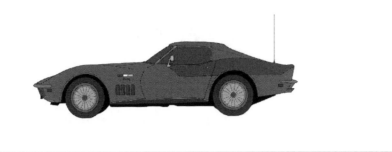

Ruby: Training Wheels

Developed in Japan in the 1990s, Ruby is a friendly language for beginners. It does not require a lot of prerequisite knowledge and reads very similar to English.

One of the main advantages of the Ruby language is the Ruby on Rails (RoR) Framework. Without getting into too much detail, RoR allows programmers to launch an interactive website quickly.

Because Ruby is easy to learn and setup, it is a popular language among tech startups - specifically those focused on web applications. Although some tech startups have outgrown the language and had to move away from Ruby eventually - most famously Twitter, moved from Ruby to Java[110] around 2002.

A downside to Ruby (and a factor likely responsible for its downward popularity) is that the language runs relatively slowly.

Example of Ruby

---

[110]https://careerfoundry.com/en/blog/web-development/10-great-sites-built-with-ruby-on-rails/

```ruby
# use the pound sign for a comment
def howdy(name) #def for a function
  puts "howdy, #{name}"
end # end of function

x = "Folks!"
howdy(x) # call function and pass in x
```

Well known companies using Ruby

- Square
- Hulu
- GitHub
- Dribble
- 37Signals

Ruby = Smart Car

If Ruby were a car, it would be a **Smart Car**. If you live in a fast-paced city, with no place to park, a Smart Car makes your life a lot easier. It gets you where you need to go and quickly, just don't take the thing onto a busy HWY - it maxes out at 55mph.

Job Descriptions

I want to get you comfortable looking at programming job descriptions, keeping an eye out on the language requirements.

By the end of this, I hope you'll have a better understanding of how to search for Programming Language requirements in a job description. Additionally, I hope this encourages you to do some additional, personalized research of your own.

In this section, we will look at the following job posting sites.

 It should go without saying that there are a lot of job posting sites out there. I choose to focus on these 3 because they post jobs specifically for developers.

- **GitHub Jobs**[111]
- **StackOverflow Jobs**[112]
- **Smashing Magazine Jobs**[113]

We could spend a whole day looking at different job postings. But I am going to assume that, depending on your level of curiosity, you can continue the following exercise for as long as you'd like. I am just going to get you started, focusing on where to find information about Programming Languages.

Frameworks And Libraries

To get in front of what might later become confusing, I want to stop and quickly talk about **Frameworks and Libraries**.

You'll often hear people refer to *Frameworks*, *Libraries*, and *Programming Languages* in the same breath.

I want to clarify with you that **they are different things**. To make it more difficult, the lines between a "library" and a "framework" aren't always clear.

---

[111]https://jobs.github.com/
[112]https://stackoverflow.com/jobs
[113]https://www.smashingmagazine.com/jobs/

For example, you may come across a job post requiring skills in PHP, React, and Angular.

- PHP is a Programming Language
- Angular is a Framework (made of up several Libraries)
- React could also be considered a Framework, even though there is a specific `React` library.

Frameworks and Libraries are a collection of tools that support writing in a particular Programming Language. For example, the popular Library called React was built by Facebook. Facebook built[114] React to help manage data and make maintenance of their codebase more manageable.

React extends JavaScript, but it does not replace it. Therefore React isn't a Programming Language, just a tool that in many ways, makes JavaScript more powerful.

Frameworks and Libraries have become a crucial part of web development, and something you will need to learn more about as you continue in Web Development. For now, know they exist and are often mentioned in the same space of Programming Languages.

Learn the Programming Language First

Learn the Programming Language First. Once you have a handle on the language, then explore Libraries and Frameworks.

I wrote a blog post on Frameworks and Libraries. I actually wrote the post from a removed section I had originally written for this book. However, as this Chapter is already quite long, I removed the section. You can read that blog post here[115].

---

[114]https://reactjs.org/blog/2013/06/05/why-react.html
[115]https://www.newline.co/30-days-of-webdev/day-21-frameworks-and-libraries

Exercise 2 of 3: Looking at active job postings

1. Let's start on the GitHub Jobs site. Later in the book, in the Git chapter, we will cover GitHub in much more detail. For now, we will only use it to focus on jobs.

Navigate to the GitHub Jobs website[116].

Feel free to type in any Job Description and Location you'd like. For our example, I typed in "Web Developer", and a job for Coretechs Consulting firm came up.

 Your job search experience will result in different job postings.

The following is a screenshot from Coretechs job posting. I have highlighted with pink boxes some things we'll discuss.

---

[116]https://jobs.github.com/

Full Time / Kensington, MD
Web Developer

Full time employment with many benefits - get paid for every hour you work!

Coretechs Consulting is looking to add web developers to its growing team. Our projects with various clients can involve a diverse array of different platforms and frameworks. The most common is Python with Django, Custom PHP, .NET and Java - plus we also build iOS and Android apps. We're looking for developers who want to learn new systems, while having a strong base of experience with at least one web based platform.

We are based in Kensington, MD and have many clients in the DC Metro area and beyond. You'll be able to work flexible hours and grow your role within the company as a valued part of our team.

Some of the Benefits of working for Coretechs:

- Competitive pay, 401k, health care, paid vacation and bonuses
- Hourly Pay - Get paid for every hour you work - Avoid Salary Burnout
- Ability to grow your position and role within the company
- Work remotely - After your introductory period you can work some days remotely
- Work for a locally owned, locally managed, US based company

Job Requirements:

- Proven experience with either Python, PHP or .NET and its various flavors. We want developers who know at least one language / framework very well, and who are looking to broaden out their experience
- Experience with HTML, CSS, Bootstrap and jQuery
- Some Database experience with either MySQL, PostgreSQL or SQL Server.
- Knowledge of various repository systems such as Git and Subversion
- Previous development or exposure to iOS or Android app development is a plus.
- Comfortable interacting with clients via email, phone or in person if needed.
- Ability to work independently and productively, but also to work well in a collegial, team atmosphere
- A degree is preferred, but individuals with comparative experience may apply
- At least 2 - 5 years industry experience
- Ability to work in our Kensington, MD office

If working for a fast growing, local company sounds like a step in the right direction for your career,

Coretechs Consulting Inc.

https://www.coretechs.com

How to apply

Apply with this link:
https://hire.withgoogle.com/public/job
trackingTag=gitHub

Under Job Requirements, it becomes clear that knowledge in **Python and PHP** are a must. Here the overlap between Python *and* PHP makes sense because this company is hiring a programmer to work on client code. It's a consulting firm, not an in-house gig.

The comment,

> "... .NET and its various flavors...",

suggest that you'll be using the **C#** language (remember C# is used for all things Microsoft and the .NET platform).

The comment,

> *"we want developers who know at least one language/Framework very well...",*

is a great reminder that even if the posting list more than one language, the employer is not always expecting you to master every language listed. They just want to see that you can master one language and are assuming you will pick up others quickly; something to keep in mind if you get overwhelmed by trying to learn every language listed on a job posting.

> *"...with HTML, CSS, Bootstrap and jQuery...",*

This line suggest they are using an older toolset. jQuery is a Library, and Bootstrap is a Framework. Both expand the JavaScript language. However, many companies today may not start with jQuery, as it's considered a little out-of-date, having been outpaced by newer technologies like React or Angular.

The comments about database knowledge,

> *"Some Database experience ...",*

indicates that you should be familiar with Database languages, something we will cover later.

> **In summary**, this company is looking for a developer whose main strengths are in Python, PHP, and likely C#. They should have experience using the SQL languages (databases) and be able to walk themselves through client-side frameworks/libraries that are built off of JavaScript.

2. Now let's look at StackOverflow's job listings[117]. I clicked on the first job that came up, and it was for a Frontend (React.js) Engineer[118].

---

[117]https://stackoverflow.com/jobs
[118]Checkout Chapter 8 to learn more about what a Frontend Engineer/Developer is.

Frontend (React.js) Engineer (m/w/d)

Alasco | München, Germany

€50k - 80k   Visa sponsor   Paid relocation

Overview   Company   Developer Culture   More Jobs

About this job

Job type: **Full-time**

Experience level: **Junior, Mid-Level, Senior**

Role: **Frontend Developer**

Industry: **Construction, SaaS**

Company size: **11-50 people**

Company type: **VC Funded**

Technologies

javascript   reactjs   twitter-bootstrap   amazon-web-services   webpack

Job description

Your Responsibilities

- Together with your team, you ship new features for our cloud platform. Thereby you actively participate in delivering the best software possible for our customers.
- You learn about the customers needs and processes and strive to solve them as quickly as possible.
- You work directly with our UX/UI Designers in your team and bring their designs to life.
- You strive to deliver the best possible experience for our users by empowering them through an effective and intuitive UI.
- You build features with an "you build it, you run it" mindset and are responsible for testing, deployment and monitoring of your code.

Your Profile

- Profound knowledge of JavaScript, especially React.js (2+years).
- Experience with testing and bundling of JavaScript code (e.g.Webpack, Jest,...).
- You treat CSS as a first class citizen and have deep knowledge in CSS Frameworks (e.g. Bootstrap) and Preprocessors (e.g. Sass).
- You have been part of an agile development team and experience in collaborating with UX/UI designers. You favor open communication, constant feedback and short decision paths.
- You have a "Never-stop-learning" attitude and a desire to develop and grow.
- You are fluent in English.

Again, I've highlighted in pink boxes a couple of things to note. The first is under "Technologies" where they put JavaScript alongside a bunch of things that are *not* Programming Languages.

- React is a Framework/Library,
- twitter-bootstrap is a (CSS & JavaScript) Framework
- Amazon-Web-Services is a "cloud-based" services platform.

Really, the only Programming Language these folks are asking for is **JavaScript**!

I can tell right away, just by the technologies they want, that this company does something with websites. I've never even heard of Alasco before, but a quick Google search[119] shows me they are a Software as a Services Company (SaaS). They provide web-based software solutions, i.e., a website that does things for their clients. Just like Facebook is a SaaS company, providing social networking services through a website.

Under "Your Profile" they want *"Profound knowledge of JavaScript ..."* - the translation might be better as *proficient*, but the idea is they want you to know JavaScript well. By saying *"... especially React.js..."* they are adding to the confusion that JavaScript and React are both Programming Languages. They are not, which we already know.

> **In summary**, this company is looking for a developer who has proficient JavaScript Programming Language skills, and experience using the React Library.

3. For this step, we are going to search Smashing Magazine's jobs page[120]. However, to speed things up a bit, I just took snippets from different job postings and have provided a quick analysis.

Software Engineer - JavaScript[121]

You have 2+ years of related experience in Front-End development with JavaScript and the Angular 2+ framework.

---

[119]https://www.linkedin.com/company/alasco-gmbh/about/
[120]https://www.smashingmagazine.com/jobs/
[121]https://www.smashingmagazine.com/jobs/2018-11-06-javascript-developer-san-francisco/#main

These guys did a better job at separating Language from Framework. They want you to know JavaScript but also be familiar with the Angular 2+ Framework which is built off JavaScript.

> *You know the subtle nuances of JavaScript - e.g., hoisting, the difference between "undefined" and "null", not being surprised that "typeof []" returns "object".*

This comment seems to say - "nope we *really* do you want you to know JavaScript!" In your future studies, a comment like this might make more sense. Basically, the comment is saying, don't just kind of know JavaScript, we want you to know it better than most.

Front End Developer - WordPress[122]

> *4+ years of work experience in front end development roles using Javascript, HTML, CSS, PHP, and WordPress.*

This is a classic WordPress job requirement. As we mentioned earlier, if you're going to be working with WordPress, you should know PHP. On top of that, they are saying you need to know the basics: HTML, CSS, and JavaScript.

Robotic Process Automation Developer[123]

> *2+ years of professional experience coding in any OOD language (C# / Java / C++/ etc.).*

No surprise here. It's a robotics company, and they want you to know the C languages (C#, C++ and by "etc.", I'm guessing C).

Hopefully, this brief look at job postings has given you some sense of what languages are required to get a job. And maybe what languages fit best with whatever industry you're looking at.

---

[122]https://www.smashingmagazine.com/jobs/2018-11-16-front-end-developer-wordpress-remote/#main
[123]https://stackoverflow.com/jobs/221544/robotic-process-automation-developer-orbis-consultants?so=i&pg=1&offset=6&q=robotic

Tech Stacks

Before we wrap up, I want to show you how to look up tech stacks. I am going to briefly introduce you to the concept here. Looking at a company's tech stack can provide key insights into the Programming Languages you need to learn.

A tech stack is all the software products and programming languages a company uses to operate. To make a legit hotdog, you need a hoagie bun, beef hot dogs, and spicy mustard. These ingredients would be the equivalent to a hotdogs "tech stack"; everything it needs to be a hotdog.

Several websites provide information on companies' tech stacks, but we are going to use Stackshare[124]. Stackshare allows you to search for companies by Programming Language, and also search by company. We'll do both.

Exercise 3 of 3: Tech Stacks

1. Let's first search by Programming Language. For no reason other than I would currently like more coffee, let's search by Java. Here is a quick link[125] to Stackshare's listing of companies using Java.

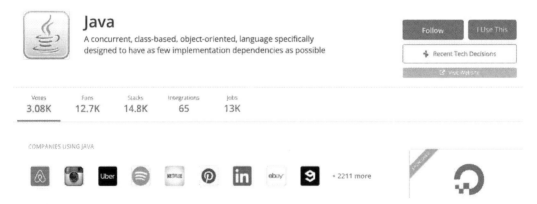

Stackshare shows over 2000 companies that use Java, and it has highlighted some of the more popular companies like eBay or Netflix.

---

[124]https://stackshare.io/google/google
[125]https://stackshare.io/java

Notice also the stats like Jobs and Fans. These stats are relative to the data on this website, so keep that in mind. However, comparing stats like this between the different languages can provide insight.

Please go ahead and search for other Programming Languages[126].

2. Now let's search by company. In the upper-right, search for "Netflix" in the search field. After you click on the company in the results, you should land here[127].

One thing that might surprise you is the number of technologies Netflix uses. Of all these technologies, only two of them are Programming Languages - Java and Python. You'll learn more later about what some of these technologies are and do, but for now, I think it's helpful to see where Programming Languages fit among the rest of the tech stack.

Continue to poke around, search for companies that interest you.

---

[126]https://stackshare.io/languages-and-frameworks
[127]https://stackshare.io/netflix/netflix

Key Takeaways

- Programming Languages are formalized instructions. A programmer is someone who writes those instructions.
- Frameworks and Libraries are often grouped together with Programming Languages, but they are not a language, rather a collection of tools whose main purpose is to make a programmer's job easier.
- Learn the Programming Language *before* learning any related Framework or Library.
- JavaScript is a Programming Language that you should know to become a Web Developer.
- The most popular Programming Languages include: JavaScript, Java, Python, PHP, C, C++, C#, TypeScript, Shell Script, and Ruby.
- The popularity contest among all groups, Programming Languages, but Frameworks and Libraries as well, is dynamic. Something may be popular today, but fade away in a couple of months or several years.
- Stack Overflow, Smashing Magazine, and GitHub are good resources to view jobs for programmers.
- When looking at Job postings, it's not always obvious what languages you'll need to know, as Frameworks and Libraries are often thrown in the mix.

Considerations for Further Study

Over your career you're going to learn multiple Programming Languages, tagging on some Frameworks and Libraries in there as well.

But don't make the Programming Language decision quite yet. Put it in your back pocket for now. If you have any lingering questions, explore them, but don't feel like you should pick a language or path now.

 Don't be Overwhelmed

That was a lot to cover. You don't need to learn it all – no one knows it all.

Further Readings

If you like to do some additional research on the languages we've covered, below are resources I recommend. Because each language mentioned is "popular," there are plenty of available resources. Don't limit your search to my list here.

- **JavaScript**: See the Further Reading section in the JavaScript Chapter.
- **Java**: Oracle, which now owns Java, has its own Java tutorials - see here[128].
- **Python**: The Python Software Foundation has a good tutorial series here[129]. It will likely need to be augmented by a more beginner-friendly tutorial as well.
- **PHP**: PHP.net is a great resource for learning more about PHP - see here[130].
- **C**: There is a good YouTube video series by Free Code Camp on the C Programming for Beginners - see here[131].
- **C++**: Udemy has a *free* course on learning C++ for beginners - see here.[132]
- **C#**: Udemy has a reputable course on C# for Beginners - see here[133]. Hint: wait for Udemy sales, in which the price reduces by as much as 94%.
- **TypeScript**: I would recommend only learning TypeScript *after* you learn JavaScript. And many of the TypeScript tutorials will assume you have done just that. But if you're curious what TypeScript and the hype is all about, I recommend reading this article series[134] by Free Code Camp on the Medium Website.
- **Shell Script**: The book "From Bash to Z Shell" is one of the books on my bookshelf I have revisited many times. It's been around a while now so used versions can be found at reasonable prices.
- **Ruby**: There are lots of tutorials out there, but Lynda.com has a collection of some very helpful ones. See their collection of Ruby tutorials here[135]. The Ruby Docs also list some useful - and free - resources[136].
- In addition to individual Programming Languages, one of my favorite instructors, Simon Allardice, has a great 5hr video course discussing Programming

---

[128]https://docs.oracle.com/javase/tutorial/getStarted/index.html
[129]https://docs.python.org/3/tutorial/
[130]http://php.net/manual/en/getting-started.php
[131]https://www.youtube.com/watch?v=KJgsSFOSQv0
[132]https://www.udemy.com/free-learn-c-tutorial-beginners/
[133]https://www.udemy.com/csharp-tutorial-for-beginners/
[134]https://medium.freecodecamp.org/want-to-learn-typescript-heres-our-free-22-part-course-21cd9bbb5ef5
[135]https://www.lynda.com/Ruby-training-tutorials/303-0.html
[136]https://ruby-doc.org/gettingstarted/

Language Syntax, and covers in more detail some of the topics we've discussed here. Simon is an instructor for Lynda.com. If you are interested, you can preview the course here[137].

- The programming community abounds with opinions on Programming Languages, and for fun, I would recommend looking at StackOverflow's tag "programming-languages" and the postings by most votes[138]. You'll get an understanding of commonly asked questions, and a look at the lively debate behind a lot of these topics.

What's Next?

That was, admittedly, a lot of information to throw at you. And not all the information may be useful quite yet. Bookmark this chapter, and revisit it as you get closer to looking at Job Descriptions or making a decision about your next steps.

In the next chapter on the terminal, we'll jump back into our more traditional Exercise format. The terminal is a crucial tool that you will need to know and somewhat "master" as a future Web Developer.

I can also promise you, however, that you'll feel a whole lot cooler after making it through the terminal chapter. Read on to find out why.

---

[137]https://www.lynda.com/JavaScript-tutorials/Foundations-of-Programming-Fundamentals/83603-2.html?utm_medium=viral&utm_source=youtube&utm_campaign=videoupload-83603-0101

[138]https://stackoverflow.com/questions/tagged/programming-languages?sort=votes&pageSize=15

Chapter 6: Terminal

The terminal is a program that you use to type in commands. It is a text input/output environment. Not knowing how to use a terminal as a Web Developer would be like a writer not knowing how to use a computer; sure they could use a typewriter or good-old pen and paper, but how effective would they be?

In this chapter, we'll cover what a terminal is, introduce you to some of the more common and useful commands, and hopefully give you a sense of the efficiencies the terminal makes available. This chapter is a required read before going into the Git chapter.

Opening the terminal

The default terminal is usually white, but you've probably seen black terminals in movies. Featuring a geeky hoodied-hacker doing something like "running an algorithm" or "extinguishing the override" or some other nerd'ish lingo nonsense. Take for example, the terminal making an appearance in these well-known movies:

From left to right, these images are from *Girl With The Dragon Tattoo*, *The Fifth Estate*, *Snowden*, and *The Matrix*.

Let's start things off by opening your terminal; every major computer comes packaged with a terminal program.

 Because macOS and Windows OS users have different default terminal programs, the commands differ slightly. I will start each Exercise with macOS instructions, followed by instructions for Windows OS users (specifically Windows 10 users).

Exercise 1 of 9: Opening the terminal

 When talking about the actual Terminal program that comes packaged with macOS I'll capitalize the "T," otherwise terminal with a lowercase "t" will refer to any terminal program that interfaces with your Shell - more on that shortly.

1. macOS users: There are several ways to open the Terminal on a Mac. I will use Spotlight. To use Spotlight, press cmd + spacebar. Then type in "terminal." You should see the terminal app come up. Click on it.

There is a good chance that your terminal looks slightly different than mine. That's OK. There are appearance settings you can play around with, but regardless our terminal programs do the same thing.

2. macOS users: Once open, type the command say bananas.

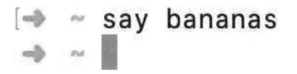

You should hear your computer say "bananas".

 Your mouse does not work in the Terminal or in the Window's PowerShell program. To navigate, you'll need to use the left and right arrow keys. If you want to delete something, move the cursor in front of the character and press the delete key.

1. Windows OS users: The dominant Shell-CLI environment for Windows 10 users is PowerShell[139]. To navigate to PowerShell, search for the "PowerShell" in the Windows Explorer and open it up.

The say command that macOS users entered in their Exercise is a shortcut command that comes default with macOS. You will be making a shortcut command also called "say." To do this, copy-paste the following command into your PowerShell.

```
Add-Type -AssemblyName System.Speech
$say = New-Object -TypeName System.Speech.Synthesis.SpeechSynthesizer
```

---

[139]We are using PowerShell and not Command Prompt, in part because since Windows 10 PowerShell is considered the more prominent CLI-Shell. The other part is that it is much more powerful. If you are curious, here is a good article describing the differences.

2. **Windows OS users**: The code snippet you copy-pasted in the previous step creates a command called $say. The dollar sign in PowerShell indicates a variable. Because we are assigning a script to this command, we have to use a dollar sign.

Now, to use the "$say" command, enter the following into your PowerShell:

```
$say.Speak("bananas")
```

You should hear your computer say "bananas".

macOS and Windows OS users

3. Congrats! You just entered your first terminal command - also called a Shell Script. Remember the Shell Scripting Language from the Programming Languages chapter?

If Shell Script were a car, it would be the **Corvette**. It is the quintessential Hollywood car, everyone knows what it is, but only the well trained can drive it. It is a rear-wheel drive trying to kill-you-sports-car. Once mastered, it can go around a race track faster than most, but it's intimidating and requires years of practice.

Before we start typing in Shell commands, let's take a closer look at what is happening behind the scenes.

What is Shell?

To understand the terminal, you first need to know what a Shell is.

A Shell is an interface that gives you access to your computer's Operating System. Think of it as a wrapper[140] that wraps around your Operating System's kernel. Hence the name *Shell* - a shell/protective barrier - around the brain/core of your computer.

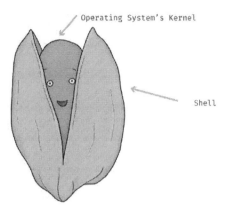

Shells come in two forms:

1. **Command Line Interface**: CLI for short, pronounced C. L. I.
2. **General User Interface**: GUI for short, pronounced "gooey."

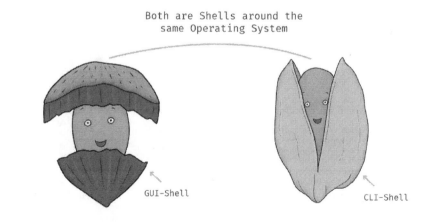

---

[140]https://en.wikipedia.org/wiki/Shell_(computing)

CLI

An example of a CLI is the Bash Shell or PowerShell that comes default with macOS and Windows OS, respectively.

Here's a screenshot of the macOS Terminal. Notice the "bash-3.2$"? That's the Terminal saying, "Hey, I'm interfacing with the Bash Shell."

```
● ● ●              angel — /bin/bash — /bin/bash — bash — 56×6
bash-3.2$ ▐
```

 ### macOS Users

In the previous Exercise, though you were interfacing with a program called "Terminal," you were interacting with your Bash Shell.

 ### Windows Users

PowerShell is a complete environment, acting as both the Shell and the terminal application. Compare this to macOS, which has both the default Shell called Bash, as well as the Terminal application (with a capital "T") that allows the user to interact with Bash.

We'll explore CLIs in much greater detail, but first, let's look more closely at GUIs.

GUI

Though you may not know it, you're very familiar with GUI's. These are programs designed to make it easy for the everyday computer user to *do* things with their computer. They use graphics, icons, and menus to make navigation and executing commands easy.

An example of a popular GUI is the Finder program (the equivalent program in Windows is "Finder Explorer").

GUIs evolved to make it easier for computer users to do things and navigate around the computer. GUIs are on smartphones, smartwatches, anything computer-based you'll find GUIs.

Here is an example of a GUI on the iPhones iOS. The GUI provides the icons, and menus you use to navigate or *do* things on your iPhone.

Here's one more example of a GUI on a smartwatch that starts your Tesla - wouldn't that be nice!

Before GUIs, computer users only had a keyboard and computer screen as tools. To do anything on the computer the user had to type out commands via a CLI. This process is not intuitive for today's average computer user. As a reaction, GUIs were built. GUIs - for the majority of computer users - make navigation and actions easier to figure out.

In the following Exercise, we are going to spend time with the Finder program, doing simple, everyday navigation.

Exercise 2 of 9: Playing with a GUI

 Windows users: This process will be the same for Windows users. Your GUI will just look a little different. Instead of using the Finder program, you'll be using your Windows Explorer[141] program.

1. Open the Finder program on your mac (cmd + spacebar, type "Finder")

2. Once open, navigate to your Downloads folder.

---

[141]https://support.microsoft.com/en-us/help/4026617/windows-10-windows-explorer-has-a-new-name

3. In your Downloads folder, go to the Finder menu at the top of your computer screen and click File -> New Folder.

4. Name the folder and move some files into it.

We will be using this same folder later. If you'd like, name it the same as my folder here - "nuts" - otherwise name it whatever you'd like. Just remember the name for later exercises.

Ta-da you just used a GUI! You used the Finder's menu dropdowns to do things like make a folder and move stuff into it.

GUIs are everywhere. If you find yourself navigating, clicking, or selecting graphical elements (icons, menus, etc.) to *do* something to the device you're using, then it's a safe bet that you are using a GUI.

CLI

Unlike a GUI, a CLI only takes commands that we type. It does not accept mouse inputs, nor does it have icons and buttons to help you *do* things. Instead, you command it to do things via your keyboard.

We've established that a Shell is a wrapper around a computer's Operating System and that a GUI is a type of Shell. The other type of Shell is a CLI - for our purposes, we will refer to this type of Shell as a Shell-CLI.

> When computer folks are talking about Shells, they are likely referring to a Shell-CLI. However, because we know a Shell can be both a GUI or CLI, we will differentiate them here as either Shell-GUI or Shell-CLI.

The standard Shell-CLI shipped with macOS is **Bash**. Bash has been the standard Shell-CLI shipped with the majority of computers since the early 1990s[142]. The standard Shell-CLI for Windows 10 users is PowerShell.

Though Bash and PowerShell are the default Shell-CLI for macOS and Windows users, you can install *other* Shell-CLIs if you'd like. For example, Zsh (pronounced z Shell) is a popular Shell-CLI alternative. There is a variety of different Shell-CLIs available. The only restriction is that the Shell-CLI you use must be compatible with your computer's Operating System.

You don't have to know the differences between these other types of Shell-CLIs. I only pointed this out so that you were aware that there were other types of Shell-CLIs out there.

Summary

The Shell is a wrapper around your Operating System. There are Shell-GUIs and Shell-CLIs, but typically when people talk about Shell, they are referring to the Shell-CLI. A Shell-CLI accepts only text commands and does things in response to those commands. An example of a Shell-CLI is Bash or PowerShell. A Shell-GUI takes inputs from graphical components like icons, menus, and buttons. Examples of Shell-GUI are the macOS's Finder program or Windows OS's Windows Explorer program.

---

[142]https://en.wikipedia.org/wiki/Bash_(Unix_shell)

How does the terminal fit in?

 Windows Users

When you see the word "terminal" used, that is the equivalent of your PowerShell program. It's confusing, but the macOS terminal program is called Terminal (with a capital T). The macOS Terminal is the application macOS uses to interact with its Shell-CLI, Bash.

Exercise 3 of 9:

- Windows users will install bash
- MacOS users will find out what shell the Terminal.app using

1. Windows users: PowerShell is both the terminal app and the shell. Thus, the answer to the question, "What Shell does the PowerShell use?" is PowerShell.

PowerShell, however, *can* use another Shell-CLI. For example, it is very common for Windows developers to install and use the Bash Shell-CLI; the same one macOS users use by default.

In fact, it's common enough, that I am going to have install the Bash Shell-CLI. I would prefer you not have to install anything, but the reality is, your life and mine will be easier if you install and start using the Bash Shell. I promise you this won't be a futile effort. If you continue in Web Development, you will want to have the Bash Shell-CLI installed.

Go ahead and follow **these instructions**[143] on downloading and installing Bash. I will assume for the remaining Exercises that you'll be using the Bash Shell-CLI.

1. macOS users On your Terminal program, navigate to Preferences.

---

[143]https://www.howtogeek.com/249966/how-to-install-and-use-the-linux-bash-shell-on-windows-10/

2. Once you have the Preferences open, look towards the middle of the General settings page, and find the area that says "Shells open with:".

I suspect your settings will have the radio button "Default login shell" selected. It's here that the computer is telling the Terminal program to use the Standard shell, though it gives you the option to use another Shell program if you'd like.

You can see from the Terminal Preferences option that I can select what Shell I want to use. Thus, right away, we can confirm that Terminal uses a Shell, but Terminal itself is not one. I know that might seem a little pedantic, but the reality is that a lot of people don't understand they are different things; we will.

With that in mind, understand that a terminal is a program that runs a Shell-CLI like Bash or Zsh. The Shell is just a wrapper around your operating system. The Terminal is what allows us to use the Shell-CLI.

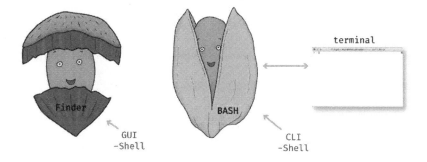

Shell Scripting

In the very first Exercise of this chapter, you typed the following command in the Terminal:

```
say bananas
```

The say command is a Shell Script. The Terminal reads and translates the Shell Scripting Programming Language. But you can't just type these commands everywhere. If you went ahead and tried to type say bananas in the DevTools Console, you'd get an error.

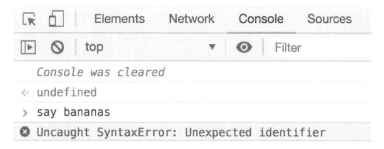

As I alluded to in the Programming Languages chapter, Shell Scripting is a language you use to interact with your computer. Common operations done in Shell Scripting include moving/creating files, opening/closing programs, and printing text. We will cover how to do some of these things throughout the remainder of this chapter.

Command Syntax

Shell Scripting commands are often followed by Arguments and/or Options.

Arguments[144] tell the command *what* to act on. For example, in the previous example, say is the command and bananas is the argument; I'm telling the computer *what* to say.

Flags are a kind of option. A single dash - or double dash -- precedes flags. Options (e.g., flags) tell the command *how* to act.

For example, the say command allows us to specify a type of voice we'd like it to use. To do this, we'd use the -v flag followed by a name our computer associated with a voice type.

 Windows Users

The PowerShell commands are slightly different, and we'll walk through how to do this in the next Exercise. But instead of adding a -v flag you would add the .SelectVoice(voice-name) command.

We will enter this command later, but for example, if I wanted the computer to talk in a Scottish women's voice, I would use a voice flag -v followed by name fiona. Fiona is the name the computer associated with a Scottish women's voice.

- The **command**: say
- The **flag**: -v fiona
- The **argument**: A nods as guid as a wink tae a blind horse

---

[144]https://unix.stackexchange.com/questions/285575/whats-the-difference-between-a-flag-an-option-and-an-argument

"A nods as guid as a wink tae a blind horse" is a Scottish saying that in English translates to "A nod is as good as a wink to a blind horse". The proverb[145] suggests that if you blink at a blind horse then it is time to get a new horse.

```
say -v fiona "A nods as guid as a wink tae a blind horse"
```

Now you might be wondering how I knew I could add the voice (-v) flag. The good news is that nearly every command comes with an **instruction manual**. How do we read this instruction manual? The manual is itself a command!

The manual command is called man (short for **man**ual page).

Exercise 4 of 9: Using the man command to understand the syntax

1. Open your terminal application (Terminal for macOS users, or Powershell for Windows OS users)

2. Type the following command.

The man command opens the manual for whatever command follows it.

 Windows Users

The man command also works in PowerShell. However, there is no man page for the say. Instead try something like: man ls, where the ls command list files in the current directory. A command you will be using later. This way, you can get familiar with using the man command.

---

[145]https://www.scottish-at-heart.com/scottish-sayings.html

In previous chapters, I've encouraged you to either type or copy-paste a code snippet. Here, however, I want you to type the commands. In fact, I am passively going to force you by using screenshots instead of code snippets, which for the digital readers will make it impossible to copy the command. I am doing this because typing commands is the first step to learning them. You are welcome.

3. Once you press enter, you'll be directed to another view. This view is the "Manual" for the command say.

```
●  ●  ●              ⬆ angel — man say — man — less ◂ man say — 80×24              ▮

SYNOPSIS
          say [-v voice] [-r rate] [-o outfile [audio format options] | -n name
:port | -a device] [-f file | string ...]

DESCRIPTION
          This tool uses the Speech Synthesis manager to convert input text to
          audible speech and either play it through the sound output device
          chosen in System Preferences or save it to an AIFF file.

OPTIONS
          string
              Specify the text to speak on the command line. This can consist of
              multiple arguments, which are considered to be separated by spaces.

          -f file, --input-file=file
              Specify a file to be spoken. If file is - or neither this parameter
              nor a message is specified, read from standard input.

          -v voice, --voice=voice
              Specify the voice to be used. Default is the voice selected in
              System Preferences. To obtain a list of voices installed in the
              system, specify '?' as the voice name.

:▮
```

man pages exist for nearly every command on almost every common system, so learning how to read them is an extremely valuable skill.

man pages can be a little intimidating to read. To help you navigate them, I've included a break down of the sections I find most helpful.

Synopsis: Where you can figure out the basic syntax for the command. It's a little cryptic at first glance, but two quick tips will make it clearer. 1. Anything inside of brackets **[ ]** is optional. 2. The vertical bar | indicates "or".

Description: The descriptions are quite useful. I usually read the descriptions first and then scan over the synopsis and then the options.

Examples: If you scroll down (using your down arrow key) to the bottom of the manual, you'll see an Examples area. Examples sometimes make more sense to me than the Synopsis section, so I'll always check here for clarification.

In the say command's man page, under "Examples," there is an example for using the -v flag followed by the name Alex. Alex is the United States male voice.

```
EXAMPLES
          say Hello, World
          say -v Alex -o hi -f hello_world.txt
          say --interactive=/green spending each day the color of the leaves
          say -o hi.aac 'Hello, [[slnc 200]] World'
          say -o hi.m4a --data-format=alac Hello, World.
          say -o hi.caf --data-format=LEF32@8000 Hello, World
```

4. To exit the manual view press q.

5. The Scottish voice is too good not try yourself, plus it gives us practice using a command flag. To use it, however, we first need to add the Scottish Fiona voice to our computer.

Windows Users

Jump to the **Windows users step** - #5. The steps for PowerShell are a bit different.

Using Spotlight (cmd + spacebar), search for "accessibility." Once open, navigate to the Speech option via the left-hand menu.

Under the voice area, click on the "System Voice" dropdown and select "Customize…". Add whatever voice you want, but for Fiona, scroll down to English (Scottish

Standard English), and select Fiona. It will take a moment to download the voice after pressing OK.

6. Now back to the Terminal. Type in the command that I did earlier, and make sure you have your computer's volume up.

➡ ~ <u>say</u> -v fiona "A nod's as guid as a wink tae a blind horse"

The point of this exercise is not to play with accents, though that is a fun aside, but to show you how to use the `man` command to learn a command's syntax.

5. **Windows users**: The Scottish Standard accent is not freely available for PowerShell. So instead, we'll be playing with an Italian accent.

First, we need to download the Italian accent. In your Windows Explorer search for "languages." Open the "Edit language and keyboard options."

About halfway down the page, select "Add a language." Search for the Italian language. Add the "Italiano (Italia)" language. It may take a moment to download. You will also likely have to restart your computer so that PowerShell recognizes the new language. If you're like me and hate restarting your computer, give the following series of commands a try first. If you hit an error, then give restarting a try.

Back in PowerShell type in the following commands:

```
$say.SelectVoice("Microsoft Elsa Desktop")
$say.Speak("Why don't you get yourself a nice girl?")
```

Of course, you can replace the text here with anything you would like, but I'm partial to the Goodfellas[146].

 If you hit a "Cannot call a method on a null-valued expression" error, make sure you go back and add the $say method that we did in the first exercise.

The Terminal & PowerShell Programs

All computers come with a default terminal application. MacOS comes with the Terminal.app (Terminal for short), which I think is an unfortunate naming choice; they named the terminal program "Terminal." This is equivalent to calling the soup of the day "Soup Of The Day".

Windows OS comes packaged with the terminal application: PowerShell[147].

For all our examples, we've been using the Terminal.app (macOS) or PowerShell (Windows OS).

Lots of programmers use the default terminal programs that come with their computers, but many programmers, myself included, prefer to use different terminal applications. Some other terminal applications that you may hear about are listed below:

---

[146]https://www.youtube.com/watch?v=r8MhDEOswo8
[147]Default for Windows 10

Description	Logo
iTerm2 works on macOS, and adds functionality on top of the default Terminal.app.	
Hyper is a fancy looking terminal, focused on style and also added functionality. It's works any LinuxOS	
cmder is a terminal app for Windows, adds functionality and styling.	

All of these programs are just different ways to talk to the same Shell-CLI.

There is a rabbit hole awaiting you if you wanted to find the pros-and-cons of each terminal program. It's a programmers party trick to have fancy looking terminal programs, with fancy capabilities. At the end of the chapter, under the Party Tricks Exercise, I include links on different terminal configurations and appearance settings. Aside from impressing your friends, you'll be using your terminal a lot so configuring it, in my opinion, is worth the time and vanity.

Tips for Learning the terminal

The terminal is very flexible and powerful. But it's only as powerful as your memory. I say that because you have to *remember* the commands. Some you'll memorize by habit and use. For the commands, you don't memorize you should have a cheat sheet or system for keeping track of them.

For example, Nate Murray a co-founder of newline[148] - this book's publishing company - has kept what he calls a "Command File" for the last 10+ years. In this file are *all* the commands Nate uses or has used. Nate says about this file,

> *"If I were ever to lose that file, I would lose at least three years of experience."* –
> Nate Murray

---

[148]https://www.newline.co

I couldn't agree more with Nate. I feel strongly enough about having a note-keeping system for commands that before we go any further, I am going to have you make a *Command File* - paying tribute to Nate's "Command File" - that you can use to start keeping track of commands.

Exercise 5 of 9: Make a Command File

 Windows Users

Most of the following commands work the same in PowerShell. For those that don't, I've added the correct command.

1. Whatever system you use for taking notes is ultimately the best system. Thus, if you already have a preferred method for taking notes, use that system and browse over these next couple of steps. If you do skip ahead, check out step #7 as I link to a starter "Commands File" that you might find useful.

2. We are going to create a note-taking system using our terminal application. The first thing we are going to do is make a folder on our Desktop that will hold our "Command File." We are going to call this Folder *notes*.

3. In your terminal application, type the following command and press enter.

 The first tilde ~ is generated by my Terminal.app, you do not need to type this; just type cd ~/Desktop.

```
⇢  ~ cd ~/Desktop
⇢  Desktop ▮
```

In the Finder, this action would be the same as navigating to your Desktop.

The **cd** command means **change directory**. The cd command moves you to the file path specified - we'll learn more about file paths later in the chapter.

The tilde ~ indicates the **home directory**. The tilde key can be found in the upper-left side of your keyboard.

The home directory is the home of the user who's executing a command. For me, this translates to users/angel for you, it will be something like users/yourComputersUserName.

The following is a screenshot of my home directory via my Finder[149].

---

[149]For more information on tilde's in file paths I recommend this article by LifeWire

4. Next, in your terminal application, type the following command and press enter.

```
→ Desktop mkdir notes
→ Desktop ▮
```

In the Finder, this action would be the same as making a new Folder and giving it the name *notes*.

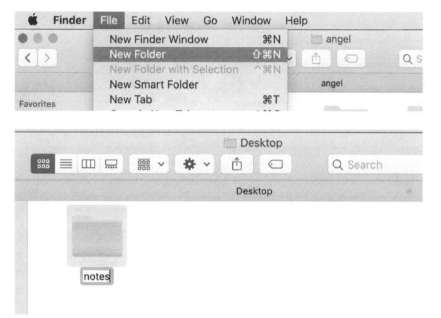

The `mkdir` command **makes a directory** (a.k.a., a Folder). With the `mkdir notes` command, we created a new folder on our Desktop called *notes*.

5. Now that we have the *notes* folder, we need to cd (change directories) into it. Type the following command to navigate into it.

```
→ Desktop cd notes
→ notes ▮
```

In our Finder, this action would be like opening our *notes* folder from our Desktop.

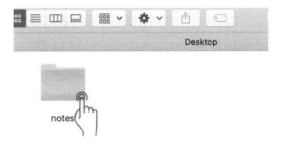

6. Next, we're going to create a **Command-file** and put it in our new *notes* folder. In your terminal application, type the following command:

Windows Users

If you are using the Bash shell, the `touch` command will work. If you are not, use the following command instead of `echo $null >> Command-file`. Where `$null` indicates a blank file. The **echo** command is used to send an output. In the previous command, we combined the `echo` command with the `>>` operator. This is a redirection operator, which tells PowerShell to move the output from the PowerShell to the file you are choosing, in this case, your new "Command-file."

The **touch** command **makes a new file**. What you put after the command, is the name you'd like to give the file. With the previous command, you just made a new file called "*Command-file*," which lives inside the *notes* folder on your Desktop.

 If you hit the up arrow key while in the Terminal *or* PowerShell, it will return your last command. Continue pressing the up key to cycle through the commands. The up arrow is very handy if you're repeating similar commands.

7. I know nothing happened when you hit enter after that last command, but if you type the command `ls`, which **lists all the files and folders** in your current location, you'll see your new file.

In the Finder, this would be like viewing all the files in a folder.

8. Let's open up the *"Command-file"* from the terminal application. Type the following **open** command to open the file.

In the terminal: `notes open Command-file`

Windows Users

Instead of the open command, type the name of the file path and press enter. You will then be prompted to open the file with a program of your choice.
`~\Desktop\notes\Command-file`

The *"Command-file"* will open in whatever default program you have that opens .txt files. You are now ready to start taking notes.

```
  TextEdit   File   Edit   Format   View   Window   Help
● ● ●                    Command-file — Edited
The beginning of my Command-file.

Let the note-taking commence!!!

cd :  Change Directory command.

mkdir : Make Directory (folder) command.

touch : Make a file

ls : List files in current directory
```

 Later on, I would recommend you make it, so your text editor (e.g., VSCode) becomes the default program to open files from the terminal application. Here's a Stack Overflow link[150] on how to do that[151].

I have gone ahead and made a *"Command-file"* that includes all the commands we've used so far, as well as the ones we will use later in this chapter. If you'd like to look at this file or copy-paste from it, you can find the file here: 6-terminal/Command-file.txt[152].

Now that we have our *"Command-file,"* we can move on and add commands to it as we go. Again, make this your own, add to it, amend it, and use whatever system - sticky notes, text file, note-taking software, etc. - that you will use.

File Paths

To effectively use your terminal application, you need to know how to navigate around it. The reason is, unlike the Finder or Windows Explorer programs, there are no menus or icons you navigate. Rather, in your terminal application, you have to *tell* the computer via directions - in the form of file paths - where you'd like to go.

To learn about file paths, we'll start with a quick command - **pwd**, which stands for **Print Working Directory**[153]. The pwd command tell you *where* on your computer

---

[150]https://stackoverflow.com/questions/46687865/how-to-change-visual-studio-text-editor-to-default
[151]I'm using Stack Overflow as it's likely that any VSCode settings change will be captured by an updated comment.
[152]code/src/6-terminal/command-list.txt
[153]https://en.wikipedia.org/wiki/Pwd

you are.

Directories and Folders are the same thing

The word Directory comes from the CLI environment and precedes the term Folder. Hence why it's pwd and not pwf. The word Folder came about from the GUI environment. In practice, when you're talking about a container of files, a Folder[154] is probably the better word choice.

1. In your terminal application type pwd.

What returns is your current location. For example, if I'm inside my Desktop on my terminal application, the return of that statement would look like the following:

```
➜  Desktop pwd
/Users/angel/Desktop
➜  Desktop ▮
```

And this is what that would look like if I were in my Finder:

So that's how you find out where you are on your computer. But how do you go from where you are to somewhere else? The answer is **file paths**. You use file paths to tell the computer where you'd like to go (i.e., computer speak for directions).

For example, say I was on my Desktop, and I wanted to move into the "nuts" folder in Downloads. The shortest file path to do this would be as follows:

---

[154]https://stackoverflow.com/questions/5078676/what-is-the-difference-between-a-directory-and-a-folder

```
../Downloads/nuts/
```

Breaking this down, the file path is saying:

"go up a folder, then move into the Downloads folder, and next into the nuts folder."

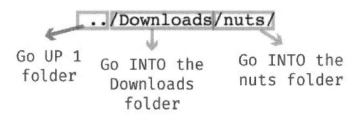

If you're a bit confused, that's OK. Learning file paths can be a bit tricky at first, but once you get them, terminal life will become a lot easier. Let's dig into it more.

There two types of file paths you can use: **absolute path** and **relative path**.

Relative File Paths

We will start by defining a **relative file path**. The key to understanding relative file paths is in the name; it means **relative to where you are**.

To understand what this means, we'll do a quick Exercise in our terminal application.

Exercise 6 of 9: Terminal and Relative File Paths

1. In your terminal application, navigate to the Desktop using the following command:

cd ~/Desktop

2. Now that we are *in* our Desktop, let's use a relative file path to move to another location on our computer. Remember, wherever we go is relative to where we currently are. Right now, we are in our Desktop.

Let's say we want to go to our ***notes*** folder we created earlier. We know it's on the Desktop, so it is just a short jump into that folder (Desktop -> notes). Using the cd command followed by the following relative file path gets us there.

```
➡ Desktop cd ./notes
➡ notes █
```

3. And what if we wanted to move into our Downloads folder from our Desktop? That would look like the following:

```
➡ Desktop cd ../Downloads
➡ Downloads █
```

The commonality between both of these is that they start with a dot . the same keyboard symbol for a period. All you have to do to indicate you want to use a relative file path is to start the path off with a dot.

If you use one dot, like our first example, that means you want to look in the same folder you are currently in. In our case, we were looking for the *notes* folder while we were inside our Desktop.

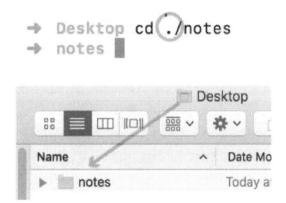

If you use a double dot .. that means you want to move up one folder.

```
→ Desktop cd ../Downloads
→ Downloads ▮
```

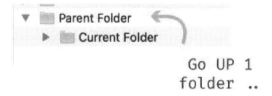

You can see in the screenshot that I moved up one folder into the angel directory. I did this by using the double dot. Then, (highlighted in blue) I moved into the Downloads folder by using /Downloads.

Both of these moves were **relative** from where I was on my Desktop.

You might be asking yourself what exactly does "up" mean? Up is easier to show than it is to explain, and hopefully, the following screenshot helps you visualize it. Essentially, "up" means to move into the parent folder of where you currently are.

```
▼ ▣ Parent Folder
   ▶ ▣ Current Folder

           Go UP 1
           folder ..
```

4. One more quick command to help bring this home. You can chain double-dots together to move up several folders at a time. Try it out. In the following screenshot, I moved from my *notes* folder on my Desktop to my angel directory - two folders up.

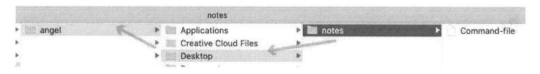

```
[➡  notes cd ../..
[➡  ~ pwd
/Users/angel
➡  ~ ▮
```

Here's what it looks like in my Finder. The first .. moves me into my Desktop. The second .. moves me into my angel directory.

 Let's Review

Relative file paths start from where you *currently* are. You must start the file path out with a dot . to indicate you are using a relative file path. If you use one dot that means you are looking in your current folder. If you use two dots .. that means you are moving up a folder. You can chain double-dots to move several folders at once.

Absolute File Paths

Absolute file paths use the **root directory** to figure out navigation. The root directory ("root" to elicit the image of a tree's beginnings) is the topmost folder of your file system.

"Users" is the root directory of my mac. It is the topmost folder/directory. Macintosh HD is a disk, not a folder/-directory.

The absolute file path starts at the root directory.

The absolute file path starts at the root directory.

Windows Users

The root concept is the same for Windows users. The only difference is that instead of "Macintosh HD" the drive is "C:/Windows". If you tab as you enter in the file path, PowerShell will automatically correct any potential errors in your file path. I recommend using this auto-complete feature.

To indicate you are using the absolute file path, you start the file path off with a forward slash /. No dot. The following is the absolute file path to our Desktop.

⇥   ~   **/Users/angel/Desktop/**

Here is what that file path looks likes on the Finder. (The tree on the screenshot indicates the "root").

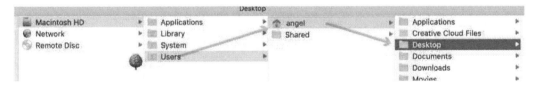

Let's use a directions analogy to help clarify. Imagine for a moment you are giving a friend directions to your house. Say your friend is at their home. Your directions will start from their house (let's call this the "beginning") and go to your home. The directions might sound something like:

"Out of your apartment, head East on Main street until you reach 4th street. Take a right on to 4th street. I'm the last house on the right."

Let's call that an absolute path - your directions are starting from the beginning - or at least how I've defined beginning here.

But later, another friend is already at Starbucks on Main street and needs directions. You might say to them:

"Take a left out of the Starbucks onto 4th street. I'm the last house on the right."

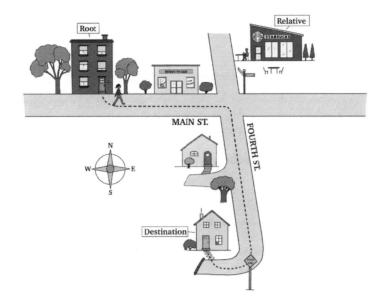

Your first friend is starting from the "beginning," and thus you are giving them directions akin to an absolute file path. Your Starbucks friend is starting somewhere else, and you give them directions relative to where they're at, much like a relative file path.

Let's get more familiar with Absolute File Paths using the terminal application.

Exercise 7 of 9: Terminal and Absolute File Path

1. In your terminal application, navigate to your root directory. A quick way to do this is to use the **change directory** command followed by the tilde: cd ~

2. Using an absolute file path, let's move into our "nuts" folder.

Remember, using the absolute file path means we start from the root directory, and omitting a dot start with the first Folder we want to move into.

replace with your computer's name

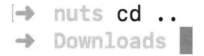

```
➜  ~  cd /Users/angel/Downloads/nuts
➜  nuts ▮
```

And just like that, we moved into our nuts folder using an absolute file path.

3. Now using an absolute file path, let's navigate to our Downloads folder.

```
➜  nuts cd /Users/angel/Downloads
➜  Downloads ▮
```

If we had used a relative file path, the command would have been much shorter. Relative to where we were - in the "nuts" folder" - the Downloads folder is only a folder up. And if you remember, to move a folder up using a relative file path requires us to use two dots. Here is what it would have looked like if we had used a relative file path.

```
➜  nuts cd ..
➜  Downloads ▮
```

 Relative File Path

Is relative to where you are. The file path will always start with a dot .

 Absolute File Path

Starts at the first folder in your system. The file path will always start with a forward-slash /

You should now have a better sense of how to move around the terminal application using relative and absolute file paths. Keep practicing with it. Things will get easier.

 The **tab** key triggers an autocomplete feature built into most all Shell-CLIs. It's an essential trick when working with file paths. To use it, begin typing the folder or file name, and press tab mid-way through. Based on what you typed, it will try to complete the name for you.

File System

We now have a better understanding of how to navigate around our computer. But what exactly are you navigating *in*? If you were the captain of a ship , I basically just showed you how to sail a ship, but did not tell you if you'd be in the Atlantic, Bering Strait, or a bathtub.

Your computer uses a File System to organize everything on it, and it is this File System that you're navigating around when inside the terminal. Whenever you are moving files, creating folders, or deleting things you are doing those things on the computer's File System.

The File System is your terminal's equivalent of the captain's bathtub.

File Types

The File System is made up of two types of files:

1. **Data files**. Think anything that contains data, text files, word docs, images, mp3, etc.

For example, all the files that you've downloaded for this book are data files. Some are .html files, some are .png, but they all are data files.

2. **Executable files**. These are files that when you open them, they execute something. It's a good bet that any file in your Applications folder is an executable file.

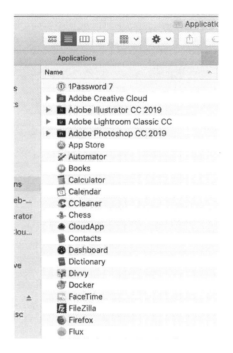

All of these files run a program on your computer. When you open *Adobe Illustrator* or the *Calculator* application, you are running executable files[155].

 Another, less obvious, example of an executable file are the commands we've been running in the terminal. Think about it; every time we executed a command in the terminal, the commands *do* something. Behind the scenes, these commands are linked to executable files.

Now we know there are two types of files on our computer - data files, and executable files. Additionally, we understand that the computer has a file system it uses to keep things organized. Let's move onto the fun part: writing commands.

Let's run some commands!

The best way to get comfortable with Shell Scripting and the terminal is to type commands and run them. I'll give you some of the more popular commands, and

---

[155]https://medium.com/@jalendport/what-exactly-is-your-shell-path-2f076f02deb4

handy tricks that will make working in the terminal easier.

Here is a quick summary of the commands we've already used to get to this point:

Command	What the Command Does
cd	change directories (a.k.a. folders)
pwd	print working directory (where you are located on your)
ls	lists all the files and folders
man	manual command
mkdir	make a directory (a.k.a. folder)
touch	make a file
echo	returns an output. It can also be used to make a file
say	MacOS - make the computer say whatever comes after the command
$say	A script we made for Windows OS. Does the same thing as the macOS say command

Windows Users

I recommend keeping the Microsoft PowerShell website bookmarked, which lists all the commands available to PowerShell and gives great examples of how to use them. Here is the link[156] for PowerShell version 6. You can change the version with the dropdown in the upper right. To see what version of PowerShell you're running, enter the following command $PSVersionTable.PSVersion

Exercise 8 of 9: Commands that manipulate files

For this exercise, we'll be using the "nuts" folder located in our Downloads. We've learned how to make folders, and make files. In this Exercise, we'll learn how to copy, delete, and move files.

---

[156]https://docs.microsoft.com/en-us/powershell/scripting/overview?view=powershell-6

1. In your terminal application, make sure you are inside your "nuts" folder. If you have moved all over the place and are unsure where you are, the following set of commands should get you where you want to be. We used this same file path in the absolute file path Exercise.

replace with your computer's name

```
→ ~ cd ~
→ ~ cd /Users/angel/Downloads/nuts
→ nuts
```

2. Let's copy the cashew image. To copy a file, you use the **cp** command, followed by the filename and destination.

 I suspect you don't have a cashew.png in your "nuts" folder. No worries. If you're a macOS user, use the **touch** command: touch cashew.png. If you're a Windows OS user (not using Bash), use our **echo** command echo $null >> cashew.png.

If we wanted to copy the cashew image from our Downloads onto our Desktop the command would look like the following:

```
→ nuts cp cashew.png ../../Desktop/
Desktop/     Documents/   Downloads/
```

A couple of notes:

- I used the tab auto-complete feature to double-check that I was using the correct file path, which is why you see the red "Desktop" "Document" "Downloads" options below the command.
- The ../../ of the file path indicates that I want to use a relative file path and that I want to go up *two* folders.

If I look at the following Finder screenshot you can see one folder jump up gets me to the Downloads folder. One folder jump more gets me to the parent folder holding both Desktop and Downloads. I then used the tab key to confirm that yes, indeed, I was in the parent directory holding the Downloads and Desktop folder.

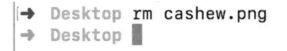

Try this yourself, and use that tab key!

You can confirm that you copied the cashew image by using the cd command into your Desktop. Then using the ls command to list the files there. There we can see our cashew.png image.

```
[➜  nuts cd ../../Desktop
[➜  Desktop ls
cashew.png notes
➜  Desktop ▊
```

3. Now let's delete that copied cashew image. The command **rm**, which stands for remove, will delete files. If you are in the location of where the file is located, then you can name the file you want to remove. Otherwise, you can specify a file path to where the file is you want to delete.

```
[➜  Desktop rm cashew.png
➜  Desktop ▊
```

4. Now let's move our "nuts" folder from our Downloads to our Desktop. We can move either a folder or file using the **mv** command.

To move a file, you need to follow the mv command by the file name and destination.

Let's first navigate over to our Downloads, and then move the "nuts" folder to the Desktop. This is how we would do that:

```
➥ Desktop cd ../Downloads
➥ Downloads mv nuts ../Desktop
➥ Downloads ▮
```

Go ahead and navigate over to the Desktop. Then ls the items there to confirm that you have indeed moved the "nuts" folder.

```
➥ Downloads ../Desktop
➥ Desktop ls
notes nuts
➥ Desktop ▮
```

5. The mv command both moves files/folders but can also rename them as well. Now let's use the renaming feature of the mv command. This is also very helpful.

Let's say we wanted to rename the "nuts" folder to "NUTS!". Easy, follow the mv command by the file or folder you want to rename, which is then followed by the new name you want to assign it.

```
➥ Desktop mv nuts NUTS
➥ Desktop ls
NUTS   notes
➥ Desktop
```

Done, and I confirmed using the ls command to show the folders/files on my Desktop. Pretty neat.

I've only skimmed the surface of available Shell commands. And I didn't even enter into the world of Shell Scripts. Hint: Shell Scripts, are essentially commands chained together to execute a more complex series of operations. However, the commands we practiced are very helpful and commonly used. Consider yourself sufficiently introduced to Shell Commands.

Exercise 9 of 9: Party Tricks

The following are what I call "terminal Party Tricks." All but one of these are relatively worthless, but entertaining nonetheless. This section is entirely optional.

1. **Dancing party parrot**. Type the following command and be entertained. To exit, hit ctrl + c.

```
curl parrot.live
```

 Windows Users

This command should work. However, if you run into errors, it's likely you have not set up your default Internet Explorer. See an article here[157].

You'll come across the curl command later in your programming career, but for now, know that the curl command is calling the parrot.live from a server. If you scroll up on the terminal while the parrot is dancing, you'll see it's a bunch of text, that together makes the illusion of a dancing parrot.

2. **Jazz up your terminal application**. A quick change to your terminal's theme will go a long way. By no means do you *need* to do this, but honestly I think it's worth it. You'll spend a lot of time in your terminal, so why not make it pretty.

- For those who'd like to continue using Bash as their Shell-CLI and MacOS Terminal app, I recommend this article by Free Code Camp[158][159]. It will give you a couple of quick steps to modify the look of the Terminal.
- If you're on a macOS and want to try a different terminal application and Shell-CLI, I'd recommend iTerm2 or Hyper for a terminal app, and zsh for a Shell-CLI. Before you go this route, make sure you understand why you want to do this. I've included some links to help you weigh your options.

   - iTerm2's website[160] does a great job of giving an overview of the benefits.
   - Hyper[161] sure looks good - there's no denying that. I don't personally use this

---

[157]http://wahlnetwork.com/2015/11/17/solving-the-first-launch-configuration-error-with-powershells-invoke-webrequest-cmdlet/

[158]https://medium.freecodecamp.org/jazz-up-your-bash-terminal-a-step-by-step-guide-with-pictures-80267554cb22

[159]Operating systems update so frequently, there is a chance this article could be out of date by the time you get to it. If that's the case, a simple Google search for "jazz up your bash terminal" should get you started.

[160]https://www.iterm2.com/features.html

[161]https://hyper.is/

one, but I might have had I done more research before getting familiar with iTerm2.

– zsh, I'm a big fan of zsh. Its autocompletion is more powerful than Bash and that alone is enough for me. Another benefit of zsh is the oh-my-zsh project - learn more here[162], which provides theme'ing and plugin support. Here's a good article[163] on the benefits of zsh, scroll down to "Why I like it."

- **Windows users**, the customizations are endless. I recommend this article[164] as a first step.

3. Playing emacs games. Yes, games, like Tetris, pong, and more. I won't go into how to do it here, other than to say your first step is to run the `emacs` command from the terminal.

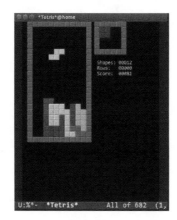

There are lots of tutorials and games you can play directly from your terminal. Here is a good start up article[165], and here is a wiki[166] listing all the available games. Here are some[167] games just for PowerShell users.

Have fun!

---

[162]https://github.com/robbyrussell/oh-my-zsh

[163]https://justin.abrah.ms/dotfiles/zsh.html

[164]https://www.gngrninja.com/script-ninja/2016/3/20/powershell

[165]https://lifehacker.com/5984870/unlock-old-school-arcade-games-in-your-macs-terminal

[166]https://www.emacswiki.org/emacs/CategoryGames

[167]https://gallery.technet.microsoft.com/Games-in-PowerShell-89dd585e

Key Takeaways

- The terminal is the interface for you to interact with a Shell-CLI. The default Shell-CLI is Bash for macOS and PowerShell for Windows OS.
- A Shell is a wrapper around your computer's Operating System. There are two types of Shells: CLI and GUI.
- The Terminal (with a capital T) is the default macOS terminal application. PowerShell is the Windows default terminal app, acting as both the Shell-CLI and the terminal app. You can use other terminal applications like iTerm2 or Hyper. All of them are interfaces to interact with your computer's Shell-CLI.
- Shell Scripting is a Programming Language you can use to either type commands or link commands together to execute scripts.

  // Example: mkdir notes
- File paths are what you use to point your terminal towards a location on your computer. There are two types of file paths:

  // 1. Absolute file path. Start at the root of a computer's file system, and begin the file path with a forward slash.
  // 2. Relative file path. Start at where you currently are in your file system. Begin the file path with a dot. If you use two dots in a row that means you want to move up one folder.
- Your computer uses a File System to keep track of all its files and folders. This is the system you are navigating around when using File paths. There are two types of files: data and executable files.
- All the commands we covered can be found in the `3-terminal/Command-file.txt`[168].

Considerations for Further Study

I don't think the terminal deserves a separate course like JavaScript or HTML & CSS do. Instead, I would make sure you generally understand how it works - we covered about as much as you *need* to know here.

In the next chapter on Git, we'll get even more practice using your computer's terminal. Hopefully, through practice, you'll start to get more comfortable.

---

[168]code/src/3-terminal/command-list.txt

There is a learning curve. It will take you more time initially to use the terminal application than say the Finder but stick with it. Look up commands or things you might want to do and stay curious. Don't stop adding to your "Command-file" with everything listed here; that file is just a starter list.

Further Readings

I recommend playing with the commands in this article[169]. Many we have covered, but some we haven't. Additionally, they list more resources at the bottom if you'd like to go even deeper.

For Windows users, I would recommend spending time reading Microsoft's Power-Shell[170] documentation.

If you're interested in learning more about the history of Bash and Zsh, I recommend this slide presentation[171]. It does a great job covering the history and major differences and requires very little time.

I mentioned this book in the previous chapter, but "From Bash to Z Shell," is a great book, with lots of tidbits and history lessons squeezed in.

For Windows users, Microsoft's Virtual Academy[172] is a great resource. They have a lot of free classes on PowerShell.

If you *do* want to jump more into Shell Scripting, I would recommend spending some time on this tutorial[173]. It starts you out working through commands and eventually moves you into more complex Shell Scripts.

Additionally, the Bash Shell Scripting WikiBook[174] is free, and an easy to navigate online book resource.

Though Shell Scripting is not a required skill for many Web Developer positions, I promise you no time will be wasted building up this skill set.

---

[169]https://medium.com/the-code-review/top-10-bash-file-system-commands-you-cant-live-without-4cd937bd7df1
[170]https://docs.microsoft.com/en-us/powershell/scripting/overview?view=powershell-6
[171]https://www.slideshare.net/jaguardesignstudio/why-zsh-is-cooler-than-your-shell-16194692
[172]https://mva.microsoft.com/training-topics/powershell
[173]https://ryanstutorials.net/linuxtutorial/
[174]https://en.wikibooks.org/wiki/Bash_Shell_Scripting#What_is_shell_scripting?

What's Next?

The next chapter is all about Git. Git is a version control tool and is something you will use daily as a future Web Developer. Though you *can* use a GUI to interact with Git, the industry standard is to use your Shell-CLI, e.g., your terminal application.

This chapter on the terminal is required reading before moving into the next chapter on Git.

Chapter 7: Git and Version Control

Have you ever run into file saving hell? You started with good intentions, telling yourself you'd stick with an organized system of v1, v2, etc., but a couple spelling mistakes, and recovered files later you've got a file system like the screenshot on my right?

You're not alone. This problem is universal: developers, grandmas, your mail-person, anyone who has touched a computer. Thankfully, software platforms of all sorts have come together to create a variety of solutions. Google docs, for example, let's you look at your document's revision history, even allowing you to restore old versions.

Developers are especially demanding when it comes to version control. They are continually making small tweaks, revising, sharing code, and looking at changes done to code in the past. Today, Git is the technology that programmers use to solve for their onerous version control needs.

Git is open-source[175], meaning that it is free to use and may be redistributed or modified. Released in 2005, Git become popular very quickly and had wide-sweeping impacts on the programming community. There were Version Control Systems before Git came along, but Git's unique approach to tracking changes was an industry game-changer.

There has been and still is no real competitor[176] to Git. As a future web developer, you will need to know how to use it.

In this chapter, we come to understand what Git does and what problems it has solved. We will cover basic Git commands, using them to illustrate how Git works. We will then look at GitHub, a very popular software platform that uses the Git technology.

 I will be introducing a lot of Git commands in this chapter. If you'd like, add these commands to your Command-file, but don't focus too much on syntax. This chapter is about introducing concepts, not an instructional on Git syntax. That will come with practice and study done outside of this book.

Version Control

We've all been there. You saved a file on your computer, but accidentally removed something you wanted to keep. Maybe you thought ahead and have a previous version of the file you can search through, or more likely you didn't. Version management sucks and its suckiness grows exponentially larger when you're a developer working on a huge codebase.

Subsequently, developers have been trying to solve for the version control nightmare since there started being developers. Working on codebases present several consistent challenges, regardless of the size of the codebase or the number of people working on them. These challenges are - generally - as follows:

- Version control

---
[175]https://en.wikipedia.org/wiki/The_Open_Source_Definition
[176]https://rhodecode.com/insights/version-control-systems-2016

- Keeping an accurate history of file changes
- Logging information about file changes
- Allowing different people to make changes to the same codebase at the same time

Version Control Systems (VCS)

At first, developers tried to solve some of these problems with simple Version Control Systems (VCS). These were OK, but they only helped developers keep track of files that had changed. They didn't solve for any of the other issues mentioned above.

Additionally, these VCS were local. Meaning the whole codebase was on the developers' machines. Google's codebase is over 2 billion lines of code[177]. Keeping a codebase that large on your computer without it exploding isn't an option.

Local VCS also didn't come close to solving the issue of different developers collaborating on the same codebase. If the code was on your computer, how could you easily share it with another developer?

Meet Bob. He's a programmer in the 1980s.

Co-worker: *"Hey Bob, can you email that file version again, I think it's from the change you made on Friday, but I can't be certain. I know you already sent it, but I'm too lazy to look. Thanks!"*

Bob: *"I quit."*

I would too Bob.

Centralized Version Control Systems (CVCS)

Next came Centralized Version Control Systems (CVCS). CVCS improved upon the process enough that they were the industry standard through the 90s up until Git was released.

---

[177]https://www.wired.com/2015/09/google-2-billion-lines-codeand-one-place/

Unlike VCS, CVCS stored the codebase in a single place, not on individual computers. Whoever needed to work on something would just check out that file to work on it; similar to checking out a book from a library. The problem, what happens if the place with your codebase burns down, or the library floods?

Developers couldn't sleep at night knowing that all their work had a single point of failure.

Meet Kat. She's a programmer from 2003.

Co-worker: *"Hey Kat, did you hear there was a massive hail storm in Aurora, Nebraska? They recorded 7-inch diameter hail[178]! Isn't that where we have the computer that holds all of our code?"*

Kat: *"I quit."*

I would too Kat.

Distributed Version Control System (DVCS)

The third times a charm. Building off of VCS and CVCS, developers created Distributed Version Control Systems (DVCS). Git is a DVCS.

In DVCS, programmers check out a fully mirrored[179] version of the codebase. If this were a library, instead of checking out a book, you'd be checking out a mirrored image of the library, the book included[180]. Thus, if the library burned to the ground, anyone who checked out a mirrored version of the library could restore it with their version.

---

[178]https://en.wikipedia.org/wiki/List_of_costly_or_deadly_hailstorms#North_America

[179]https://en.wikipedia.org/wiki/Distributed_version_control

[180]As mentioned earlier, Google's codebase is huge. Under the DVCS you wouldn't have a mirrored version of the entire codebase, but rather only the areas you wanted to work on. In practice, this means that the codebase is spread across different repositories, and you only grab a mirrored version of the repository you are interested in.

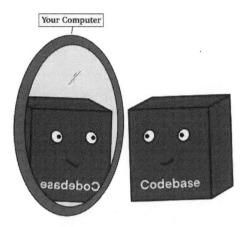

DVCS also allow for branching and merging. Branching here means to duplicate. With Git, this often means you are duplicating the codebase you are looking at. You make a branch - a duplicate of the codebase - then you make changes on that branch. Merging comes in when you want to *merge* the changes on your branch back to the original codebase. We will discuss both topics in more detail later.

Meet Ivan. Ivan is a programmer from 2006.

Co-worker: *"Hey Ivan, we made a change a year ago, and I think we need to merge that change back into the codebase. Can you help me?"*

Ivan: *"We can do it, no problem. Go learn some Git, and you can do it sans my help."*

Ivan's a bit of a jerk for not helping, but at least he's not quitting.

Git

There are other DVCS, aside from Git out there, but Git is the world's most popular[181], and the one we will cover in this book.

---

[181]https://en.wikipedia.org/wiki/Distributed_version_control

There are two main ways to use Git. Through your terminal, or a Git GUI[182]. We will interact with Git via the terminal.

I am happy to boast about Git all-day, but Git toot's its own horn the best. Here is what Git has to say about itself, taken directly from the Git Website[183]:

Before we start introducing Git commands and the Git workflow, we need to set up a GitHub account and install Git.

Exercise 1 of 5: Setup GitHub account & Install Git

1. Open the GitHub website[184] and sign up for an account.

We will review GitHub in much greater detail later in this chapter. I am having you set up an account now because it makes the install process for Git a bit easier.

Choosing a GitHub username

The username you use will appear on most-all of your GitHub activity. People won't see your name so much as - in my case - see Monkeychip, my GitHub username. It's probably best not to choose a username like "annita-diaper" or "joemama."

When you set up your GitHub account, take note of your GitHub username and email. You will use these in the next step when installing Git.

---

[182]https://git-scm.com/downloads/guis/
[183]https://git-scm.com/
[184]https://github.com/

2. Next, let's navigate back to our terminal and install Git. You will be installing Git globally (e.g., on your computer, not in any particular location). Thus, it does not matter where you are in your terminal when you install Git.

Windows Users

Jump to the next step for your Git installation guide.

Git itself has a wonderful installation guide, which you can find here[185].

If you're on a macOS, you may be asked to install Xcode Tools while running the Git install commands. If you are prompted, go ahead and install. Xcode[186] is Apple's developer tools, and you'll need it to use Git.

During the installation process, Git will ask you for your GitHub username and email. By giving Git your GitHub username and email, you're connecting your local Git with your GitHub account. If you miss this step or run into issues, follow the instructions here for[187] setting up your Git username, and here for[188] your Git email.

2. **Windows users** You will be downloading Git for Windows. Click here[189] to begin the download process.

Select the defaults during the installation process. This download is going to set up a Git Bash for your Windows machine. What this means is that it will emulate the Bash shell so that you can run Git on it. It will also install a GIT GUI, which we won't be using.

Once installed, you can search for Git Bash, and it will pop up.

---

[185]https://git-scm.com/book/en/v2/Getting-Started-Installing-Git
[186]https://developer.apple.com/xcode/
[187]https://help.github.com/en/articles/setting-your-username-in-git
[188]https://help.github.com/en/articles/setting-your-commit-email-address-in-git
[189]https://gitforwindows.org/

This application will look very similar to PowerShell. The difference is that it's emulating the Bash shell. For the rest of the chapter, you will be able to follow along using the same commands as a macOS user because you are both running Git on the Bash shell. When I say something like "in your terminal," for you that "terminal" will be Git Bash.

Windows Users

Similar to the macOS installation process, while installing Git you *should* be prompted to enter your GitHub username and email. Missing this step will cause errors later on. If you were not prompted to enter these credentials during the installation process, click here for[190] setting up your Git username, and here for[191] your Git email.

General Git Workflow

To help explain the Git Workflow, I will be using a nature-watching analogy to describe Gits features. While working through the analogy, we will also be typing out Git commands.

---

[190]https://help.github.com/en/articles/setting-your-username-in-git
[191]https://help.github.com/en/articles/setting-your-commit-email-address-in-git

Exercise 2 of 5: Basic Git Workflow

Step 1: `git init`

Imagine Git is the name of your friend. You are both out enjoying nature. You ask Git - your friend - to keep an eye out for anything interesting that happens. Git pulls out his binoculars and commences watching.

1. In the code that comes with this book, navigate to the folder: `7-git/nature-watch`[192] in your terminal.

```
cd ~/Desktop/7-git/nature-watch
```

 The previous command assumes you downloaded the "7-git" folder containing all the code examples for this chapter onto your desktop.

2. Once in the nature-watch folder we are going to initialize git using the **git init** command.

```
git init
```

This command initializes an instance of Git, effectively making a Git repository (repo for short). Running this command tells Git to focus on the folder and all the files inside it where you have initialized Git.

---

[192] code/src/7-git/nature-watch

In our analogy, `git init` is similar to how we asked our buddy Git to "keep an eye out for anything interesting."

```
→ nature-watch git init
Initialized empty Git repository in /Users/angel/Desktop/nature-watch/.git/
```

When you initialize a Git repository, Git adds hidden files in your folder. These files are apart of Git setting itself up to watch any files in the folder you just initialized.

You can see these files by using the `ls` command with `-a` flag. This command list all the files in the current directory. The `-a` flag indicates "all" files, including any files that start with a dot.

```
→ nature-watch git:(master) × ls -a
.           ..          .git        bird.txt fox.txt  worm.txt
```

 You may also have noticed the `git:(master)` added in the last screenshot. This is added to your terminal when you initialize a Git repository. We will talk more about what master means later in the chapter.

Step 2: `git add`

If Git spots a change, it will keep its eye on it, but that's it. It won't start recording changes and documenting anything until you tell it to.

Back to the nature-watch example. You're a big fan of foxes. In fact, your favorite song is "What did the fox say," and you think everyone - readers included - should watch the music video[193].

You ask Git to keep an eye on the fox. Your friend, Git, noticed that a bird and worm were also doing some things, but you don't care about them so you tell Git not to worry about them. In the following screenshot, I've greyed out the worm and bird because we've asked Git to not worry about them.

---

[193]https://www.youtube.com/watch?v=jofNR_WkoCE

3. Back in the terminal, we're going to use the command `git status` to check-in and see what Git is seeing.

Let's run the `git status` command on our recently initialized nature-watch folder.

```
nature-watch git:(master) git status
On branch master

No commits yet

Untracked files:
  (use "git add <file>..." to include in what will be committed)

        bird.txt
        fox.txt
        worm.txt
```

What Git is telling us is that we have 3 files - fox, bird, and worm - that it sees, but it hasn't been told to watch.

For now, we're only interested in keeping an eye on our fox.

To tell Git to keep an eye on a file, you use the **git add** command. This command **stages** the file. Adding a file to the staging area tells Git that you want to include updates to that file in the next commit - committing is an action we'll learn about shortly. Staging a file is similar to when you asked your friend Git to "watch the fox."

4. Let's use the `git add fox.txt` command to stage our fox file.

```
nature-watch git:(master) git add fox.txt
```

When you run `git status` again, you'll see that the `fox.txt` file is now staged, but the `bird.txt` and `worm.txt` are not.

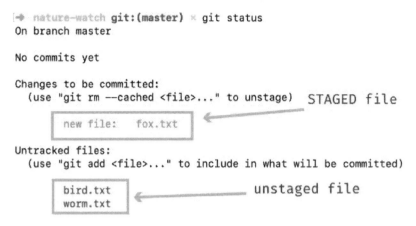

Step 3: `git commit`

Your friend Git is faithfully keeping an eye on everything in your nature-watch area but knows you specifically want to focus on the fox. Something crazy happens then, the fox starts to say something!

That's significant, and you want to document that change; put it down in writing so that you can refer to it later.

You tell your buddy Git, "OK Git, let's take a picture of that!" Git does, and asks you, "do you want me to add a comment in our log about it?" And you say, "yes, let's add the following note: 'The fox just said Wa-pa-pa-pa-pa-pa-pow!'" Just like[194] in your

---

[194]https://youtu.be/jofNR_WkoCE?t=47

favorite song.

Git writes the comment down as well as noting the time of day, the date, and that it was you who asked to take a picture of it. All of that information stays with the picture on Git's log.

Taking a picture and journaling about what you took a photo of, in Git, is akin to committing a file.

5. Let's make a similar change to our fox.txt file and commit that change.

Open the fox.txt file in your text editor. The fox.txt file lives inside the nature-watch folder that you downloaded.

The file is blank, but go ahead and add whatever it is you'd like, you just need to make a *change* of some sort to the file.

Sticking with our analogy I've added: "The Fox just said 'Wa-pa-papa-pa-pa-pow!"

```
1    "The Fox just said 'Wa-pa-papa-pa-pa-pow!".
```

 It's important to understand the git commit command only records the area on the file that changed and does not save a new version of the file itself. So if you had a file with 10 lines of code, but only changed one line, it would only take a snapshot of the one line that changed.

After pressing save on the fox.txt file, we are now ready to commit the change.

In your terminal use the `git commit -m` command. I have appended the `git commit` command with the -m flag, allowing me to append a message right after the command. If I did not use this flag, Git would prompt me to enter the commit message in another window.

```
↦ nature-watch git:(master) × git commit —m "The fox just said Wa-pa-pa-pa-pa-pa-pow"
[master (root-commit) 4849d62] The fox just said Wa-pa-pa-pa-pa-pa-pow
 1 file changed, 0 insertions(+), 0 deletions(-)
 create mode 100644 fox.png
```

Once Git takes the snapshot, that event is recorded in history. Anyone else can come along, and ask to see that snapshot again.

Summary

If a file changes, Git notices. If you want to record that change, you use the `git add` command to add that file to the staging area. Then, when you're ready, you use the `git commit -m` to commit the change with a message.

This is the general flow of how Git keeps track of file changes. Next, we are going to take a closer look at what happens on the `git commit` step. The details of what Git is doing during the `git commit` step is one of the reasons why Git is so revolutionary.

Commit, a snapshot of the change

When you make a change to a file, and you commit that change, Git takes a snapshot of that change. This process is called a **commit**. When you check out a file from a Git repository, you are not looking at the latest version of the file, instead, you are looking at a montage of Git commits (a.k.a., Git snapshots).

If you don't ask a file to be committed, it won't end up in the montage. This was the case for the bird and worm in the nature-watch example. We never asked Git to watch the bird and worm (we never ran the command: `git add bird.txt worm.txt`).

To help illustrate how this works, let's go back to our nature-watch example. Let's take more snapshots (a.k.a. `git commits`) to get a better understanding of what is happening.

Exercise 3 of 5: Making more Commits

We've already made a commit that the fox said "Wa-pa-pa-pa-pa-pa-pow!" Now, there's some action happening with the bird and the worm that we want to record; the bird is trying to eat the worm.

1. To keep up with the analogy, back in your text editor, add text to both the bird.txt and the worm.txt file. I went ahead and added text that went with the analogy. You don't have to do the same thing, just add something and save it.

bird.txt ✕	↻ ⊓ ⋯	worm.txt ●
1 🦉: I'm going to eat you worm!		1 🐛: Try me!

Next, we're going to *add* the worm and bird into the things Git is keeping track of.

2. Back in the terminal, use the `git add bird.txt worm.txt` to stage those two files.

```
➜ nature-watch git:(master) git add worm.txt bird.txt
```

3. Back in our nature-watch folder, in the terminal, let's commit these changes and make a note about it. `git commit -m "the bird is trying to eat the worm."`

```
➜ nature-watch git:(master) ✗ git commit -m "the bird is trying to eat the worm"
[master d4dbe28] the bird is trying to eat the worm
 2 files changed, 0 insertions(+), 0 deletions(-)
 create mode 100644 bird.txt
 create mode 100644 worm.txt
```

In the analogy, our friend's journal would now look like the following:

4. But wait, now the Fox begins speaking again. He appears to be saying, "Hatee-hatee-hatee-ho!" Yep, that's going in the record books.

Because we already committed the last thing the Fox did, we have to re-stage the fox.txt file, and then add and commit it.

Back in your text editor, add something new to the fox.txt file. I've added "Hatee-hatee-hatee-ho." Make sure to save the change.

5. Then in your terminal add the file and commit it using the following commands:
git add fox.txt git commit -m "the fox is now saying Hatee-hatee-hatee-ho".

```
➜  nature-watch git:(master) git add fox.txt
➜  nature-watch git:(master) ✗ git commit -m "the fox is now saying Hatee-hatee-hatee-ho"
[master ed7eb14] the fox is now saying Hatee-hatee-hatee-ho
 1 file changed, 1 insertion(+)
```

Here's the commit in our buddy Git's journal:

We've taken 3 pictures so far, each with a commit message. Git allows us to view a log of commits using the `git log` command.

→ nature-watch `git:(master)` `git log`

Once you enter the `git log` command, you'll be taken to another view. Here you can see all the commits. Notice that in addition to our commit messages, the log includes a timestamp and author information for each commit, just like our buddy Git's photo album.

```
commit ed7eb143ff073d325ba8d28cadce7c5953b36f35 (HEAD -> master)
Author: Monkeychip <argarbarino@gmail.com>
Date:   Sun Apr 14 20:55:44 2019 -0600

    the fox is now saying Hatee-hatee-hatee-ho

commit d4dbe28b08e23cffa829ababd680d9224f87248c
Author: Monkeychip <argarbarino@gmail.com>
Date:   Sun Apr 14 19:56:53 2019 -0600

    the bird is trying to eat the worm

commit 70f7f50de4e3ccf8cbaaf97605e4ea5a44de3a13
Author: Monkeychip <argarbarino@gmail.com>
Date:   Sun Apr 14 19:40:13 2019 -0600

    the fox just said Wa-pa-pa... 🐵
(END)
```

The key about how Git manages version control is that Git doesn't save "files", it saves snapshots of changes (commits) and puts them all together to create a file.

Additionally, Git does you a solid by allowing you to attach a message about the commit and date/time/author information. This information isn't displayed, but it's there, just like if you were looking through an old fashioned photo album with subtitles and date stamps on it.

Git Branching

Another key feature of Git is its branching feature. I mentioned earlier that when developers work on Git repositories, they are checking out a mirrored version of the repository.

Imagine for a moment that you have a mirrored version of a repository on your computer, and you want to make some changes to it. That mirrored version by default is named "master", and "master" is a branch.

I find it helpful to think of branches as silos of work. You can copy them and then work on changes on just that branch independent of your other branch.

The "master" branch is what Git, by default, makes when you `git init` a folder. After you `git init`, you may have noticed the git:(master) added to your terminal prompt.

```
➜  nature-watch git:(master) ✗
```

 If you don't see the `git:(master)` added to your terminal, it's because of your terminal settings. I highly recommend having this show, especially for the Exercises we do later in the chapter. Feel free to Google "add Git prompts to terminal", or use the instructions in this article[195], which details how to add Git prompts - as well as other theme options.

You could make changes to your master branch, but it's generally good practice to create a side branch and do changes there. Then either merge those changes back into your master branch or push them to a remote repository (we'll talk about that process a little later).

There are several reasons for using side branches. The main reason is to keep your changes organized. You may find yourself with several side branches at once, each focused on changing or fixing one specific thing. It's easier to keep track of them if they are on their own branch.

You could rename your master branch to anything you want, but the convention is to stick with "master." There is nothing special about the master branch, other than it's the first branch made when you initialize Git.

When you make a side branch from your master branch, the side branch is a copy of the "master" branch.

To get more familiar with branching, we are going to make a side branch where we determine the end of the worm's story. We'll then compare this new branch to our master branch and merge in the changes.

Exercise 4 of 5: Branching

1. Back in your terminal, still on the nature-watch folder, let's make a side branch.

---

[195]https://medium.freecodecamp.org/jazz-up-your-bash-terminal-a-step-by-step-guide-with-pictures-80267554cb22

To make a branch in Git, all you have to do is type the command `git checkout` with the -b flag and name the branch. Let's name our new branch `worms-story`

➜ nature-watch git:(master) git checkout -b worms-story
Switched to a new branch 'worms-story'

This new branch "worms-story" is a copy of the "master" branch that you can modify as you'd like.

2. When working with branches, it's often helpful to see the branches you currently have. To do this, use the git command `git branch`. Try this command out. You should see the "master" and "worms-story" branches listed.

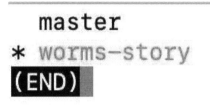

  If you are directed to another window, press "q" to return to the main terminal window.

3. Let's edit the worm.txt file and give the worm's story an ending. You can add whatever you'd like, but I'm partial to the worm. Make sure to save your changes.

```
 worm.txt  ✕
 worm.txt
   1   🐛: Try me!
   2
   3   Nice try.  Be a little earlier next time.
```

4. Back in the terminal, add and commit the change.

```
git add worm.txt
git commit -m "the worm has lived to see another day."
```

→ nature-watch **git:(worms-story)** git add worm.txt
→ nature-watch **git:(worms-story)** git commit —m "the worm has lived to see another day"

5. Now our "worms-story" branch is different than our "master" branch. Let's view these differences using the git command `git diff`.

There are a lot of options you can use with this command. For our purposes, where we just want to see the differences between the two branches, we'll follow `git diff` with the name of the branch we want to compare against (e.g., "master").

```
git diff master
```

You should see an output which highlights the differences between the two branches.

```
diff --git a/worm.txt b/worm.txt
index 12fa54f..90b9545 100644
--- a/worm.txt
+++ b/worm.txt
@@ -1 +1,3 @@
-🐛: Try me!
\ No newline at end of file
+🐛: Try me!
+
+Nice try.  Be a little earlier next time.
\ No newline at end of file
(END)
```

5. Let's try and merge the changes we made in the "worms-story" branch into our master branch.

We want to merge our "worms-story" branch *into* our "master" branch. Thus, we need to checkout the master branch and then run the `git merge worms-story` command.

To checkout master again, you run the `git checkout master` command. We used this branch earlier to *create* the "worms-story" branch. The difference with that previous command was the addition of the -b flag. That flag indicates a new branch. Without it, you're telling Git you want to checkout the branch rather than make one.

```
 nature-watch git:(worms-story) git checkout master
Switched to branch 'master'
```

6. Next, let's merge the "worms-story" branch into the "master" branch using the git merge worms-story command.

```
 nature-watch git:(master) git merge worms-story
Updating d624706..ccb05d7
Fast-forward
 worm.txt | 4 +++-
 1 file changed, 3 insertions(+), 1 deletion(-)
```

7. Next, let's delete the branch we no longer need as we've merged in the changes.

To delete a branch, you use the command git branch -d worms-story. If you haven't merged in your changes, Git will prompt you to merge in any changes first.

```
 nature-watch git:(master) git merge worms-story
Updating d624706..ccb05d7
Fast-forward
 worm.txt | 4 +++-
 1 file changed, 3 insertions(+), 1 deletion(-)
```

8. One last step, let's confirm that our ending of worm's story was merged in.

In your text editor, navigate to your worms.txt file. You should see the changes even though the branch where you made those changes was deleted.

We've kept our branching example pretty simple. But you can imagine how useful it might be to have these silos/branches of work where you can eventually merge your changes back together.

In most companies, you'll have lots of developers all working on the same code base. By making side branches and working on their code changes in these side branches, the developers avoid stepping on each other's toes. Then, when a developer is ready, they can "easily" merge their changes into the master branch[196]. This is a

---

[196]I added quotations around easily because merge conflicts can make things less easy.

very simplified summary of how companies manage this kind of workflow, but the point is: branches make this all possible.

The benefits of branching deserve more consideration than I have given them here. However, I think branching is something you learn to appreciate as you gain more experience with Git. In other words, Git's branching benefits will make themselves known as you spend time with them in the wild. For now, just understanding the basic concepts of branching is sufficient.

Git in the Cloud

We mentioned earlier that pre-Git developers didn't have a good solution for preventing a single point of failure, or allowing multiple developers to work on the same codebase at the same time.

Git solves for these two issues by communicating with Git repositories stored in the "cloud." These repositories are referred to as **"remote"** repositories. As we'll learn later, GitHub is the world's most popular, in the cloud, hosting service for Git repositories.

Whenever anyone says "cloud," they mean a computer, not near them. The computer in question is called a **server**. It is called a server because it is a computer with special properties that make it adept at "serving" up content.

You'll come to recognize the GitHub logo, but in case you didn't recognize it, it's the cat-like thing inside the black circle in the following illustration.

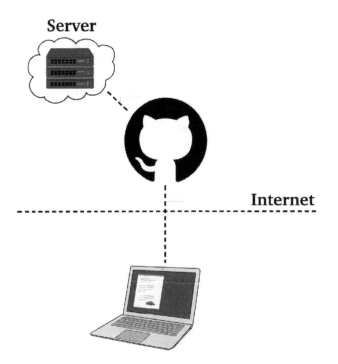

To help us understand how having repositories in the cloud is beneficial, we will work through a typical Git workflow using GitHub.

We will spend a whole section on GitHub later in this chapter. For now, know it is the cloud solution we are using to share and communicate with our Git repositories.

Exercise 5 of 5: Workflow between Git and GitHub

The following illustration is the Git to GitHub workflow we will be working through.

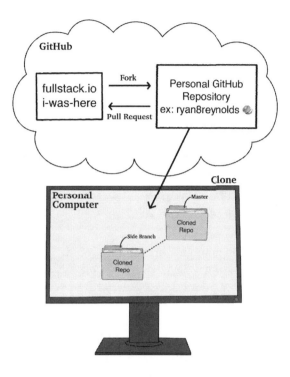

The process is as follows:

- Step 1. **Fork** a repository onto your personal GitHub account.
- Step 2. **Clone** the Forked repository onto your computer.
- Step 3. Make a **side branch** on your computer's Cloned repository.
- Step 4. Make changes and **commit** them.
- Step 5. **Push** the changes to your remote Forked repository.
- Step 6. Open a **Pull Request** to merge the changes from your Fork into the original repository.

We'll go through this process in the Exercise and review it again at the end of the Exercise.

Step 1: Fork

The first step is to **fork** a remote repository onto your GitHub account.

Forking means to make a mirrored-version of a remote repository onto a specific server[197]. In this example, that server is the GitHub platform.

What makes Forks special is that they are independent of the repository they copy. For example, if a devastating hail storm destroys the server holding the codebase, your Fork is unaffected. Your Forked version of the codebase could seamlessly become the "original" codebase.

For this Exercise, I will pretend to be the GitHub user "ryan8nolds." I will show you screenshots and commands from ryan8nolds, and you will follow along using your own GitHub account. We will also be using a GitHub repository called "i-was-here" that is hosted on the Fullstack.io GitHub account.

 "ryan8nolds" is a pseudonym for Ryan Reynolds, who is my favorite tweeter[198]. His well-known bagel tweet is a classic, and I use this tweet in the example.

1. Before we begin, let's confirm that our Git and GitHub account are set up correctly. Earlier, when you installed Git, you connected Git to your GitHub account by setting up our username, and email during the Git install process.

To confirm that this looks correct, let's quickly checkout out `git global config` file. To look at this file, run: `git config --global --list`

```
➜ Desktop git config --global --list
```

Once you enter this command, you'll be taken to another view that lists what's in your Git config file. This is what my `git global config` file lists.

```
user.name=ryan8nolds
user.email=⸱⸱⸱⸱⸱⸱⸱⸱⸱⸱⸱⸱@gmail.com
```

What's important here is that your user.name and user.email match your GitHub account.

---

[197]You don't have to Fork a repository to get it onto your computer. You could skip this step entirely and Clone the repository onto your computer (step 2). However, if you plan on contributing to a repository, you'll need to make a Fork first, and then Clone your Fork

[198]https://twitter.com/vancityreynolds

Make sure this is set up correctly. Failing to do so will result in errors later when you try and push your changes.

To exit this view hit **q**.

If your user.name and user.email do not match your GitHub account information follow these instructions for setting up your Git username[199], and here for your Git email[200].

2. Now, let's Fork the "i-was-here" GitHub repository. To do this, login to your GitHub account.

Then, navigate to the "i-was-here" repository here[201], which is hosted on the Full-stack.io GitHub account. By Forking, we are going to make a copy of the repository onto *our* GitHub account.

 Make sure you are logged into GitHub before you Fork.

Next, click on the Fork button, just like Ryan did. This will Fork the repository onto your GitHub account.

![Screenshot of the GitHub page for the fullstackio / i-was-here repository showing Watch, Star, and Fork buttons, with tabs for Code, Issues, Pull requests, Projects, Wiki, and Insights.]

Step 2: Clone

After Forking, the next step is to **clone** the Forked repository onto your computer.

---

[199]https://help.github.com/en/articles/setting-your-username-in-git
[200]https://help.github.com/en/articles/setting-your-commit-email-address-in-git
[201]https://github.com/fullstackio/i-was-here

3. To Clone a Forked repository onto a computer, navigate back to your own GitHub account. Find the repository section.

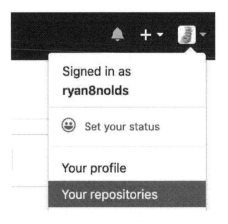

When you get there, you'll see the "i-was-here" repository.

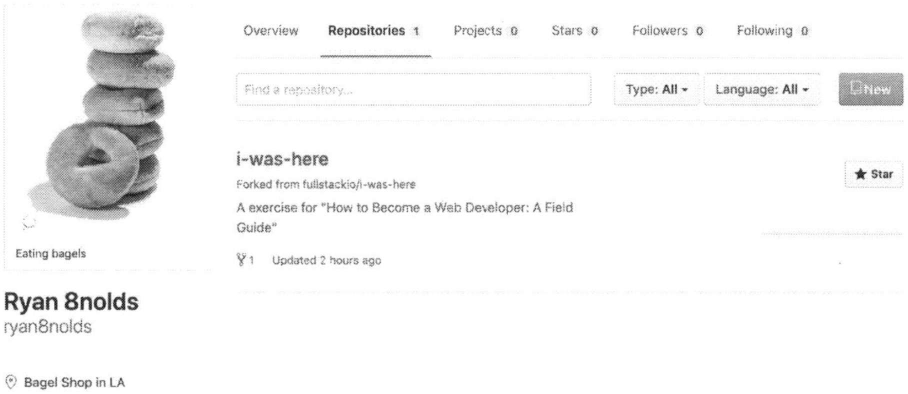

4. Once there, click on the "i-was-here" repository and click on the green "Clone or download" button. Make sure you're on the https, not ssh clone type. Once clicked, GitHub will provide you with a URL of the repository. Copy this URL.

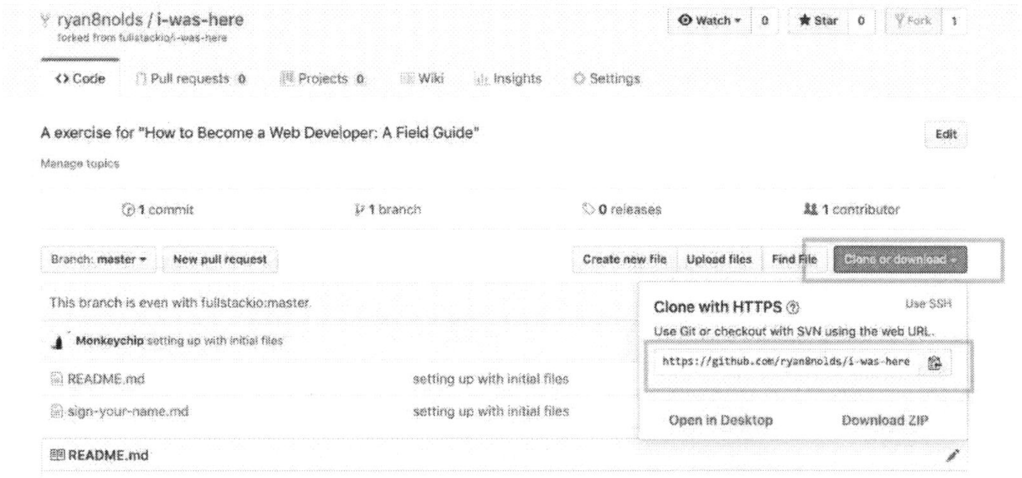

5. Now back in your terminal, navigate to the place on your computer where you want to Clone the "i-was-here" repository. In the following screenshot, Ryan is on his Desktop.

To Clone the repository, use the `git clone` command followed by the Forked repository's URL.

```
⇥ Desktop git clone https://github.com/ryan8nolds/i-was-here.git
Cloning into 'i-was-here'...
remote: Enumerating objects: 4, done.
remote: Counting objects: 100% (4/4), done.
remote: Compressing objects: 100% (4/4), done.
remote: Total 4 (delta 0), reused 4 (delta 0), pack-reused 0
Unpacking objects: 100% (4/4), done.
```

 Forking and Cloning are different.

Though it's not entirely obvious how. Forking means to create a copy of the repository on a remote server (e.g., your GitHub account). Cloning means to copy the repository onto your computer.

Now you've got a mirrored version of the codebase cloned onto your computer.

The next step is to navigate into the cloned repository[202]. Use the `cd i-was-here` to do this.

```
⇥ Desktop cd i-was-here
⇥ i-was-here git:(master) ▌
```

Step 3: Side branch

By default, a "Master" branch was created, and Ryan is on it. But if you remember, best practices tell us that when we want to make changes, it's best to make a side branch and make changes there.

6. Go ahead and make a side branch called "add-my-name."

```
⇥ i-was-here git:(master) git checkout -b add-my-name
Switched to a new branch 'add-my-name'
⇥ i-was-here git:(add-my-name) ▌
```

In this screenshot, Ryan adds his name to the file alongside his most famous tweet about bagels.

---

[202]Unlike in our nature-watch example, where we had to initialize a Git repository using the `git init` command, the Cloned repository is already initialized as a Git repository.

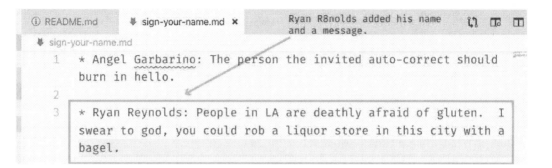

7. Now it's time to add your name - yes *your* name to the file. This will be the name that gets posted to the live repository that is public. If you'd like to use a different pseudo name, please feel free. Just be creative, no "John Smiths." Also, if you'd like, add a message, quote, whatever you'd like.

To do this, open the "sign-your-name.md" file in your text editor. The file is a format called "Markdown" (hence the .md ending). Markdown syntax is similar to HTML in that it is a type of Markup Language. Here is a cheat sheet[203] on how to write in Markdown. However, if you'd rather copy-paste one of the names and replace with your own, that works too.

 I will be reviewing your change. Needless to say, if it's not appropriate, I will reject it.

Step 4: Commit

8. Now that you've made the change let's head back to our terminal and add that file we just changed to Git's stage using the git add command we learned about earlier.

Make sure to include a commit message, as Ryan did.

```
 → i-was-here git:(add-my-name) × git add sign-your-name.md
 → i-was-here git:(add-my-name) × git commit -m "Added Ryan Reynolds
name and a funny bagel message."
[add-my-name 4eb68e1] Added Ryan Reynolds name and a funny bagel mess
age.
 1 file changed, 1 insertion(+), 1 deletion(-)
```

Step 5: Push

---

[203]https://github.com/adam-p/markdown-here/wiki/Markdown-Cheatsheet

9. Now that the file with your name and comment has been staged and committed, let's push the change to your Forked repository. Remember the Forked repository lives on your GitHub account. So in this step, you won't be pushing the change to the "i-was-here" repository on the Fullstack.io account. It will only be pushed to your account.

I am going to paste the command here for you to copy. I am hesitant to describe too much of what this command does as it opens a whole can of worms. You will learn about the Git HEAD, Remotes, and pushing in your continued Git studies. It's a bit much for us here, so bear with me and paste the command as is.

```
git push -u origin add-my-name
```

"Origin" is the default remote name that GitHub gave your Forked repository when you Cloned it. You can confirm this by typing the `git remote -v` command, as Ryan did below.

The "add-my-name" is the name of the side branch you made the change on. If you used a different branch name, use that name instead of the "add-my-name" example.

For Ryan, that command looked like the following:

```
➜  i-was-here git:(add-my-name) git remote -v
origin  https://github.com/ryan8nolds/i-was-here.git (fetch)
origin  https://github.com/ryan8nolds/i-was-here.git (push)
➜  i-was-here git:(add-my-name) git push -u origin add-my-name
Counting objects: 3, done.
Delta compression using up to 4 threads.
Compressing objects: 100% (3/3), done.
Writing objects: 100% (3/3), 342 bytes | 342.00 KiB/s, done.
Total 3 (delta 1), reused 0 (delta 0)
remote: Resolving deltas: 100% (1/1), completed with 1 local object.
To https://github.com/ryan8nolds/i-was-here.git
```

If all goes well, you'll get a success message.

If you have any issues, first try Google'ing the error message Git returned. If you are unable to figure it out from there, reach out to us.

Step 6: Pull Request

10. We're almost done. Right now the changes sit on your Forked repository on *your* GitHub account.

To get these changes onto the original repository - the Fullstack.io GitHub repository, you need to create a **Pull Request**. Submitting a Pull Request is like submitting your homework to your teacher. A Pull Request is a request to the original repository of the changes you'd like to merge into it. The Pull Request shows the details about what files you changed, lists all your commits, and allows the reviewers to give you feedback.

GitHub is smart. When you pushed your changes via the last step, GitHub noticed that. If you now navigate back to your GitHub account, you'll see a yellowish indicator asking you to make a "Compare & pull request." Click on it.

ⓘ **1 commit**	**2 branches**	◇ **0 releases**	👥 **1 contributor**

Your recently pushed branches:

add-my-name (1 minute ago)   ⨝ Compare & pull request

By default, GitHub will set you up by saying you want to merge your branch "add-my-name" into the master branch on the Fullstack.io repository. And that's exactly what we want.

Go ahead and add a quick message about the change. Then click the "Create Pull Request" at the bottom of the page.

Tada! You did it. Full Circle! You Forked, Cloned, Committed, Pushed, and then made a Pull Request. This is a very common workflow between Git and a cloud-hosting service like GitHub. This process is a process you'll be repeating on an almost-daily basis as a developer.

And because this is such a common workflow between Git and a Cloud hosting service like GitHub, we'll summarize the process one more time.

Step 1. **Fork** a repository onto your personal GitHub account.

Step 2. **Clone** the Forked repository onto your computer.

Step 3. Make a **side branch** on your computer's Cloned repository.

Step 4. Make changes and **commit** them.

Step 5. **Push** the changes to your remote Forked repository.

Step 6. Open a **Pull Request** to merge the changes from your Fork into the original repository.

The ball is now in my court. I will review the change. If I approve the Pull Request and merge it, your name and message get added to the file. You will also receive an email notification from GitHub that your change has been made.

Aside from giving you hands-on-experience doing this very common workflow, I wanted to show you how Git works with a Cloud hosting service. Git works so seamlessly with these Cloud hosting services that people often mistake them for the same thing. Git is not GitHub; Git works with GitHub. GitHub is the Cloud hosting services, and Git is the Version Control System. Think of them as best friends; not the same person; they just hang out together all the time.

Most software companies use GitHub or a comparable Cloud service provider.

Google, and all of its services like maps, email, calendar, YouTube, etc. take up about 2 billion lines of code, all of which is stored in GitHub! Google's GitHub account is available to all of Google's 25,000+ developers. And because Git works with Cloud service providers - like GitHub - everyone can work on all of Google's codebase at the same time all over the world, pushing and pulling changes thousands of times a day with little to no conflict.

A Git Never Forgets

Another significant feature of Git is that it never forgets. If Git had a motto, it might be something like:

Always add, never delete.

The general flow of Git is to move forward, adding things, while keeping a detailed record of the change history. At any time, you can go back and review the history of a file, and even revert files to a certain point in time.

That's not to say it's impossible to delete or change Git's history, it's just generally discouraged. And for a good reason. You never know when you might need to revisit something.

Also, who wants to be the person on the Google team that accidentally deleted the file SUPER_IMPORTANT_NEVER_DELETE.txt?

Maybe it was Monday, and you were out of coffee , it happens to the best of us, filename warning notwithstanding.

Not to worry, Git has your back. Each Git commit comes with a hash, which you can use to open up the state of your project at that commit's time in history. In Git, the hash is used as a unique identifier assigned to each commit. You can find the hash by running git log.

Once back in time, you can revert that file back to what it looked like at the time. If it was recorded by Git, it's forever available to you.

I know when I first started programming, the elephant mentality of Git gave me some reassurance. Even if I broke something, which I did and still do, I knew that I could always un-break it.

Git Summary

We've covered some of the core Git features: committing, branching, cloud communication, and Git never forgetting.

As a future Web Developer, Git will become apart of your day-to-day workflow. The more familiar you are with Git, the more powerful and efficient programmer you'll be.

GitHub

I've already introduced you to GitHub; we've even set up a GitHub account, Forked, Cloned and submitted a Pull Request. However, I want to spend more time talking about what makes GitHub so special.

GitHub is the single largest host for Git repositories, with over 100 million repositories on its platform. Not only is GitHub a powerful cloud hosting service provider, but it has also become a social media platform of sorts for millions of developers.

This last statement might seem a little strange: how does a software platform that host code repositories provide social media-type interactions? Good question. The answer, "open-source", meaning that code is available to view and improve upon. A rising tide lifts all boats, right[204]?

The open-source ethos fly in the face of mainstream business norms. How many scientists do you see openly sharing their findings? Or have you ever heard about industry R&D giving away their trade secrets for free, and financial companies asking the public to help them improve their services? You don't, but sharing, no-entry cost, and asking for contributions are the foundations of open-source development.

GitHub plays a significant role in fostering open-source collaboration. It does this by making it very easy to contribute, share, and communicate with each other.

GitHub allows users to make repositories, which can either be set to private or free. It also enables repositories to claim a license type, which is a certified sharing standard if you will. If you'd like to learn more, here is GitHub's[205] documentation on how to choose and add a License.

In addition to making the repositories easy to access and claim a license type, GitHub makes it very easy for other developers to make changes to a repository's code. We covered this process in the Git in the Cloud section.

Culture of GitHub

Before we wrap up our discussion on GitHub, I want to quickly talk about the culture of GitHub as a resume builder and community resource.

GitHub: the new resume

Your GitHub activity, profile, and repositories will be much more valuable to any prospective employer than your resume. It's also likely that any project you take as part of the application process will be done using the Git / GitHub workflow.

---

[204]https://en.wikipedia.org/wiki/A_rising_tide_lifts_all_boats
[205]https://help.github.com/articles/licensing-a-repository/

Employers will use your GitHub profile to determine what if any projects you are contributing to, what projects you have made yourself and if you are actively using Git. In the developer world, it's less about what school you went to, and more about what you've created or are contributing to. If you have an active presence in the GitHub community, your future employer will be sure to take notice.

Use GitHub whenever you can

Ask advice from any senior developer, and they will recommend you try and contribute to a GitHub repository.

It's a little tough (and intimidating) as a beginner to contribute to a repository. Thus, before contributing to someone else's repository, create your own repository, and play around with that first.

Continue to use best practices even if it's only yourself contributing to your repository; make side branches, open pull requests, and leave helpful commit messages.

Embrace the community

GitHub is huge, and the community loves contributors. Take social cues from previous Pull Request. Make sure to read the README.md file, and explore.

Here are some of my favorite GitHub repositories. Let these encourage your explorations. Star repositories and maybe start thinking about a project you are currently working on that would benefit from the Git / GitHub workflow.

- 30-seconds-of-code[206]
- Scripts to Rule the All[207]
- GitHub-cheat-sheet[208]
- Frontend-dev-bookmarks[209]

---

[206]https://github.com/30-seconds/30-seconds-of-code
[207]https://github.com/github/scripts-to-rule-them-all
[208]https://github.com/tiimgreen/github-cheat-sheet
[209]https://github.com/dypsilon/frontend-dev-bookmarks

Git and GitHub usage statistics

Before we wrap things up, I want to talk more about who uses Git and GitHub, as well as back up my sprinkled statements of how popular Git and GitHub are with some statistics.

 Feel free to skip this section if you feel comfortable accepting my claims - at face value - that Git and GitHub are the kings of their respective industry.

Git: Who uses it

Any serious software company, large and small use Git. It is an industry-standard. Poke around Stackshare[210] - a website we used in the Programming Languages chapter - to get a sense of all of the companies using Git.

It is only fair of me to note, however, that there are other Version Control Systems out there. Subversion is probably Git's closest competitor.

Subversion is pre-git, and for a long time, it was the standard VCS. For companies still using Subversion, it's a good bet that they are using a hybrid of Git and Subversion. There's a plugin that you can use with Git that allows you to use Subversion.

A quick look at Google Trends comparing Git to Subversion[211] paints a clear picture of Git's rise to dominance.

---

[210]https://stackshare.io/git

[211]https://trends.google.com/trends/explore?date=all&q=%2Fm%2F05vqwg,%2Fm%2F012ct9

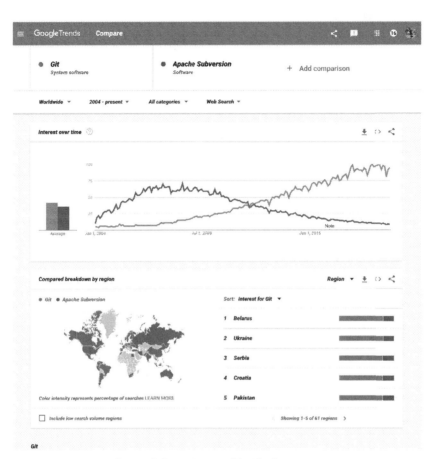

Git vs. Subversion worldwide, last 5 yrs

GitHub: Who uses it

GitHub's success story is similar to Git's. Though GitHub does have a few more serious competitors than Git does. Mainly Bitbucket and GitLab. It's less certain the GitHub will remain as dominant as it currently is, as there is some shuffling and true competition going on between the companies in this space. For example, Microsoft recently purchased GitHub[212], which had lots of developers jumping to GitLab.

---

[212]https://www.reuters.com/article/us-github-microsoft-gitlab/gitlab-gains-developers-after-microsoft-buys-rival-github-idUSKCN1J12BR

This book was written using GitLab, and I'm a fan. If you care to read more about GitHub-vs-GitLab, I recommend this article[213]. The best part is probably the comment section.

A quick look at Google Trends[214] comparing GitHub with it's two closest competitors - Bitbucket and GitLab - helps us see that GitHub is still a safe bet.

GitHub vs. Bitbucket vs. GitLab worldwide, last 5yrs

One more stat before we wrap this up. According to GitHub's website[215], there are more than 31 million registered users worldwide - you just added to that list by one when you signed up for an account.

---

[213]https://hackernoon.com/github-vs-gitlab-which-is-better-for-open-source-projects-31c45d464be0

[214]https://trends.google.com/trends/explore?date=today%205-y&q=%2Fm%2F04g0kcw,%2Fm%2F05mx6p6,%2Fm%2F0125_4f0

[215]https://github.com/about/facts

Key Takeaways

- Git is the preferred Distributed Version Control System, used by individuals, small and large companies alike.
- When you commit changes to Git, it takes a snapshot of the difference and attaches a message and metadata along with the image.
- When you view a file in Git, it is a montage of Git commits.
- Git uses branches to keep projects organized.
- Git works with Cloud hosting services like GitHub, making it easy for developers to work on the same codebase at the same time.
- When you Fork a repository, you are making a mirrored version of the repository, and effectively making a backup of the repository.
- GitHub is the most popular Cloud hosting service for Git repositories.
- GitHub has had a large influence on growing the open-source community by making it easy to share and collaborate on projects.
- Git and GitHub are essential tools for any modern developer.

We covered a lot of Git commands. Though I don't expect you to understand each of these in detail, I wanted to make it easy to see them all at once for easy reference.

Summary of Git Commands

Command	What the Command Does
git init	This initializes a Git repository. You use this command on the folder on your computer that you want to use Git on.
git add	This command followed by the file name, adds the file to Git's staging area. A file must be staged before it can be committed.
git status	This command lists the files that have changed, and the ones that Git has staged or those that are not staged.
git commit -m	The command used to commit the staged file(s). The -m flag ► allows you to append a commit message.
git log	Shows the log of commits, including the commit hash, author, and timestamp.
git checkout -b	The Git checkout command with the -b flag ► sets you up to make a new branch. Follow this command by the new side branches name.
git branch	List all of your local Git branches.
git checkout	The Git checkout command without the -b flag gets you ready to checkout a new branch you've already made. Follow this by the name of the branch you want to checkout.
git clone	Cloning a repository onto your computer. You follow the Git clone command by the URL of the repository. You can find this URL on the repository, either your forked version or the original repository.
git remote add	Adding a remote repository to your local Git repository. Use this command followed by the GitHub account you're connecting to and the remote repository's URL.
git remote -v	List remotes you have set up.
git diff	Shows the differences between branches. use-case
git push --set-upstream	Set's an association between the branch on your Git repository and the GitHub remote you want to push.
git push	Pushes changes to your remote repository, you have to set the association first, and then you can use this command whenever you want to push a change.

Considerations for Further Study

This chapter was an introduction to Git and GitHub. Mastering the workflow and commands will only come with practice. Find reasons to make a Git repository, and/or explore different GitHub repositories.

Further Readings

In addition to practicing Git or exploring GitHub repositories, I highly recommend reading or skimming the relevant sections of the Pro Git book provided by Git itself. This book is free online - see here[216] - or you can purchase the printed version. The book covers both Git and GitHub. It's not a book you have to read all the way through, rather the kind you keep bookmarks in and return to often.

Git, unlike a lot of other topics, doesn't require a separate course or video tutorial. Instead, it just takes practice. With the Pro Git book resource open, get your feet wet and find the questions you still have by working through the process and participating in the GitHub community.

What's Next?

The next chapter is the last chapter we introduce new topics and work through exercises. We have covered the main subjects of Web Development to the point of a fork in the road. It is this fork we will discuss in the next chapter on Frontend vs. Backend development.

---

[216]https://git-scm.com/book/en/v2

Chapter 8: Frontend and Backend Web Development

Instagram[217] is a platform built on quickly scrolling through loads of photos. But have you ever wondered where those photos are stored? Is Instagram downloading those photos to your device, or maybe it's saving them somehow to the browser?

If you've ever seen the "Storage Almost Full" message on your phone, you know that photos devourer storage space. It's unlikely Instagram is downloading *all* the photos to your device. Additionally, it's no secret that downloading photos takes time, much more than it does for the next Instagram photo to show up as you scroll.

So how does Instagram do it? Instagram accomplishes this feat by storing all of the photos on remote servers (remember our cloud discussion in the Git Chapter), and requesting those photos as you scroll.

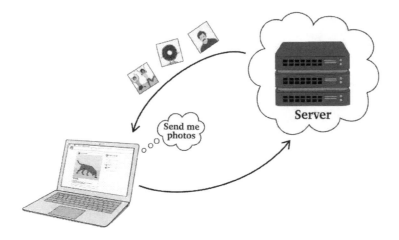

---

[217]https://www.instagram.com/about/us/

I have grossly oversimplified an impressive feat of engineering to describe "how" Instagram works. I have done this to help set up the following conversation about data storage and the transfer between the Frontend and Backend. With this goal in mind, I feel it is OK that I have left out the details. If you *do* desire more, I encourage you to subscribe to the Instagram Engineering blog[218], or read this dated but still helpful[219] article written by Instagram engineers.

At the time of writing, there are over 40 **billion**[220] photos on Instagram's servers; that's about 5 photos per person on earth!

Holding all of these photos means Instagram uses a whole heck-of-a-lot of servers. The number of servers Instagram uses is not public information, but Facebook - who owns Instagram and houses the Instagram servers - has been building server farms constantly since 2011[221]. Each of Facebook's server farms houses tens-of-thousands of computers.

A server farm is a term used to describe the building holding servers (also called a Data Center). To help you understand just how massive these "farms" can be, here is a picture of a server farm in small-town Prineville, Oregon. Facebook is *still* adding square footage to this facility. Taking into account the plans for new construction, this server farm will eventually take up 3.2 million square feet. That's a lot of computers, storing a lot of data. This server farm[222] is just one of many owned by Facebook.

---

[218]https://instagram-engineering.com/

[219]https://instagram-engineering.com/what-powers-instagram-hundreds-of-instances-dozens-of-technologies-adf2e22da2ad

[220]https://instagram-press.com/blog/2018/12/12/instagram-year-in-review-2018/

[221]https://www.wired.com/2014/06/facebook-instagram/

[222]https://www.datacenterknowledge.com/data-center-faqs/facebook-data-center-faq

Let's recap. As you merrily scroll through your Instagram feed, your phone or browser is making requests to a server farm, and the server farm is sending back photos. Photos are being downloaded and stored on your browser and device, but only the ones you have viewed, and a good chunk of that data is removed once you close the app.

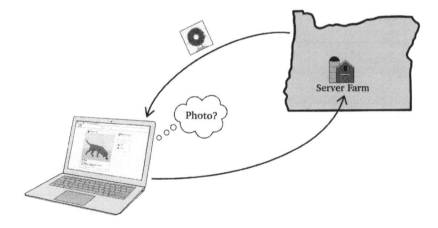

Terminology: Frontend, Client-side, Backend, Server-side, UX, UI

The reason we're discussing how Instagram delivers content is that this process for delivering images illuminates an important separation in Web Development between the **Frontend** and the **Backend**. It's worth noting that all the exercises and examples in the book so far have been of Frontend programming.

 You'll sometimes see the Frontend spelled front-end or Front End. Similar spelling differences exist for the Backend. Ultimately, the spelling doesn't matter, but I think "front end" and "back end" conjure up different topics, not related to programming. I think formally the "correct" spelling is Front-End, but that's a little too formal for my taste.

Frontend

The **Frontend** in the Instagram example is what the user interfaces with; all the HTML, CSS, and JavaScript you interact with to use Instagram. That includes the scrolling, any menu buttons you use, the ability to edit photos, etc. Additionally, the Frontend is responsible for the short-term storage of data. Instagram is downloading a minimal number of photos to your browser or device as you scroll, but all of this data is temporary.

Backend

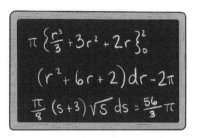

The **Backend** in our Instagram example are the servers, storing data, receiving requests, and responding to those requests. As well as all the code that manages the logic around returning the data and processing it.

When talking about Frontend vs. Backend development, you will also read or hear the term "client-side" and "server-side." These terms are so closely linked to Frontend and Backend that they are often talked about as if they were synonymous; client-side the same as Frontend and server-side the same as Backend.

But they are different. Client-side and server-side describe the *where*; Frontend and Backend describe the *what*. Let's take a closer look.

Client-side

As discussed earlier, the Frontend is concerned with all things the user interacts with. The term client means your device. If you're playing Solitaire on your computer, your computer is the client. If you're on your browser Googling, the browser is the client. If you're scrolling through your Instagram feed on your phone, your phone is the client.

With that in mind, the term "Client-side" refers to everything that is displayed or any processes that happen on the client.

Take, for example, our Exercises with HTML, CSS, and JavaScript. For all of those examples, we relied on a browser to interpret and display our work. All of this is done on the client, i.e., the browser. Remember our event listeners in the JavaScript example? The client, i.e., the browser handled those event listeners. In all three of those chapters, we never once used a remote server to help us process the code. It was all done by the client. It was all Frontend development.

To recap, the term Frontend describes all the responsibilities and processes that run on the client. Client-side refers to *where* the Frontend runs its processes, e.g., the browser, smart-phone, computer, etc.

Before jumping into the Backend and server-side discussion, I want to take a small sidestep to review two crucial Frontend terms; UX and UI. Understanding these terms will also clarify what "responsibilities" the Frontend is concerned with.

User Experience (UX) and User Interface (UI)

UX stands for **User Experience**, and UI stands for **User Interface**. You'll come to see that these terms are self-explanatory after working through some examples.

UX is how the user *experiences* the platform. If you find yourself frustrated at how Instagram feels as a platform, then you're having a bad UX. Let's use a non-computer example to expand on this concept. Think about the coffee mugs in your home. Do you have a coffee mug you always use? If yes, then for whatever reason - maybe it's sentimental, or you like how it holds heat - you have associated a positive UX with that mug.

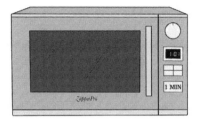

UI, on the other hand, is about how you *interact* with the web page or app. For example, maybe you really dislike how Instagram uses the heart icon to indicate a like. You don't love the picture, you just like it, and you dislike that you are forced to either do nothing or express your love for a photo. That is bad UI - at least in your opinion. Or maybe you like your microwave because of that instant 1 minute button. It's an easy one-click action; your microwave has a good UI.

UX and UI are essential concepts for Frontend development. They both deal with how the user interacts with all things Frontend.

Server-side and Backend

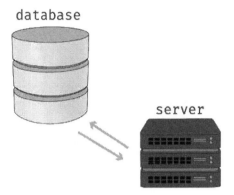

Given our earlier discussion on server farms, it shouldn't surprise you that "server-side" is paired with Backend. The term server-side clarifies the *location* of the Backend processes rather than defining what the Backend is responsible for.

The term server-side reinforce that the Backend code is running somewhere on a remote server, and *not* on the user's computer; not on the client. In our Instagram example, the server-side - the location - is the remote servers at Facebook's server farms.

In general, the Backend is responsible for logic. So for example, if you enter a discount code while checking out on Amazon, the processes that validate the discount code and recalculate the price should be done by the Backend - on remote servers, and not on the client.

The Backend is also generally responsible for managing data. For example, when someone signs up for an Instagram account, their login information, profile information, and photos are organized and managed by the Backend, all on remote servers.

We've covered a lot of terms here, so let's do a quick recap:

- **Frontend**: the part of the development process responsible for everything the user interacts with. It's safe to generalize that everything written in HTML, CSS, and JavaScript are apart of the Frontend development process.

- **Client-side**: the location of where the Frontend code is run. The client includes things like your computer, browser, or smartphone.
- **UX**: How a user feels about using an application or web page. The user's overall experience.
- **UI**: How a user interacts with an application or web page. Is it easy to use, intuitive, or are things hard to read or click on?
- **Backend**: the part of the development process responsible for data management, data processing, and receiving and responding to requests from the Frontend.
- **Server-side**: indicating the location of where the Backend is run, on servers, not on the client.

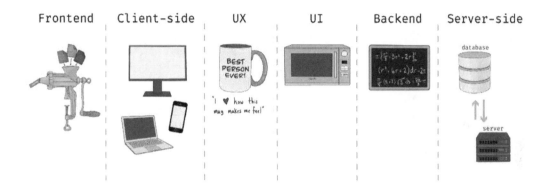

Frontend and Backend balance of responsibilities

Back in the day, nearly all web development was the Backend's responsibility. Development was done on remote servers, and not on the client. This was because personal computers and browsers were not capable of handling all the processing and rendering that web pages or applications required. Additionally, HTML, CSS, and JavaScript were just not as powerful as they are today.

In the last 5-10 years, however, the Frontend has taken on a considerable amount more responsibility all because of the advancement of Frontend technology. Browsers, smartphones, personal computers, etc. (all examples of "clients") have become much more powerful, meaning they can now run a lot more code or processes than they could before.

While we saw advancement in the clients, the Frontend languages - HTML, CSS, & JavaScript - were also going through a growth spurt. They continue to keep growing, but there were some game-changing updates to the languages along the way. I won't go into detail here, but if you're curious about exactly how these languages have become more powerful, I encourage you to read about HTML5[223][224], CSS3[225], and ES6[226].

All of this to say, the Frontend can now handle a lot more than it used to. As a result, today it's very common to define yourself as either a Backend, Frontend, or Fullstack developer. This differentiation between types of developers is relatively new.

 Fullstack Developers work in both the Frontend and Backend space. If you think of a hamburger, where the buns are the Frontend and the Backend everything in the middle, you would be the full burger - Fullstack!

Let's consider some statistics. In 2019, Stack Overflow reported in its annual Developer Survey Results[227] that Frontend Developers made up 32.8% of Developer Roles, with Backend making up 50%.

---

[223]https://developer.mozilla.org/en-US/docs/Web/Guide/HTML/HTML5

[224]HTML5 wasn't just released and then became what it is today; there was a process. I found this Mashable illustration very helpful in understanding the history.

[225]https://developer.mozilla.org/en-US/docs/Web/CSS/CSS3

[226]https://developer.mozilla.org/en-US/docs/Web/JavaScript/New_in_JavaScript/ECMAScript_2015_support_in_Mozilla

[227]https://insights.stackoverflow.com/survey/2019/

👥 Developer Roles

Developer Type

All Respondents	United States Unweighted	⭐ United States Weighted by Gender

Developer, full-stack **51.9%**

Developer, back-end **50.0%**

Developer, front-end **32.8%**

Developer, desktop or enterprise applications **21.3%**

Compare this to just three years earlier, when Stack Overflow reported[228] that Frontend Developers made up only 5.8% of Developer Roles, with Backend Developers at 12.2%.

II. Developer Occupations

Full-Stack Web Developer — 28.0%

Back-End Web Developer — 12.2%

Student — 11.4%

Mobile Developer (Android, iOS, WP, and Multi-Platform) — 8.4%

Desktop Developer — 6.9%

Front-End Web Developer — 5.8%

Other — 5.2%

The lower percentages in 2016 highlight the division happening in web development. People are becoming *specialized*.

It used to be that you were a "Fullstack" developer, meaning that you do both Frontend and Backend development. Though this position is still very relevant today,

---

[228]https://insights.stackoverflow.com/survey/2016/

there is a good portion of developers who are curating specialized skills in either Frontend or Backend rather than having a generalized "jack-of-all-trades" skill set. The Frontend is taking on more responsibility and complexity such that it is getting tougher to keep up the skills required to do both Frontend *and* Backend, hence the specialization.

I think it's important to stop and clarify that it's not just that the Frontend is *taking* responsibilities away from the Backend, but the Frontend is also *making* and *giving* itself new responsibilities.

Yes, the Frontend has absorbed some of the Backend's workload. Such as taking on some of the rendering, validation, and preferences work, things you don't need to be concerned with right now. However, the more recent surge in Frontend work-load is due to growth in the impressive things the Frontend can do.

For example, the CSS language is *way* more powerful than it was just ten years ago. You can do all sorts of things with CSS that folks wouldn't have dreamed the unassuming markup language would have been capable of. One of the flasher CSS advancements is its ability to do complex animations. Here is a very slick CSS animation[229] of our solar system, complete with scaled rotation speeds and moons - all done in CSS and HTML, no Backend required.

Animations like this - made entirely on the Frontend - were not possible before 2010[230]. Previously all animations were handled on the Backend by things like Adobe Flash, and they weren't that great relative to today's animations. And though you still may see Adobe Flash notifications - like in the following screenshot - animations that used to be done by Backend processes can now be done by the Frontend.

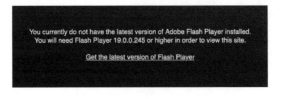

---

[229]https://codepen.io/tadywankenobi/pen/QbWNGR
[230]https://en.wikipedia.org/wiki/CSS_animations

Notifications like this pop up because you have to *download* Adobe Flash; it's a Backend Process and can't be run by your browser alone as CSS can. Adobe Flash[231] is set to be retired by 2020, thank-goodness. "I love Adobe Flash notifications," said no one, ever.

You'll eventually need to decide what kind of web developer you would like to become. Do you want to focus on the Backend, or Frontend, or try your hand at Fullstack. Though it's not a decision you need to make today, be aware that as the balance of responsibilities changes so too will the type of developers employers will be looking for.

Why Split the Difference?

> *"It's all the choosing sides that made everything so horrible."*

– Stannis Baratheon from George R.R. Martin, A Game of Thrones

Frontend and Backend are the most significant split in web development. The separation was made to help filter down a vast - and growing - tech space into more manageable groups.

 As Stannis Baratheon from Game of Thrones warns, don't choose sides. Yes, it is possible that you find yourself specializing in either Frontend or Backend Development, but the Frontend and Backend work together. If you specialize, you will still need to understand the fundamental concepts of the other group.

Now that we have a sense of what each group is responsible for let's look at the flow of information between the Backend and Frontend, and why the division is made where it is.

The following diagrams the communication flow between these two groups:

[231]https://elmlearning.com/is-adobe-flash-going-away/

Frontend / Backend

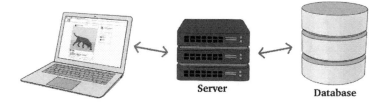

As we saw earlier with our Instagram discussion, it's not practical to assume your phone can store all the photos you want to view as your scroll. The same data storage situation happens all across the web.

Imagine you have signed up for a GitHub account. When you do this, your profile, username, and password are pieces of data that the Frontend sent to the Backend. That data is now stored somewhere on a remote server.

Next time you go to sign-in to your GitHub account - on a browser (the client) - through a login screen like the following, you are interacting with the Frontend.

Sign in to GitHub

Username or email address

ryan8noids

Password   Forgot password?

••••••••••••••••

Sign in

New to GitHub? Create an account.

When you press the green "Sign in" button, the Frontend sends your username and password (the data is sent in an encrypted format, meaning it can't be read by anyone/thing intercepting it) to the Backend. Once the Backend receives and decrypts this data, it confirms that you have an account. That account information and whether it exists or not is data the Backend stores and is responsible for. Next, once confirmed, the Backend sends a message to the Frontend saying something to the effect of, "yes they are a real person with an account, and here is their account information."

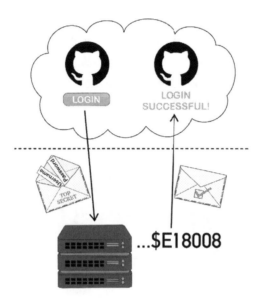

If we step back and think about what's happening, we can see that the split between the Backend and Frontend has naturally occurred on the line where data management is handed off. The Frontend is essentially defined on the line where the management of data is no longer relevant; the Frontend is concerned with only the presentation of data.

If and when the data changes, because you updated your password or added another photo to your Instagram account, that becomes the responsibility of the Backend.

To help explain why it makes sense that data management is the burden of the Backend I am going to play devil's advocate and ask, "why shouldn't the Frontend manage and store data?"

There are lots of reasons the Frontend should *not* be the primary storage location for data. We will discuss some of the more pertinent ones: **Security**, **Scale**, **Connectivity**, and **Performance**.

Security Concerns

As a rule, you should avoid storing any sensitive information in Frontend code.

A common mistake for beginner developers is to use their Frontend JavaScript code to handle authentication or access to secret data. Without getting too much into the weeds, the Frontend JavaScript can't protect sensitive data in the same way that the Backend does.

Storing sensitive data on the Frontend - regardless of any security measures taken - would be like locking a gate, and still allowing people or porcupines to navigate around it.

Why is this? Well, remember when we used `console.log` to run JavaScript on our page? The end-user can run any JavaScript to manipulate that code. So if, for example, you were checking that a username and password pair was valid in JavaScript on the Frontend, this wouldn't be secure, because the end-user can easily circumvent that.

For example, say you had the following JavaScript code that checked the validity of a username and password.

```
var password = document.getElementById('password');
var correctPassword = 'password123';

function checkPassword(){
  if (password === correctPassword) {
    return true;
  } else {
    return false;
  }
}
```

For the record, this is a horrible password check. I wrote it to show you how if you used JavaScript like this on the Frontend, then all the user would have to do is modify the checkPassword function to return true.

Something even as simple as changing the password to equal the correctPassword would make it so the checkPassword function always returned true.

```
document.getElementById('password').replaceWith(correctPassword);
```

For the most part, all secure information is handled by the Backend; the Frontend may be involved in sending the data, but it's unlikely it will validate it.

Scale

We've touched on scale earlier in our Instagram discussion. Scale is simply the fact that your computer can't hold every Instagram photo from every one of your friends. It's too much data.

We don't need to spend any more time on this. This concept, especially when so many of us deal daily with data constraints on our electronic devices, is pretty intuitive.

Connectivity

Connectivity is the concept of catering data to a user's needs. As discussed earlier, the Frontend is constrained by the client running it (e.g., fast vs. slow internet or cell service), so the best user experience (UX) is going to be the one that only spends time on data relevant to you as a user. Uber is a great example of this.

Uber pairs drivers with riders. When you load the Uber app, you only see drivers close to your location. Why would you care about loading up data on your mobile device from drivers half-a-world away? You don't. Hence why Uber only connects you to drivers nearby. This is an example of connectivity: the Backend is helping narrow the amount of data the Frontend handles by providing connectivity through a central point that you couldn't get otherwise.

Performance

Scale and Connectivity are smaller concepts that fall under the concept of performance. Performance is essentially how fast and efficient the Frontend can display data.

Performance[232] is a term used in web development to discuss the speed and usability of a web page.

The more data or responsibilities the Frontend has, the slower it will be. Google and other search engines will actually penalize[233] a website if it loads slowly.

Additionally, users penalize slow loading sites. According to research done by Google[234], 53% of mobile users will leave a site that takes longer than 3 seconds to load.

The Frontend does not *want* to be responsible for storing data, it would much rather just make a call to the server, ask for a piece of data, display it and when you move on, it does too.

Let's use metrics to help us better understand how fast data can travel from a request -> server -> back to the requestor. Let's say you are requesting 1mb of data.

For perspective, moving around Facebook requires about 1mb of data every 30 seconds[235].

[232]https://en.wikipedia.org/wiki/Web_performance
[233]https://www.sitecenter.com/insights/141-google-introduces-penalty-for-slow-websites.htm
[234]https://www.thinkwithgoogle.com/marketing-resources/data-measurement/mobile-page-speed-new-industry-benchmarks/
[235]https://www.amaysim.com.au/blog/tips-tricks/whered-my-data-go-a-data-guide-to-common-internet-activities

Let's say you're in California on a computer, and the server farm you are pinging is somewhere in Europe. Requesting 1mb of data takes about 150ms, which means that it takes 0.15 seconds for a request made from your location in CA to Europe and back to CA. Pretty impressive if you think about it.

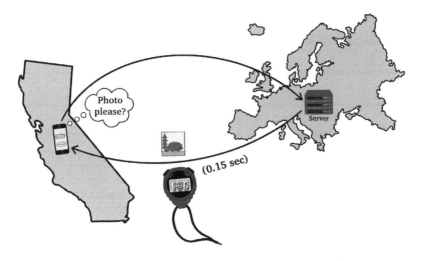

Whereas if you have the Frontend handle the data, your browser (or whatever client you are using) downloads and stores the data. And depending on your internet speed, downloading data can be faster than pinging and returning data from a server farm. *Or* it may not be as fast; the rate at which data gets downloaded onto the Frontend depends on a variety of factors, the main ones being internet speed and the client (e.g., if your using Internet Explorer as your client, your download speed will likely be slower than if you're on Chrome).

So why store any data on the Frontend at all? The short answer, because storing some specific types of data on the Frontend makes the UX better.

 The more verbose answer to why store any data on the Frontend at all includes discussions on things like state management, tracking, advertisements, and analytics. Things I am skirting around because they detract from the conversation.

Have you ever visited a web page the second time and it seems to load much faster then when you first visited it? The reason the page loads faster after already having visited it is that the Frontend has stored some data from the first visit making your second visit load faster; improving UX.

Performance can either be slowed down or speed up depending on how you manage data storage on the Frontend. If you require that the Frontend always downloads a lot of things, it will be slow. If you store the right data and only the essential data on the Frontend, then it *can* help performance. Web page performance is an art, and something any developer - Frontend, or Backend - will need to be aware of.

APIs

We've spent a decent amount of time discussing how the Backend and Frontend are different. But I have not explained *how* they communicate; how they send data back and forth between each other.

The communication between the Backend and Frontend is made possible with **Application Programming Interfaces (APIs)**, pronounced (A P I). APIs are the keystone that allows this whole system to work. Formally, APIs[236] are a set of instructions that allow you to access a different feature, data, operating system, or some other service.

APIs are used for more than communication between the Backend and Frontend. As of writing, there are over 20,000 APIs listed on ProgrammableWeb[237], and only a fraction of those are in involved in the Backend / Frontend communication process.

The formal API definition never really did it for me. Instead, I find it easiest to think of APIs like the Jeeves[238] butler; I request things, and he brings them to me. The Frontend does the same thing; it calls up its "Jeeves" and asks it to get or send data to and from the Backend. It uses different "Jeeves" (APIs) to do this. In the following Exercises, we will work with a couple of APIs to help us work through this communication process.

---

[236]https://en.wikipedia.org/wiki/Application_programming_interface
[237]https://www.programmableweb.com/
[238]https://en.wikipedia.org/wiki/Jeeves#Personal_characteristics

A more common API analogy is to think of an API like plugging into a power outlet[239]. You plugin, and you have access to power. You don't have to go and connect yourself to the power supply, just plug-and-play. The important thing to understand about APIs is that they allow you to tap into more complex code with a simpler command. So whether it's Jeeves or a power outlet that helps you grasp the concept, stick with that.

All APIs provide some service. You have to request something from them, and they in return do something for you. For example, remember the DOM from our HTML chapter? The DOM is an API. The DOM does all the work for you - it takes your HTML, and it makes the model that the browser uses to display the HTML and CSS. We won't get into details here, but the DOM is a *service* that you have plugged into. Think of it like hiring a painter; you told the painter how you wanted it to look, the painter provided their service and did the painting for you.

There are different types of APIs. The DOM is a Web API, meaning that it is an API that you use when working on web applications. But if you ever wanted to return random cat pictures, there's an API for that[240]. Or what about retrieving all of your tweets, well there is a Twitter API[241] for that.

APIs can be written in most any Programming Language, and depending on their purpose can be relatively "easy" to write.

My favorite API is the Ron Swanson API. Ron Swanson[242] is a fictional character portrayed by Nick Offerman in Parks and Recreation. If you have not seen Parks and Recreation, all you need to know about Ron Swanson is that he is full of brilliant one-liners. He is a protagonist libertarian who works for a government agency he believes shouldn't exist.

The Ron Swanson API returns his one-liners. It is simple. There are no instructions on how to use it, and there are no rules other than to request a quote from a specific URL (referred to as an "Endpoint"). We are going to be using the Ron Swanson API to get a feel for what it's like to request data from a remote server. Hint: it's easier than you think.

---

[239]https://developer.mozilla.org/en-US/docs/Learn/JavaScript/Client-side_web_APIs/Introduction
[240]https://thecatapi.com/
[241]https://developer.twitter.com/en/docs.html
[242]https://en.wikipedia.org/wiki/Ron_Swanson

Endpoints

Endpoints are one end of a communication channel you use to connect to an API. It is often a URL. You ping the URL, and you are pinging or initiating communication with the API. As we'll see in the Exercise, the Ron Swanson API endpoint is: `http://ron-swanson-quotes.herokuapp.com/v2/quotes`

Exercise 1 of 5: Watching an API communicate with a server using the Network panel

1. In Chrome, open up the Ron Swanson API.[243]

```
←  →  C  ⌂    ⓘ Not Secure | ron-swanson-quotes.herokuapp.com/v2/quotes

["Friends: one to three is sufficient."]
```

Refresh the page a couple of times to see a new quote - and remember it's satire.

The web page is not fancy. It's not supposed to be. All the web page is doing is making a request to the Ron Swanson API by hitting the

- **Endpoint**: `http://ron-swanson-quotes.herokuapp.com/v2/quotes`.

This API is set up so that as long as you hit the Endpoint, it will return a random quote. That's it. Super simple.

2. Open the Chrome DevTools and navigate to the Network Panel; the panel just to the right of the Console.

The Network panel[244] shows you the resources being downloaded or uploaded over the "network", including the communication that happens between the Frontend and Backend.

The Network tab is pretty amazing, and your best friend when working through communication between the Backend and Frontend. We won't go into details here, but the Network panel is something you'll want to get familiar with.

---

[243]http://ron-swanson-quotes.herokuapp.com/v2/quotes
[244]https://developers.google.com/web/tools/chrome-devtools/network/

With the Network panel open, refresh the page. The Network panel won't start recording activity unless it's open, hence the page refresh.

The Network panel is watching for "network request." When the Backend and Frontend are sending things back and forth to each other, they are making a network request. When you hit the refresh button, the web page immediately fires off a request to a remote server for a new quote.

The "quotes" row you see is the name of the request.

3. Go ahead and click on the "quotes" row. Once clicked, you'll see a lot of information pop up under the "Headers" tab.

```
×   Headers   Preview   Response   Timing

▼ General
    Request URL: http://ron-swanson-quotes.herokuapp.com/v2/quotes
    Request Method: GET
    Status Code: ● 200 OK
    Remote Address: 35.170.227.83:80
    Referrer Policy: no-referrer-when-downgrade

▼ Response Headers      view source
    Access-Control-Allow-Origin: *
    Connection: keep-alive
    Content-Length: 55
    Content-Type: application/json; charset=utf-8
    Date: Sat, 23 Mar 2019 23:35:17 GMT
    Etag: W/"37-ebcf7054"
    Server: Cowboy
    Via: 1.1 vegur
    X-Powered-By: Express
```

There is a lot of information here. I don't want to overwhelm you, so we'll only cover a couple of items.

Under the "General" section, the "Request URL" is telling us that the URL:

```
http://ron-swanson-quotes.herokuapp.com/v2/quotes
```

was the Endpoint used to initialize a request from the remote server. The Status code of 200 means that the request was successful.

Also, do you see the **Request Method**[245] of GET? If the Request method is GET, that means the Frontend is attempting to "get" data.

> ℹ️ If the Request Method is "POST," that means that the Frontend sent data
> - "posting data." GET, and POST are very common methods. Looking at
> the Request Method helps you understand the direction of communication.
> Down the road you'll eventually need to become familiar with the other
> Request Methods and the details on the more common ones; MDN web
> docs has a concise summary of each here[246].

Farther down, under **"Response Headers,"** we see that the server that received the

---

[245]https://developer.mozilla.org/en-US/docs/Web/HTTP/Methods
[246]https://developer.mozilla.org/en-US/docs/Web/HTTP/Methods

request is called "Cowboy." Why is it named "Cowboy," because programmers are a strange bunch. The name doesn't matter, the point is that it hit a remote server, and the server returned the quote.

Programmers naming things

You'll find in programming that there are a *lot* of strange names out there. Examples include FORTRAN, Befunge, Daemonization, Phalanger, and my favorite, Sharding. I choose to believe that programmers look at whatever is closest to them, and that's where they come up with these sometimes off-handed names. How else do you explain Cookies[247]?

4. To help bring this home, we are going to make a request to the Cowboy server, but we're going to make the request from our terminal. It doesn't matter where in your terminal you make this request.

Open your terminal, and enter the following command:

Windows Users

You can make this `curl` request from either your PowerShell or Git Bash program.

```
curl http://ron-swanson-quotes.herokuapp.com/v2/quotes
```

You should see a quote returned after entering the command.

```
⇒ ~ curl http://ron-swanson-quotes.herokuapp.com/v2/quotes
["The less I know about other people's affairs, the happier I am. I'm not intere
sted in caring about people. I once worked with a guy for three years and never
learned his name. Best friend I ever had. We still never talk sometimes."]%
⇒ ~ ▊
```

Pretty cool right? We made a request to a server just using this one line. The **curl** command can be used to request and/or send data to a server. The way the Ron

---

[247]https://developer.mozilla.org/en-US/docs/Web/HTTP/Cookies

Swanson API is set up requires that we only need to follow the `curl` command with the URL.

When attempting to return sensitive data, like an email, from an API, it's not enough to just hit the Endpoint. Typically, you'll have to include additional information that gives your request credibility; ensuring that you are who you are and you have permission to receive the data.

For example, say you want to return your tweet history from Twitter, a simple curl command like this would not be enough. The Twitter API will make you go through an authentication handshake proving that you are who you are, have access and that you specify the data you want.

To summarize, the Ron Swanson API allows you to request data from the server "Cowboy," which has access to a list of random Ron Swanson quotes. Cowboy is returning that data (a quote) every time we hit the Endpoint URL. The Backend is doing the action of receiving and returning the data. The Frontend does the requesting.

Exercise 2 of 5: Ron Swanson API with some Frontend

The previous Exercise was Backend focused. The only thing the Frontend did was provide the client; the browser. And when we hit the Endpoint using the `curl` command in the terminal, the Frontend wasn't involved at all. But let's be honest, it was a pretty boring display of quotes. There was no UI or UX to talk about.

We're going to change that by looking at an application that adds HTML, CSS, and JavaScript. The whole point of this Exercise is to drive home what the Frontend "looks" like.

1. In the code that comes with this book, open up the:

`8-fe-vs-be/ron-swanson-frontend.html`[248]

in your browser.

---

[248]code/src/8-fe-vs-be/ron-swanson-frontend.html

Ron Swanson Quotes

Turkey can never beat cow.

Quote me!

Refresh the page or click the "Quote me" button to see a new quote. Everything, but providing the quote, is done by the Frontend. The image, the style, the button functionality, that is *all* Frontend.

2. Let's take a look at this HTML document in our text editor. The style is being set between the `<style></style>` tags, on rows 9-34.

```
9    <style>
10     body {
11       font-family: Fira Mono, monospace;
12     }
13     h1 {
14       text-align: center;
15       font-size: 50px;
16     }
17     div {
18       margin: auto;
19       width: 60%;
20       padding: 0px 10px 40px 10px;
21       text-align: center;
22       font-size: 20px;
23     }
24     button {
25       background-color: #9FCEE2;
26       color: rgba(0,0,0,0.6);
27       font-family: Fira Mono, monospace;
28       display: block;
29       margin: auto;
30       width: 250px;
31       height: 30px;
32       font-size: 20px;
33     }
34   </style>
```

Scroll a little farther down, and you'll see the HTML. There's not a lot to the HTML; your basic HTML structure, a `<h1></h1>` element, and two `<div></div>` elements used to hold the image and the quote. These can be found on rows 37-43.

```
37    <h1>Ron Swanson Quotes</h1>
38    <div>
39      <img src="./ron-swanson-img.png" alt="ron-swanson">
40    </div>
41    <div id="quoteDisplay">
42        <!-- Quotes will display here -->
43    </div>
44
45    <button onclick="getQuote()">Quote me!</button>
```

3. Making the API request is JavaScript. If you navigate to the bottom between the `<script></script>` tags, on row 50, you'll see the function called **getQuote**.

```
47    <script>
48      const endpoint = 'https://ron-swanson-quotes.herokuapp.com/v2/quotes';
49
50      function getQuote() {
51        fetch(endpoint)
52          .then(response => {
53            return response.json();
54          })
55          .then(quote => {
56            document.getElementById('quoteDisplay').innerHTML = quote;
57          })
58      };
59    </script>
```

JavaScript is using an API called the Fetch API. Yep, even programming languages use APIs; they're everywhere!

The Fetch API[249] allows JavaScript to make HTTP request. What this means is the Fetch API allows JavaScript to reach over the internet and make requests to servers. Like, for example, request quotes from the Cowboy server.

---

[249]https://developer.mozilla.org/en-US/docs/Web/API/Fetch_API/Using_Fetch

Using the Fetch API is simple, especially in the case of the Ron Swanson API, which only requires we hit the specific Endpoint. This one line of JavaScript accomplishes making that request:

```
fetch("https://ron-swanson-quotes.herokuapp.com/v2/quotes")
```

All the Javascript after that `fetch` request is JavaScript handling the response. We don't need to know the specifics; I just wanted to show you how JavaScript - the Frontend code - is using an API to request a response from another API. Pretty cool right?

Everything else, the button click, the color, fonts, the Ron Swanson head-shot, is the Frontend showing off. Sending the quote and the storage of all the quotes is the responsibility of the Backend.

4. Before wrapping up, let's check back in our Network panel and see if we can find that same network request that makes calls to the Cowboy server. Remember to refresh the page or hit the "Quote me!" button once you're on the Network panel.

And there it is, our 1 network request, "quotes."

If you have "all" selected you'll see all the things being loaded on the web page, like the image, and HTML document. If you only want to see the request to a remote server - as we do - select "XHR" as I've done in the following screenshot. XHR stands for XMLHttpRequest[250], and means all request that transfer data between a browser and a webserver.

Name	Status	Type	Initiator	Size	Time	Waterfall
quotes ron-swanson-quotes.her...	200 OK	fetch	ron-swanson... Script	392 B 134 B	119 ms 118 ms	

Again we see the same Endpoint URL we used in the previous example is still being used. We also see the same GET Request Header and 200 Response. You'll also see that it's the "fetch" method making the request.

Let's now move onto to talk about *how* the Backend stores data. The data isn't just haphazardly stored on a server, under a folder-file system. Not at all. The Backend uses **databases** to store and keep data organized. Understanding how to use databases is a big part of being a Backend developer.

Backend Data: Databases

Have you ever used a Google Spreadsheet or Excel file to store information about something? Even if it was just a list of quotes from authors you like. That spreadsheet is essentially a dumbed-down version of a database. Much like bottle rockets are a dumbed-down version of actual rockets; dumbed-down in the biggest of ways.

---

[250]https://en.wikipedia.org/wiki/XMLHttpRequest

Author	Witty line
E. E. Cummings	"Unbeing dead isn't being alive."
P.G. Wodehouse, Very Good, J	"Red hair, sir, in my opinion, is dangerous."
Dr. Seuss, The Lorax	"Unless someone like you cares a whole awful lot, Nothing is going to get better. It's not."

Databases are similar to spreadsheets in that they generally use table names and columns and rows. However, databases do so much more than spreadsheets are capable of. Databases are super powerful because instead of keeping track of your favorite 10 or so quotes, they have to keep track of hundreds - billions of pieces of information. Facebook has 2.3 billion users[251], and each of those profiles are stored somewhere in a mind-boggling system of databases.

The Facebook example is extreme, but you get the gist- if you thought your spreadsheet slowed down if you have a thousand or so cells, it will explode if it had to manage what a typical Backend database handles on the day-to-day.

 Databases deserve much more discussion than I give them here. They are a key component in making the Backend what it is. However, it's too much to explore them adequately as a section of a chapter. Consequently, we will devote a whole chapter to Databases in the second series of this book "How to Become a Backend Developer: A Field Guide."

I do, however, think it's important that I at least introduce you to the most popular Database programing language, "Structure Query Language", a.k.a. SQL.

SQL

We did not cover database languages in the Programming Languages chapter, because technically they are not a programming language. Languages that deal with

---

[251]https://zephoria.com/top-15-valuable-facebook-statistics/

databases are "database management languages." SQL[252] is one of the most popular of these languages, and it's relatively easy to pick up.

Here is a quick list of the most popular database languages[253].

	Rank		DBMS	Database Model	
Mar 2019	Feb 2019	Mar 2018			
1.	1.	1.	Oracle ➕	Relational, Multi-model ℹ	1
2.	2.	2.	MySQL ➕	Relational, Multi-model ℹ	1
3.	3.	3.	Microsoft SQL Server ➕	Relational, Multi-model ℹ	1
4.	4.	4.	PostgreSQL ➕	Relational, Multi-model ℹ	
5.	5.	5.	MongoDB ➕	Document	
6.	6.	6.	IBM Db2 ➕	Relational, Multi-model ℹ	
7.	⬆9.	7.	Microsoft Access	Relational	
8.	⬇7.	8.	Redis ➕	Key-value, Multi-model ℹ	
9.	⬇8.	9.	Elasticsearch ➕	Search engine, Multi-model ℹ	
10.	10.	⬆11.	SQLite ➕	Relational	

SQL is relatively intuitive; it's easy'ish to read, and just a little harder to write. To see what I mean, let's use the W3Schools practice SQL tool.

> ⚠ This Exercise is optional. I found it helpful when first being introduced to SQL to play with it a bit. If this has the opposite effect, i.e., it confuses you, even more, ignore this section and move onto "Backend Programming Languages."

Exercise 3 of 5: Practicing with SQL on a set of data

1. Navigate to the W3Schools' SQL tutorial[254].

2. In the first example, you'll see the command SELECT * FROM Customers. What this command is saying is return everything from the "Customers" table. The * is a wildcard symbol, meaning "all."

Click on the "Try it Yourself" button.

---

[252]https://en.wikipedia.org/wiki/SQL
[253]https://db-engines.com/en/ranking
[254]https://www.w3schools.com/sql/default.asp

Example

```
SELECT * FROM Customers;
```

Try it Yourself »

Click on the "Try it Yourself" button to see how it works.

3. Per the instructions of the web page, try it out by clicking on the "Run SQL."

The representation of the Database is on the right-hand side of the web page. When you run this command, the results are displayed below. In this test database, you have 91 customers.

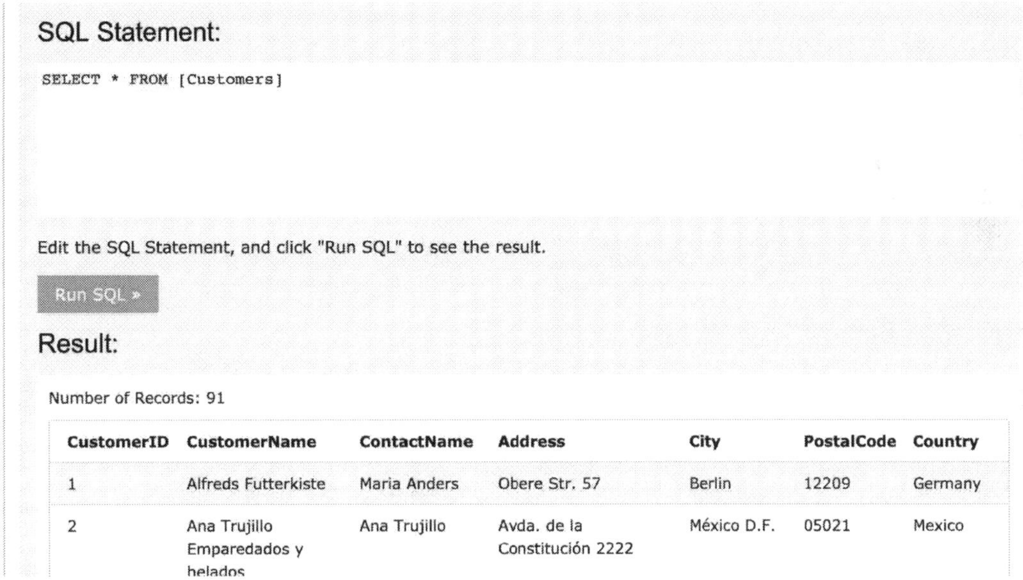

SQL Statement:

```
SELECT * FROM [Customers]
```

Edit the SQL Statement, and click "Run SQL" to see the result.

Run SQL »

Result:

Number of Records: 91

CustomerID	CustomerName	ContactName	Address	City	PostalCode	Country
1	Alfreds Futterkiste	Maria Anders	Obere Str. 57	Berlin	12209	Germany
2	Ana Trujillo Emparedados y helados	Ana Trujillo	Avda. de la Constitución 2222	México D.F.	05021	Mexico

4. The point of this Exercise is to show you a glimpse into how the SQL language communicates with a database of information. Continue to play around if you'd like. Try out some of the following SQL statements.

Returning only the City and Country columns from the Customers table

```
SELECT DISTINCT City, Country
FROM Customers;
```

Return everything from the Customers table where their country equals Spain

```
SELECT * FROM Customers
WHERE Country='Spain';
```

Return everything from the Customers table if their CustomerID is less than 10 and then order by the Country name

```
SELECT * FROM Customers
WHERE CustomerID < 10
ORDER BY Country;
```

Backend Programming Languages

Unlike the Frontend which uses HTML, CSS, Javascript, the Backend can be written in pretty much any Programming Language.

As mentioned in the Programming Languages chapter, certain languages are better suited for different types of jobs. If you're storing data for a video game, then you'll likely be writing the Backend in C. If you're working in academia, you might be writing in Python.

You can even write the Backend in JavaScript. However, instead of running JavaScript on our browser, you run JavaScript on a tool called Node.js. Remember how the browser has a rendering engine that can read and process JavaScript? Well in the Backend you're not writing code for the browser, you are writing it for a server. Thus, you use Node.js to write JavaScript instead of using the Browser's rendering engine.

Without getting into too many details, Node.js acts like a browser, doing only the things necessary to execute JavaScript. Node.js[255] is built on Google Chrome's V8 rendering engine.

So you can walk away from this chapter feeling like you did something in the Backend we are going to set up a Node.js server.

---

[255]https://www.tutorialspoint.com/nodejs/nodejs_introduction.htm

Exercise 4 of 5: Setting up a Node.js Backend

1. The first thing we need to do is install both Node.js and Node Package Manager (NPM). Think of NPM[256] as a giant online library of various software packages free to download and use.

As I alluded to earlier in the Git Chapter, programmers are all about sharing and caring. One significant way they do this is by creating software packages that other people might benefit from using. NPM is a place they can upload these software packages effectively making them available for anyone to use. NPM is, in fact, the world's largest Software Library[257].

As of writing, the most download software package in NPM is called Lodash[258], with 21 + million *weekly* downloads. Yes, you read that correctly, 'weekly downloads'!

To install NPM, you need to install Node.js, in fact installing Node.js by default also installs NPM. Strange I know, but you need both: Node.js and NPM.

There's a chance you already have Node.js and NPM installed if you've ever worked with NPM before. To check if you have Node.js and NPM installed run node -v and npm -v in your terminal. If a version number is returned, then you already have them installed.

To install Node.js, and NPM by default, the easiest thing to do is follow Node.js's install instructions - see here[259]. Make sure you install the version of Node.js that matches your Operating System (e.g., macOS or Windows).

Windows Users

To determine if you are using 32 or 64-bit version, you can visit this website[260]. Follow the instructions based on what Windows version you are using.

---

[256]https://www.npmjs.com/
[257]https://www.npmjs.com/
[258]https://www.npmjs.com/package/lodash
[259]https://nodejs.org/en/download/
[260]https://www.computerhope.com/issues/ch001121.htm

Once you have downloaded Node.js, make sure to go through the installation process. You can select all the default settings. Depending on your internet speed and machine, this could take a couple of minutes.

Note: you will need to restart your computer after going through the installation process. After rebooting you should be able to use Node.js from the Git Bash program. To test, run `node -v` and you'll see a version returned.

2. With that out of the way, the rest of this Exercise will start moving much quicker.

In the code that comes with this book, navigate to the folder called

`8-fe-vs-be/nodejs-practice`[261]

in your terminal application.

Once there, run the command `node app.js` in your terminal.

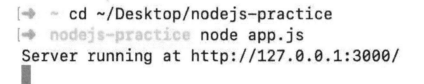

```
[→  ~ cd ~/Desktop/nodejs-practice
[→  nodejs-practice node app.js
Server running at http://127.0.0.1:3000/
```

Next, navigate to the `http://localhost:3000` on your web browser. You should see a "Howdy rockstar " printed on the screen.

`←  →  C  ⌂      ⓘ localhost:3000`

`Howdy rockstar`

Hold your horses. I know a lot just happened. First, what is `localhost:3000`? Remember, servers are special computers specially designed to serve up data. However, *any* computer can act as a server. When you see the **localhost** in your browser's URL that means your computer is acting as the server. If you'd like to learn more about

---
[261] code/src/8-fe-vs-be/nodejs-practice

localhost and get a sneak peek into computer networking, I recommend you start with an article like this[262].

Second, what was that node app.js command all about? The node app.js command starts the webserver! But how? I know that was sudden and unexpected. Let's look at how we did this.

3. Open the folder "nodejs-practice" in your text editor and navigate to the app.js file.

```
1   const http = require('http');
2
3   const hostname = '127.0.0.1';
4   const port = 3000;
                                Defining server
6   const server = http.createServer((req, res) ⇒ {
7     res.statusCode = 200;
8     res.setHeader('Content-Type', 'text/plain');
9     res.end('Howdy rockstar');
10  });
                                                    initilizing the
11                                                       server
12  server.listen(port, hostname, () ⇒ {
13    console.log(`Server running at http://${hostname}:${port}/`);
14  });
15
16  // var mysql = require('mysql');
```

Rows 6-10 are defining the server, and rows 12-14 are initializing the server; effectively saying "yep start me."

4. Right now, we can only visit the URL localhost:3000. Remember our Endpoint conversation from working with the Ron Swanson API? If we hit a specific endpoint (URL), then the API returned a quote. We're going to set ourselves up to do something similar for the next Exercise.

Back in your text editor, uncomment rows 5-7 and 11. I have highlighted the rows to uncomment in pink boxes in the following screenshot.

[262]https://www.geeksforgeeks.org/computer-network-what-is-local-host/

```
 2
 3   const port = 3000;
 4
 5   // function respondQuotes(req, res) {
 6   //    res.setHeader('Content-Type', 'text/plain');
 7   //    res.end('Show me some quotes!');
 8   // }
 9
10   const server = http.createServer((req, res) ⇒ {
11     // if (req.url === '/quotes') return respondQuotes(req, res);
12     res.setHeader('Content-Type', 'text/plain');
13     res.end('Howdy rockstar');
14   });
```

This is what the code looks like uncommented:

```
 3   const port = 3000;
 4
 5   function respondQuotes(req, res) {
 6     res.setHeader('Content-Type', 'text/plain');
 7     res.end('Show me some quotes!');
 8   }
 9
10   const server = http.createServer((req, res) ⇒ {
11     if (req.url === '/quotes') return respondQuotes(req, res);
12     res.setHeader('Content-Type', 'text/plain');
13     res.end('Howdy rockstar');
14   });
```

Rows 5-7 are setting up a function that says if this function gets called return "Show me some quotes!"

Row 11, calls this function if the endpoint (URL) is /quotes.

Save your changes. Back in your terminal, press ctrl + c to stop the server, and then re-enter the node app.js command to start it back up. Any time you make a change, you need to stop and restart the server.

Then navigate to the endpoint http://localhost:3000/quotes. You'll see the "Show me some quotes" returned. Nice work!

← → C ⌂ (ⓘ localhost:3000/quotes)

`Show me some quotes!`

Exercise 5 of 5: Create your own API

Remember how I said that APIs "can be relatively 'easy' to write"? I was telling the truth. Granted, the API we're going to write doesn't provide much of a service so it *will* be easy to write. The more complex the API service, the more complex it is to write.

Our API is going to return some random quotes anytime we hit the endpoint `localhost:3000/quotes`.

1. Back in your text editor, on the same `app.js` file we were using earlier, we are going to create a JavaScript array that holds a list of quotes.

 There is a final version of the app.js file found in the same "nodejs-practice" folder. The file is aptly called "app-final.js." It will include all the final code added via this last Exercise. Take a peek at it if you get lost or have a question.

Navigate to the end of the app.js file and on row 19 add a JavaScript array called "quotesArray." You can copy-paste my quotesArray, or make your own.

```
const quotesArray = [
  'I feel God in this Chilis tonight',
  'If You Pray Enough, You Can Turn Yourself Into A Cat Person.',
  'How would I describe myself? Three words. Hard-working. Alpha male. \
Jackhammer. Merciless. Insatiable.',
  'Sometimes The Clothes At Gap Kids Are Too Flashy, So I am Forced To \
Go To The American Girl Store And Order Clothes For Large Colonial Doll\
s.',
  'Every Little Boy Fantasizes About His Fairy-Tale Wedding.',
];
```

 In the JavaScript chapter, I used `var` when declaring a variable. Here, I am using `const`. The terms, `let` and `const` are new variable declarations introduced in ES6; a newer version of JavaScript. You'll learn about these in any further JavaScript studies you do. However, if you're curious now, here is a quick reference[263] that I believe does a good job at quickly demonstrating the differences.

2. Now that we've declared an array of quotes, we need to do something with it. Back on row 5, inside the `respondQuotes` function, I want you to modify the function so that it now looks like the following:

```
function respondQuotes(req, res) {
  res.setHeader('Content-Type', 'text/plain');
  const randomQuoteIndex = Math.floor((Math.random() * 4) + 1);
  const randomQuote = quotesArray[randomQuoteIndex];
  res.end(randomQuote);
}
```

We've added the two **const** (a.k.a. Constants). The first one, "randomQuoteIndex" using a method available in JavaScript that randomly returns a number between 4 and 1; don't worry about understanding that line of code exactly.

---

[263]https://medium.com/@josephcardillo/the-difference-between-function-and-block-scope-in-javascript-4296b2322abe

The second "randomQuote" takes the random number returned as the const "randomQuoteIndex" and returns that index of the array. So for example, if the random number returned was 3, then the const "randomQuote" now equals quotesArray[3], which is our 4th quote in the list (remember indexes start at 0).

```
5    function respondQuotes(req, res) {
6      res.setHeader('Content-Type', 'text/plain');
7      const randomQuoteIndex = Math.floor((Math.random() * 4) + 1);
8      const randomQuote = quotesArray[randomQuoteIndex];
9      res.end(randomQuote);                    We added these two
10   }                                                    lines
```

Save your changes, and stop, and restart the server.

3. Now refresh the URL endpoint localhost:3000/quotes. You should randomly see a quote from your list returned.

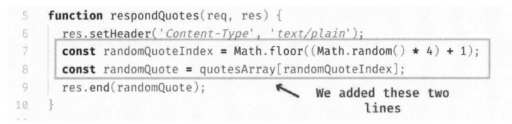

Does this process seem familiar? Yep, just like the Ron Swanson API. It's possible that the Ron Swanson API is using a giant list of quotes stored inside an Array - like us. Or more likely, it has a list of quotes stored in a database, and it's using a language like SQL to pull at random a quote from the database.

The service we created here is similar to the service provided by the Ron Swanson API. And because returning quotes like this is a service, it's fair enough to say you just created an API - nice work.

I'll admit the Backend is hard to wrap your head around because it's not as visual as the Frontend. But hopefully, this Exercise demystifies - even if just a little - what the Backend can look like.

What kind of programmer do you want to be?

The separation between Backend and Frontend can lead to a split in career paths. That or you can go the route of Fullstack developer, working in both the Frontend and Backend space.

There is also a 4th off-shoot type of developer we have yet to mention, the holly DevOps Engineer[264]. Technically these folks are not developers; they are the engineers managing all the structures that hold an application together. There are even more specific database engineers and computer systems engineers. The list goes on. Again the larger the company and codebase, the more specific engineering roles you get.

We have drawn the line at Frontend and Backend, but don't take that to mean there are no further divisions; there are.

So what does this all mean for you? Should you be a Fullstack, Frontend, Backend developer, or maybe seek out the more specific DevOps or database engineer positions? Some might say a Frontend Engineer should be more drawn to design and experience, whereas a Backend Engineer is best suited to a person that likes problem-solving and big data management problems.

I don't entirely agree, however, especially in today's technology stack. These descriptions are shallow stereotypes, much like saying there are dog people and cat people. Instead, I'd say it depends on what animal you get first, or in web development what opportunity for studying presents itself to you.

I was recently asked why I became a Frontend Developer. After a moment of hesitation, I told the truth, "it's what I could apply for." Frontend development was accessible, I fixed friends' websites, and by association learned HTML, CSS, and JavaScript. When I started to try and develop skills based on an inner-company hiring positioning, I choose the job I already had skills in, and that's the honest, unsexy reason why I'm a Frontend developer. I had no calling to improve the user experience or create elegant interfaces.

---

[264]I say "holly" here because I truly believe these folks have the hardest job. I like to think of them as the First responders of the web development world. I recommend reading the Phoenix Project, which aside from it being a great fictionally-real read, it's a wonderful perspective on the development process.

For you, your journey will hopefully have more focus, hence why you're reading this book.

Key Takeaways

- The **Frontend** is responsible for everything the user interacts with. It only stores a limited amount of data.
- The two main reasons the Frontend is not responsible for data storage is Security and Performance concerns.
- The **Backend** is responsible for data management, data processing, and receiving/responding to requests from the Frontend.
- The split between Frontend and Backend came about as a way to manage responsibilities as the technology space continues to grow.
- More and more, we are seeing developers specialize in either Frontend or Backend positions.
- APIs are what you plugin to access more complex services. Frontend and Backend use APIs as a way to communicate with each other.
- The Backend stores data in databases. One of the most popular database languages is called SQL. You use SQL to interact with the database.

Considerations for Further Study

This was a difficult chapter to reign in, and clearly, as it's one of the longest of the chapters, it still got away a little from me.

The problem is that there is a lot here to discuss, and we've arrived at a critical step - a fork in the road - if you will. I have introduced you to the most important things about web development up until the point of where you need to start considering if you'll be turning left, right, or forging a different path. Thus, that's why this chapter is the end of any new content or Exercises.

The encore, the next chapter, is a very visual chapter - it's a field guide; appropriate considering the title of this book. There will be no new information, just a guide of what we've covered and what's next.

Further Readings

There are so many topics here that I wanted to dive deeper into but had to keep short. As a compromise, I have included some of the resources for learning more on topics we just started to explore.

All of these are of course, optional. And honestly, even if you're a go-getter, only explore the ones that truly interest you.

Hey, go-getters,

Listen to me when I say you can't go-get everything. I know, you just immediately wrote me off because I don't know you or understand the depth of your go-getting personality. That may be true, but there is too much in the web development space to know it all. Shift from knowing everything to only knowing the things that move you forward towards a goal. I promise you, even in the most specialized niche of web development you won't run out of things to learn.

What is Good UI and UX? Smashing Magazine[265] I believe does a great job at putting out content relevant to anyone working in the Frontend space. I have their books and have attended their conferences. Time spent with their content is time well spent.

Web Designer? Here's a solid Medium article[266] on becoming a UX/UI designer. This is a topic I didn't spend any time talking about, but the design aspect of web development might be a career path that interests you. These are the folks that design what web developers are tasked with making.

The Network Panel in Detail The Network panel is the go-to when working on Backend-Frontend communication. Learning it in more detail will pay off in spades. I always lean on Google's "Tools for Web Developers" when learning about the DevTools - it *is their* platform - and as such, here[267] is Google's documentation on the Network Panel.

Frontend Developers Handbook Frontend Masters is my favorite online "university." It's not the cheapest, but the content is top-notch. They do, however, have a free

---

[265]https://www.smashingmagazine.com/
[266]https://blog.nicolesaidy.com/7-steps-to-become-a-ui-ux-designer-8beed7639a95
[267]https://developers.google.com/web/tools/chrome-devtools/network/

online "Frontend Developers Handbook"[268]. If becoming a Frontend Developer is the path you're leaning towards, I would check this out.

More on Node.js If you're interested in going the Backend Developer route, learning Node.js is a smart place to start. There are a ton of Node.js resources out there, but one I have an affinity towards is the Fullstack Node.js Book, which is also being published by Fullstack.io. I have had a sneak preview of this book and love the approach the author is taking. It should be released shortly after this book makes its debut and can be found on the newline.co website.

Database discussions Databases are a hard thing to read about. I recommend before going much deeper into the SQL language or making a Database you learn about Database concepts. Here is a good video[269] discussing these topics.

What's Next?

The next chapter of this book is essentially a friendly version of this roadmap[270]. In my opinion, this road map makes sense - at least most of it - once you're *already* in a developer position; so not very helpful for the audience here. It's too much and just words and lines if you reading it as a beginner. That being said, I still would have greatly appreciated seeing this when I first started.

---

[268]https://frontendmasters.com/books/front-end-handbook/2018/
[269]https://youtu.be/wR0jg0eQsZA
[270]https://github.com/kamranahmedse/developer-roadmap

Chapter 9: Field Guide

We've come a long way, and you should be proud. I did my darndest to make the content and Exercises helpful and fun, but there is no denying that the material is thick. I suspect you feel a mix of overwhelmed and exhausted, all of which is normal.

Web development, especially in the last 5+ years, has blown up and the content along with it. There is a lot to learn, and honestly, you can't learn it all. So that begs the question, what do you do next, and where do you go from here; how can you get a job as a Web Developer?

As the title of this book suggests, this is a *field guide* to web development. This book alone and its content may not get you far enough along to get a job. It does, however, get you on the most direct path to get one.

Having made it through to the last chapter, you now have the information and skills to make an educated decision about the next step; and honestly, that puts you ahead of most. Even for folks completing a computer science degree or going into a "coding bootcamp," unless they have taken the time to understand what the field of web development looks like they may not be adequately prepared to decide that next step. You are.

In this last chapter, as promised, I will not be introducing any new content or Exercises. Instead, we have created a How to Become a Web Developer Field Guide[271] (called "Field Guide" from here out). This Field Guide is a printable 11X17 PDF that can be downloaded similar to the code examples. It's under the folder "9-field-guide". I would encourage you to either bookmark or print this Field Guide if you're the poster sorts.

The remainder of this chapter takes each major content area, illustrated as a "trail-post" and discusses the four following areas:

1. **Skill Level**: The amount of skill you should have for a particular topic. Keeping with the theme of a "field guide," I use universal trail markings to indicate the recommended skill level.

---

[271]code/src/9-field-guide/map.pdf

Easy/Beginner

Moderate/Intermediate

Difficult/Expert

2. **Project Suggestions**: I am suggesting that you do a project for each of the topics covered by a trail-posts.

I know I have already had you do a lot of project-like Exercises. And in some cases, you may feel that you have adequately covered the topic. But the reality is, learning happens while *doing* things. You will make mistakes and problem solve questions you didn't even know to ask. It is during these struggles that you solidify what you've read and studied.

There is a reason why many developer positions are amended with "Engineer" – Frontend Engineer, Software Engineers, etc. It's because you are **making**, **creating**, and **designing** things. Just like you can't become an artist without making art, you cannot become a developer without developing things.

3. **Estimated Hours Spent**: Here, I will break down what I estimate to be the additional amount of time you need to spend studying and working on a project. These are subjective to the individual. I put the hours only to give you a general sense of the time commitment in front of you. Focus more on the ratio of studying to project time rather than logging hours.

In an attempt to provide the reader a sense of what lies ahead, and what that means in regards to time commitment and next steps, in the "Field Guide," I included hours and additional projects. This "curriculum," if you wanted to call it that, is not to be followed to the hour or step. Instead, it's there to give a sense of magnitude to what "next step" means. These metrics are not backed up by any quantitative, qualitative, or anecdotal findings. Take your learning into your own hands. If you feel like you're spending too much time on a topic or not enough on another, then adjust to your needs.

4. **Frontend vs. Backend**: Your decision about whether you want to be a Backend, Frontend, Fullstack or `<insert other developer occupation here>` *does* influence how much you should focus on some topics. As such, I wanted a place to add notes addressing those potential differences.

 I am not adding additional resources in this chapter as I have included these at the end of each chapter. Refer back to the "Considerations for Further Studies" and "Further Readings" sections for links to recommended resources.

1. HTML

Skill Level: Easy

Start here. This is the most natural and commonplace to start learning how to become a Web Developer. You don't need to be an expert, but learn and be comfortable with the basics.

 You'll know you're there when you can read and write ∼50% of the HTML on an average web page.

Project Suggestions

Start from scratch and build your own 1-page HTML web page. Whatever you'd like. Just make an HTML page, and open it in your browser, no additional setup needed.

Build from the examples in the book or search online for starter HTML files. Focus on HTML tags we did not cover, and try making more complex components like tables, buttons, or form fields.

Est. Hours Spent

- Time studying 5hrs
- Time working on project 20hrs

Frontend vs. Backend

HTML is foundational, the amount you learn should be similar for both Backend and Frontend developers. Some may argue that it's more Frontend focused, but it's such a foundational language of the web, I don't believe it's wise to make a difference in acuity.

2. CSS

Skill Level: Easy-Moderate

It's likely your HTML studies will mix with your CSS studies. I would, however, spend more time on CSS than HTML. There are a lot of important topics I was not able to cover in the CSS chapter, but mention in the Further Reading section.

In addition to CSS, you should spend time learning about CSS Frameworks. There are lots of CSS Frameworks; don't overdo it, just focusing on one is sufficient. Get familiar with that framework's syntax, and if you'd like, use the framework instead of plain CSS in your project.

Note: you should also spend a little time understanding what a CSS framework is. You'll run into frameworks in your JavaScript studies as well.

 You'll know you're there when you can read and write ~50% of the CSS on a web page as well as debug and modify CSS using the DevTools.

Project Suggestions

Using the same HTML page from your HTML project, add CSS to the page in all 3 ways; External, Internal, and Inline. Get comfortable with overriding styles (hint: you'll need to learn at least a little about the cascading mechanism during this process).

Having added styles, try your hand at adding a CSS animation. You don't need to build one from scratch, but try adding a pre-built one and modifying it. A quick search on Codepen.io for CSS animations[272] should get you on your way.

Est. Hours Spent

- Time studying 10hrs
- Time working on project 25hrs

Frontend vs. Backend

If you plan on going into Frontend Development, you should spend about double the time learning CSS than someone who is not planning on going into Frontend Development.

As a Frontend Developer knowing how to use your DevTools to debug CSS issues will be crucial, so make sure that your studies include modifying or debugging CSS issues.

---

[272]https://codepen.io/search/pens?q=css%20animations&page=1&order=popularity&depth=everything

3. JavaScript

Skill Level: Moderate-Advanced

JavaScript should be your first Programming Language. Though you may not end up developing using JavaScript, it will teach you the foundations of Programming Languages. JavaScript is accessible - every browser renders it - and it's extremely popular, making it an optimal first language to learn.

Take your time. Consider this the foundation upon which your understanding of other languages will come. If you don't understand a concept at first, keep chipping away at it.

 You'll know you're there when you can add functionality to a web page using plain JavaScript. The functionality should interact with DOM nodes and use several JavaScript methods.

Project Suggestions

Continue to either build off your HTML + CSS project or start anew. This project will make a great candidate for a future GitHub repository that you want to share with the world.

A good place to start is by thinking of something simple you'd like to solve. Maybe you need a calculator that calculates your average monthly bills, or you'd like to make a random name generator. Keep it simple and interesting.

A lot of examples on the web are going to use a JavaScript library or framework. There's no hiding from this, and you shouldn't avoid it. Just make sure you understand what it is you are using, and don't blindly follow tutorials. Letting a tutorial do the work for you is great - at first. But it sucks when you get blind-sided in an interview when you're asked "what is a framework, and why would you use one."

It can be a little much, even for the most organized self-learner to map out your JavaScript learning. As such, I'd recommend taking a course on just JavaScript. A video course more so than a book, something with a project. I would also strongly encourage you to choose a course that focuses on JavaScript and then optionally introduces you to a JavaScript framework.

So for example, if you had to decide between two courses, one titled "Learn React and JavaScript," or "Learn JavaScript, the fundamentals," choose the latter.

Est. Hours Spent

- Time studying 20hrs
- Time working on project 40hrs

Frontend vs. Backend

If you intend on becoming a Frontend Developer, make sure you focus on JavaScript the language. It's very likely that no matter what framework or library you end up using in your future career, JavaScript will be its foundation. Additionally, I might do two projects, one just using JavaScript and the second using a JavaScript framework like React, Vue, or Angular.

If you aim to become a Backend Developer, you should be less concerned with becoming a JavaScript master and instead focus on the concepts like functions, arrays, objects, etc. that you become more familiar with as you work with JavaScript. Once you can complete a small JavaScript project, then start thinking about the next language (ex: Python, Node.js, etc.) that you'd like to master. See the later trail-post "Programming Languages."

4. Terminal

Skill Level: Easy-Moderate

Every programmer, by nature of the day-to-day requirements of working in the terminal, will have to get familiar with it. Realistically, navigating, and knowing how to use the terminal with Git is really all you *need*.

But, and this is a big but, learning the terminal beyond what you *need*, will pay off in subtle and powerful ways. Additionally, your day-to-day as a computer user will improve. Think of it like drinking protein drinks after a workout. You'll slowly become stronger and more powerful than your peers who forgo the post-recovery routine. You'll be thankful you did when you're the only one that can remove the top from that damn pickle jar.

 You'll know you're there when you can spend a computer session just using your terminal to navigate and do things around your computer.

Project Suggestions

I have two suggestions, the first more of a "just do it," the other, "if you want to." First, use your terminal daily. And most importantly use it when working with Git and GitHub (or GitHub alternatives).

The second, create bash scripts that allow you to execute things on your computer. For example, let's say you find yourself always converting time zones because of your job, make a script that does it for you. There are lots of online resources on how to do scripting in the terminal, but playing around in this space will raise your "cool" level by at least two or three levels.

Est. Hours Spent

- Time studying 5hrs
- Time working on project 5-10hrs

Frontend vs. Backend

The terminal is a tool used by all kinds of developers. Regardless of if you spend your time with servers or clients. However, if the idea of working as a Systems Admin or DevOps person has piqued your interest, then spend more time here.

5. Git

Skill Level: moderate

The value of really understanding how Git works will not make itself evident until you f' up. If you got through the Git chapter of this book, you should have the necessary Git skills, just enough to get you by as a junior Web Developer.

However, when - not if - you find yourself in the real world facing a situation where you accidentally deleted something or broke a website, knowing how Git saves, commits and records history will be a very comforting and helpful fallback.

Think of Git like that airplane evacuation manual you've never opened. No need to expand the analogy, you get where I'm going with it. Git is there to help you. Know how it works because, unlike airplane safety stats, it's a guarantee that you will make a mistake as a developer.

 You'll know you're there when you can do and understand all the commands shown in the Git Chapter without having to rely too heavily on a cheat sheet.

Project Suggestions

Turn any of the HTML, CSS or JavaScript projects into Git repositories if you haven't already. It's overkill, for sure, but using Git is how you learn it.

Use GitHub, or an equivalent, while you're at it. Remember, GitHub will become one of the first places a future employer is going to look.

Est. Hours Spent

- Time studying 3-5hrs
- Time working on a project, use it for as many projects as you can.

Frontend vs. Backend

This is a tool used equally by all developers.

6. Programming Languages

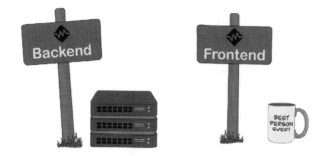

Skill Level: Moderate - Expert

Think of this as the step after the Fork in the road. You know what path you want to follow, and now is the time to specialize in a marketable language and/or framework.

It's here that you want to show off your skill, so expect to spend a good chunk of time on this step. Do a good amount of research before you choose what language or framework you want to focus on. It's also very likely you'll be using external libraries and potentially making a Backend and Frontend. Get a good sense of the tech stack you want to use, at least as much as you can, as the tech stack may need to adjust as you go.

Project Suggestions

This is the project you may use to try and get the job you'd like. So if you're looking at a company that uses Ruby as their codebase, this project should be in Ruby. Or maybe you know you want to work for a company focusing on Climate Change; then your project should focus on solving a problem in that space. In other words, make it relevant to whomever you are trying to impress.

If you are struggling to come up with a project idea, reach out to the community (think StackOverflow), or if appropriate someone at the job you're trying to get hired on with. I would also recommend seeking out Meetups, or close-to-you community events that might help you figure out the best project for your goals.

If you ever did a thesis or capstone project in school, this is that.

Est. Hours Spent

- Time studying 15hrs
- Time working on project 50+ hrs

Frontend vs. Backend

It's up to you at this point. Maybe you're leaning left, or right, or down the middle. Don't worry if you want to change paths later, you can. There is a lot of crossover between the two areas of separation. It will just be more time-efficient if you can take the most direct route on the first step.

Future Frontend Developers will likely be working with a popular JavaScript framework and APIs. If you are going to be dealing with any sensitive information - think authentication - I would recommend getting familiar with "serverless" backends. This will save you the time of having to set up a local backend environment and impress any future employer with your cross over skills.

Future Backend Developers, you might need to take an extra step and learn more about databases before trying to figure out your tech stack. There are some common pairings between languages and databases, and spending some time learning about databases first will get you set up for a more realistic project.

Happy Adventuring

Be prepared, drink lots of water, and make sure to take plenty of stretching breaks.

Changelog

Revision 4 – 01-24-2020

Fixes some headings in Programming Languages Chapter

Revision 3 – 10-12-2019

Update version log

Revision 2 – 10-09-2019

Update Video link for Jeff Malnick

Revision 1 – 09-21-2019

First Version